The Two Redeemers
of Prophecy

Biblical and Islamic End Times

John Muir

Westview Publishing

All scripture quotations are taken from the HOLY BIBLE: NEW INTERNATIONAL VERSION®. ©2008 by International Bible Society, unless otherwise noted.

Cover design: Ken Ekle
Interior design: Diane Johnson
Text Editor: Diane Johnson
Project Editor and Publisher: Jacqueline Rae, Westview Publishing

ISBN: 978-0-692-21488-6
Library of Congress Control Number: 2014941003

Published by
Westview Publishing
Mount Vernon, Washington

Printed in the United States of America

Table of Contents

PREFACE

I am writing this book as a wake-up call to every conservative, born-again, Bible-believing Christian who is looking for the "blessed hope" of Christ's return. This book is about prophecy, both biblical and Islamic. There is a startling convergence between the two that will shock you. Yet, the Christian church is mostly uninformed about Islamic prophecy, and confused about biblical prophecy. It is my hope this book will cause the conservative church in America to re-examine what it believes about the return of Christ, our redemption, and what Christ meant when he said, "he who stands firm to the end will be saved" (Matthew 24:13).

We will examine the promises made to the saints of God and the nation of Israel in the Old Testament. Then we will look at what Islam promises to the faithful of their religion. By doing so, we will discover there are two redeemers of prophecy: one who is Jewish and one who is Persian. The Bible predicts Jesus will return to earth, destroy the forces of evil at the battle of Armageddon, throw the Antichrist into the lake of fire, and reign on the throne of David forever. Islam predicts their redeemer will return to earth, kill the Jews and Christians, defeat the Jewish redeemer at the battle of Armageddon, throw him into the lake of fire, and rule the world from Jerusalem. Who is telling the truth? That is a matter of faith.

Finally, we will examine what Jesus and the apostles said in the New Testament about the future. Does it match with the Old Testament, or do they promise something that was never promised to the Old Testament saints? Many conservative Christians are convinced Old Testament saints and New Testament saints have separate futures based on separate promises. We must ask ourselves one question: Why do Jesus and the apostles refer to the Old Testament every time they give a prophecy? Are those Old Testament references important to understanding what the New Testament prophecies mean? Could it be Jesus and the apostles are saying the Old Testament promises will be fulfilled just as they were spoken?

The answer to these questions is based on your hermeneutics. How you interpret the Bible will determine what you believe about the future. In this volume, the literal, grammatical, historical, and contextual interpretation will be used with every passage without exception. No spiritualization or allegory will be allowed. The reason for this is simple: spiritualization and allegory allow for multiple meanings of the text. But any text that can have two or more meanings is meaningless. If you reject the literal, grammatical, historical, and contextual meaning, you can spiritualize the text to say anything you want. But is that proper?

The evangelist Billy Graham has written many books. What conservative Christian would dare disrespect him by spiritualizing or allegorizing one of his books to make him say something other than the literal meaning of the text? Yet, so many Christians are more than willing to do just that with the Word of God. Which text deserves more respect, Billy Graham's or God's?

The most popular theory concerning the future of the church today is called the pretribulational rapture theory. Basically, it says the Gentile church will be raptured before the troubles of the tribulation start, while the Jews will be left here on earth to suffer the trials of the tribulation. I contend that this belief is based solely upon spiritualization and allegory. The reasons for this belief will become clear as we look at the Old and New Testaments.

One further word about this book: It is intended to be read beside your Bible. All Scripture references in this book are from the New International Version (NIV), unless otherwise noted. Please check each and every reference. Verify for yourself this is what the Bible says. Then ask yourself this question: Do I believe it? If so, what will you do about it?

THE BASICS OF ESCHATOLOGY

P rophecy and *soteriology* (beliefs about how the saints of God are saved) are directly linked. Prophecy has always been God's way of communicating his plan of salvation to the saints, yet the saints have always struggled with how to understand that communication. Numerous systems of interpreting prophecy have been invented through the ages. We will look at those various systems in their historical context to better understand why they came about. But first we need to start with some basic definitions.

DEFINITIONS

The term *millennialism* is taken from the Latin word *mille* which means "thousand." It is used in the Latin Vulgate Bible, and it refers to the thousand-year reign of Jesus Christ on earth which is promised in Revelation 20:2–4, 6, and 7. Christ's promised reign on earth is also referred to as *chiliasm* because the Greek word *chilias,* which also means "thousand," is used in the original Greek text of Revelation 20.

The second word that is usually linked with end-time prophecy is the word "tribulation" (θλίψιν). This is normally used to refer to the "great tribulation," which is taken from Matthew 24:21 and

Revelation 7:14. It refers to a seven-year period of great trouble and persecution that will be experienced by the children of God. Those who believe in a literal interpretation of the Bible believe this period will immediately precede the millennium. Those who don't believe in a literal millennium do not believe in a literal seven-year period of trouble. Instead, they usually see it as symbolic of the troubles of life which are experienced by members of the church as we struggle to overcome the world.

There are three prefixes commonly attached to the term millennium. Each prefix indicates the relationship of the expected return of Christ to the beginning of the millennium.

Amillennialism

The first prefix is *a-*, which means "without." Those who believe in amillennialism believe that there will be no millennium, no literal seven-year tribulation, and no literal return of Christ. All prophecy is interpreted as being symbolic, and the "great tribulation" is seen as the struggle of the church to overcome the world. In this case, the tribulation lasts for many thousands of years, as Satan and the church do battle for the hearts of mankind. Those who hold to this view expect the church to gradually overcome the world. Since God lives in the heart of every Christian, the kingdom of God will then be established on earth, but without a literal king.

Postmillenialsim

The second prefix is *post-*, which means "after." Postmillennialism is very similar to amillennialism in that the interpretation of prophecy is symbolic rather than literal. In this scheme of things, the church will struggle to perfect the world. That struggle will eventually succeed through the progress of science, industry, medicine, education, and evangelism. Once mankind's sufferings have been conquered by progress, and every person has become a member of the church, the kingdom of God will, in essence, be established on earth. Only after that kingdom has ruled for a thousand years will Jesus Christ return to earth to take over as our king. In other words, Christ will come after the tribulation and millennium have ended.

Premillenialism

The third prefix, *pre-*, means "before." Premillennialism means that Jesus Christ will literally return to earth at the end of the tribulation and begin a thousand-year reign as king. It is sometimes known as premillennial-posttribulationalism, and it was the view of the first-century church. This view comes from a strictly literal interpretation of the Scriptures, and this is the view I contend for in this study of prophecy.

An offshoot of the premillennial view is called pretribulational-premillennialism. Some who accept this theory believe Christ will return before the tribulation to rapture the saints of God, while others believe Christ will return both before and after the tribulation. Those who believe Christ will return twice believe the first return will be in secret, and the second will be made public.

Preterism

There is another view of prophecy known as *preterism*, which believes that all prophecy has already been fulfilled; therefore, no one knows what will happen next. Preterists generally believe that many of the prophetic passages of the Bible were actually written after the events had taken place. In this view, the book of Daniel is said to have been written by multiple authors, the last one completing his work around the year 100 BC. They also believe Revelation was written early in the reign of Nero, possibly before the writing of Matthew. Many preterists accept the textual criticism and symbolic interpretation methods of the amillennialists and postmillennialists, and combine them with the skepticism of the atheists. Seminaries in America today are filled with professors who teach this view. But preterism is a mixed bag, because there are preterists who have a genuine faith in Christ.

These general categories will help us to understand the different millennial and tribulational beliefs as we take a closer look at the Bible. Before you make up your mind which system you believe, you should spend some time researching the history of each belief.

ESCHATOLOGY THEORIES

We must begin by explaining those various theories of eschatology, and see how each theory became popular with the members of the church through the centuries. Each theory of eschatology demands a different form of soteriology (beliefs about how the saints of God are saved). What you believe about the nature of God, and how the saints of God are saved, will have a strong influence on what you believe about the future. To put it in theological terms, your eschatology is shaped by your soteriology.

But there is another overriding influence on what you believe about the future and prophecy in general. Your hermeneutic (method of interpretation) will determine what you believe about God, salvation, and prophecy. How do you read the Bible? Do you believe it is the literal Word of God, or is it something else? Do you believe God uses the Bible to speak to us through mysteries and allegories that have to be interpreted by spiritualization? Are prophecies just metaphors for other hidden truths? Or, can you put your trust in the Word of God to mean just what it says in the literal, historical, grammatical, and contextual sense? Your answer to those questions will determine what you believe about the nature of God, the way in which the saints are saved, and the future of the saints. Therefore, we will attempt to explain the hermeneutic of each theory as we look at the history of eschatology.

The Fate of the Jews

Among those who have read the Old Testament, there is no doubt that a literal reading reveals God chose the Jews to be his special people, and gave them many promises concerning their future redemption. The question is: how will God keep those promises? Will they be kept literally, symbolically, allegorically, or not at all? Have the promises God made to the Jews become our promises because their forefathers rejected Christ? Have the Jews now become odious in God's sight, or is God just as forgiving of the Jews as he is of us?

The Jews were promised a miraculous gathering at the end of their "times of trouble." A literal reading means this gathering will be accomplished by the angels of God when the "last trump" is sounded—when God returns to the earth on the last day of the tribulation.[1] This promise is repeated at least a dozen times in the Old Testament.

Many Gentile Christians, on the other hand, believe that miraculous gathering of the saints will occur only for Gentile Christians, and before the tribulation begins, rather than after. So, has God reneged on his promises to the Jews and given those promises to us, or have we Gentile Christians got it all wrong? Some conservative Christians believe there will be two raptures: one at the beginning of the tribulation to remove Gentile believers, and one at the end of the tribulation strictly for the Jews. There are even those who chose to believe multiple raptures will occur at various times during the tribulation. Which theory is true? What does the Bible teach, if you accept a literal interpretation?

The Foundation of Prophetic Views in North America

Undoubtedly, you already have an opinion about God's plan for you. But do you know why you believe what you do concerning the tribulation, the rapture, the millennium, and the eternal state? Very few Christians have gained their opinion through intense Bible study. The vast majority have gained their opinion by listening to preachers—at their own church, on the radio, or on television. Others have gained their opinion from reading the many books written by proponents of those same radio and television hosts. But few Christians consider themselves to be true Bible scholars.

The truth is—if you are a typical Christian in North America— your beliefs about prophecy have come almost entirely from some form of mass media. And that mass media, for the most part, speaks with one voice concerning the future of the church. Writers and radio and television hosts expound the pretribulational rapture theory. Why? Is this the only possibility? No. Then why is there so little diversity among the Christian mass media? A little history lesson might help you understand.

Hegel and "Higher Criticism"

You may have never heard of the "search for the historical Jesus," but if you are a Christian believer you have been directly affected by that search. The "search for the historical Jesus" was proposed by nineteenth-century skeptical scholars. They believed that the Bible did not contain the true story of Jesus and his life. Instead, they believed the Bible contained distortions from those who used religion to control the behavior of the masses. Their method for determining the true findings of the search was known as "higher criticism," and was originated during the 1800s by university professors, especially those in Germany.

The nineteenth century was a heady time for mankind. The Industrial Revolution was in full swing. Science, education, medicine, and industry were making giant strides towards bettering the lives of the common man. A single machine could do the work of a hundred men, giving more time for things like education and social life in general. Medicine finally turned the corner from injurious to helpful. All these things were due to advancements in science. And so universities, where science was king, and where scholars rejected the truth of the Bible, led the "search" for the truth about who Jesus really was and why he came. G. W. F. Hegel was the prime instigator of this skeptical search. He was by far the most influential theologian of his time, taking over the Department of Philosophy at Berlin University in 1818.

His theory of the dialectic progress of human history influenced every university and seminary in Europe, and subsequently, in North America. Simply stated, Hegel's theory said that humans have progressed through the centuries through a series of conflicts. Those conflicts reflect Newton's laws of physics as they apply to anthropology. First there is an action, followed by a reaction, resulting in progress. When applied to society, it means mankind has progressed from cave-dwelling stone-throwers to scientists. When applied to religion, it means theology has progressed from superstition to humanism. Through the dialectical process of advancement, Hegel believed the spread of higher education would cause mankind to advance to the point of perfection, eventually replacing the need for belief in a mythical God. Mankind would become his own God, the ultimate form of humanism. Hegel expressed that belief by saying, "Our universities and our schools are our churches."[2]

The list of Hegel's disciples is huge, and includes such famous names as Friedrich Engels, Karl Marx, Friedrich Nietzsche, Sigmund Freud, Julius Wellhausen, David Strauss, F. C. Baur, Adolf

Harnack, Albert Eichorn, Johannes Weiss, and many, many more.[3] Because the major church denominations in North America sent their young seminary students to Europe for higher education in the nineteenth century, Hegel's philosophy began spreading to North America. Pastors and seminary professors who returned from their education abroad began "demythologizing" the Bible, casting doubt on the Word of God. By 1860, Harvard Seminary had rejected the literal reading of the Bible and elected to teach biological evolution, social evolution through the dialectic process, and Unitarianism.[4] Many other universities in America were quick to follow suit.

Niagara Bible Conference Movement

However, among conservative pastors in North America, there was a reaction to this liberal teaching called the Niagara Bible Conference movement. It was a one-week pastor's retreat held every year at Niagara, Ontario, Canada. James Hall Brooks, pastor of the Walnut Street Presbyterian Church of St. Louis, Missouri, was the president and organizer of the Niagara movement from 1875 until his death in 1897. His influence on the Niagara Bible Conference movement has left an indelible imprint on the face of conservative churches in North America.

Brooks scheduled the speakers at the conferences and controlled who said what. In 1840, John Nelson Darby, a Plymouth Brethren pastor from England, proposed his theory of pretribulationalism. Because Brooks was a convert to the views of Darby, Darby's views on prophecy were given center stage at these conferences. At first, speakers with various views on prophecy were chosen. But as Darby's view became more popular, only pretribulational pastors were allowed to speak at the conferences. By 1890, every speaker was pretribulational.

The names of those who attended the Niagara Bible Conferences read like a *Who's Who* among nineteenth- and twentieth-century

Christians. C. I. Scofield, the producer of the Scofield Reference Bible, got his financing to print the Scofield Reference Bible from Lyman Steward. Steward, co-owner of Standard Oil of California, was a regular conference attendee. Lewis Sperry Chafer, founder of Dallas Theological Seminary, was a regular; as were Dwight L. Moody, founder of Moody Bible Institute, and A. C. Gaebelein, founder of Biola Bible College. Leaders of Christian publishing companies such as Eerdmans were also regulars at Niagara. The names of the famous Christian leaders who attended Niagara Bible Conferences would fill this entire page.

The end result of the Niagara Bible Conference movement was the formation of the fundamentalist movement in North America just as WWI was beginning. There was no middle ground in the mind of the fundamentalists: either you accepted the ideas of Hegel and the demythologizers, or you accepted the teaching of Niagara, Brooks, and John Nelson Darby. The pretribulational rapture theory had become inseparable from conservative Christianity.

To this day, that thinking holds sway among conservative Christians. That is why Christian radio, television, and publishing are dominated today by pretribulationalism when it comes to prophecy. The pretribulational rapture theory is nearly universal in conservative circles. Yet there is another reason for this: the pretribulational rapture is what people want to hear, and therefore, it sells. And that is probably why you believe what you believe about prophecy today.

AN ALTERNATE VIEW

This book will offer another opinion: an opinion that believes the literal meaning of the Word of God without resorting to metaphor, allegory, spiritualization, or any other device to persuade you to think the text means something other than what it says. I do not accept anything that casts doubt on the veracity of the Word of

God. I do not believe God is an anti-Semite who has rejected the Jews and now loves only Gentiles. Nor do I believe that he reneges on his promises.

Likewise, I do not accept the pretribulational theories of John Nelson Darby. I believe in the truthfulness of the Word of God just as it was written, without distortion. That is the simple message I will endeavor to get across as we search the Scriptures to find the true plan of God for the redemption of the saints. If you dare to come along, you will discover things that no one on Christian radio or television will tell you.

For a history of the church and eschatological views, see the Appendix for an overview of what have the saints of God believed in past centuries, and why.

For many of you, this will be a scary trip. I will not make promises that you will never see tribulation in this life, as others do. Nor will I promise that you will be raptured so you can have a front row seat in heaven to watch as those evildoers suffer at the hands of an angry God. I will simply demand that every verse of Scripture be interpreted according to the principles of good *exegesis*. Those principles demand that every verse be understood in its literal, historical, grammatical, and contextual sense. Anything else is *eisegesis*.

Why am I so dead set against eisegesis? There is one simple reason: eisegesis allows you to interpret the Scriptures as having plural meanings (the literal meaning plus spiritual meanings). This kind of biblical eisegesis got out of hand with the Pharisees. Philo of Alexandria taught that every verse of the Law of Moses had forty meanings, and all forty meanings must be obeyed perfectly.[5] Likewise, when we see the text as an allegory, or see the text as a metaphor for something else, it allows for multiple meanings of the text. But any text that can have multiple meanings is meaningless. Therefore, we must stay with the literal historical, grammatical, and contextual meaning of the Bible.

ENDNOTES

1 This will be well documented by the many biblical quotes from the Old Testament.

2 John Edward Toews, *Hegelianism: The Path toward Dialectical Humanism*, pg. 66

3 Horton Harris, *The Tubingen School*, pg. 156

4 Ibid., pg. 156 Also see Clark Butler, *G.W.F. Hegel*

5 Bernard Ramm, *Protestant Biblical Interpretation*, pg. 20

Section One

Old Testament Prophecy

CHAPTER ONE

Prophecy From the Beginning

The first mention in the Bible of redemption for the saints of God is found in the story of Adam and Eve. Satan lied to Eve and tempted her to eat the forbidden fruit, which she passed along to Adam. In Genesis 13:13, Eve told God what had happened, and God said to Satan, the serpent:

> "Because you have done this, 'Cursed are you above all livestock and all wild animals! You will crawl on your belly and you will eat dust all the days of your life. And I will put enmity between you and the woman, and between your offspring and hers; *he will crush your head*, and *you will strike his heel.*"
>
> — Genesis 3:14–15

If we understand this passage in a literal way, we see that God promises an offspring of Eve will champion the cause of mankind against the serpent, Satan. Without giving any indication of timing, we are told the offspring will be victorious, but will be wounded by Satan in the process. The issue was not that mankind was innocent and in need of a white knight to defend his innocence, but that mankind was terribly guilty and had no defense for his actions. So God would do for him what he could not do for himself. This is grace. God has granted to mankind his undeserved favor and forgiveness through faith because of the promised actions of a future redeemer. As Paul said in Romans 1:17, the first man (and woman) to be saved were saved by faith in the grace of God.

Moses used the Hebrew word *zera* in Genesis 3:15, which is translated as "offspring" in the NIV. In other verses, it is also translated "seed," "descendent(s)," "son(s)," or "posterity." There is no plural form of *zera*; like bear, deer, or moose, the same form applies to both singular and plural. Furthermore, there is no implication of immediate descent with *zera*. It can be the direct descendant or a descendant a thousand generations removed: all are considered to be *zera*. Therefore, it is the context that determines the meaning of *zera*. In the context of Genesis 3, the woman, Eve, would have a child (the number of generations separating them does not matter), and that child would be our redeemer by conquering Satan on our behalf.

In other words, a redeemer of mankind would emerge from the children of Eve. He would destroy Satan, even though Satan would wound the redeemer in the process. Notice that Satan is the first one in the Bible to tell a lie. That is why Jesus called him the father of lies (John 8:44).

REDEMPTION AND THE WORSHIP OF FERTILITY GODS

Adam and Eve were driven from the Garden of Eden, and their children began to multiply on the earth. And on their heels was Satan, the liar. The evidence of archaeology shows that from the very beginning of human civilization, mankind worshipped idols. There is evidence of fertility god and goddess worship in every ancient culture on earth. Why is that, and how do you suppose it happened?

It happened like this: The father of lies restated, ever so slightly, the story of the Garden of Eden. Eve was promised a son who would redeem the world, but *zera* can be plural as well as singular. Satan's lie was that the woman would redeem the world by producing many children. In an agrarian world, having many children equals prosperity—the more hands to do the work, the more food there is to go around. Having more children also equals more defenders against enemies. And so, in a world that depends on manual labor and walls for defense, fertility equals prosperity, and prosperity equals the "redemption" of mankind. So, through the lie of Satan, fertility became the key to the redemption of mankind.

What better way to become fertile than to worship gods or goddesses of fertility? Ancient male fertility gods were gods of protection and provision, as well as gods of male virility. A male fertility god was usually depicted as a giant with lightning bolts or a spear in his hand. His agrarian symbol was a bull, and his celestial symbol was the sun. The female fertility goddess was a very beautiful woman, very fertile, and always naked. Her agrarian symbol was a cow, and her celestial symbol was the moon. Together, the pair could provide everything mankind needed, as long as they were appeased with offerings.

Satan's distortion became orthodox theology as sin multiplied. The Nephilim were the ones who spread this theology in the world before the flood. The word *Nephilim* means "giants."[1] There are two theories as to the identity of the Nephilim. In traditional Jewish belief, they were fallen angels.[2] This explains why they produced children who were giants and "men of renown." The other theory is they were the sons of Seth who married the daughters of Cain. The reasoning behind this belief is that angels cannot father children because they are spirit beings. Jesus said the angels "in heaven" do not marry (Matthew 22:30); however, these fallen angels were on earth (Jude 6). Furthermore, they forget the Holy Spirit (a spirit being) fathered the God-Man Jesus Christ, so spirit beings are not bound by our laws of nature.

Regardless of whether you believe the Nephilim were fathered by fallen angels (as I do) or by the sons of Seth, the Nephilim were giants who ruled the earth before the flood. The problem was the fallen angels who fathered the Nephilim were not all destroyed by the flood. Genesis 6:4 says, "The Nephilim were on the earth in those days—and afterward also—when the sons of God went to the daughters of men and had children by them." The phrase "and afterward also" indicates the Nephilim continued as the rulers of the earth after the flood as well. This could only happen if the fallen angels continued producing children with human women after the flood. That means some of Noah's female descendants must have married fallen angels and produced children who were Nephilim. And so Satan's lie continued unabated after the flood through the Nephilim.

Other descendants of Noah, such as Canaan, demonstrated an attitude that sympathized with Nephilim theology. And there is one descendant who is singled out in Genesis 10 as having gone far astray.

Nimrod appears to be the one who spread Satan's version of the Garden of Eden story throughout the postdiluvian world. According to Jewish tradition, Nimrod is the one who built the Tower of Babel.[3] He is called a "mighty hunter before the Lord" in Genesis 10:9. The Hebrew preposition *before* means "to stand in front of" and can refer to someone opposed to, or against, that which he is standing before. That is the way Jewish tradition interprets this verse.[4] Nimrod was *against* the Lord. He was a follower of Satan's version of the Garden story. When God stopped the building of the Tower of Babel, confused the tongues, and scattered mankind, Satan's story went with them, thanks to Nimrod. Satan's version of the redemption story became the revised standard version of religion in the ancient postdiluvian world.

What does that have to do with the study of prophecy? Everything. If the redemption of mankind was to come from fertility, what need is there of a future redeemer? The one thing a future redeemer can provide that fertility gods cannot is grace to forgive our sins. But if there is no such grace, what good is a redeemer? And there is no grace in Satan's religion.

The *Epic of Gilgamesh* is important at this point because it taught Satan's theology, and it is what Abram learned as a child. The *Epic of Gilgamesh* tells the story of a Nephilim who became the fifth ruler of Uruk, the city-state that eventually gave its name to modern-day Iraq. The Assyrian Kings List records that Uruk had divine kingship at that time.[5] In other words, the king of Uruk was the ruler of all the city-states in southern Mesopotamia. Gilgamesh was an actual person who lived about 2600 BC, about six hundred years before Abraham's time.[6] His *Epic* records the standard theology of ancient Mesopotamia, illustrated by the many trials Gilgamesh experienced in life and colored by the theology of Satan.

The *Epic* taught that when you died your soul-body traveled to the underworld. There were many entrances to the underworld, but no exits: once you entered, you could never escape. In other words, there was no such thing as resurrection or reincarnation. You did not stop existing; you simply went to the underworld where you would face judgment before the gods.[7] If you had lived a good and upright life and honored the gods with sacrifices, you would live in the upper reaches of the underworld. Your relatives could bring food to your sepulcher, and you could continue to live as you did when you were alive, with wives, cattle, vineyards, and slaves. Furthermore, your relatives could communicate with you through the use of a shaman, or medium.

The underworld was divided into upper and lower regions. If you were a bad person during your life, you would be condemned by the gods to go to the lower reaches of the underworld. The Greeks called it Tartarus, to the Jews it was Gehenna; we call it Hell. There your only food would be mud from the floor of Gehenna, all your possessions would be taken from you, and your days would be filled with toil and torment. There was no salvation, no forgiveness, no escape, and especially no grace. This was strictly a works-retribution system. What you did in this life would directly affect what you got in the next.

This basic story, or a similar story with the same theme, has been found in the earliest religious writings of every nation in the ancient world. Only minor details and the names of the gods were changed from culture to culture. It is the theology derived from Satan's version of the Garden of Eden story and spread throughout the earth after the Tower of Babel incident recorded in Genesis 11.

A NEW COVENANT WITH ABRAHAM

At this point, it would seem that God had lost the battle with Satan for the hearts of mankind. Anyone less than God would have given up and walked away, but that is contrary to the very nature of God. *"His love endures forever"* (Psalm 136). If it did not, none of us would be here. Instead, God chose a man, a sinful Gentile from southern Mesopotamia, to begin a new generation of believers. He was an Amorite named Abram. God changed Abram's beliefs and his name. In Genesis 15:5–6, the Bible says:

> He took him outside and said, "Look up at the heavens and count the stars—if indeed you can count them." Then he said to him, "So shall your offspring be."
> Abram believed the LORD, and he credited it to him as righteousness.

There was grace with the Lord that was not known among the worshipers of the gods. This marked a dramatic shift in the religious thinking of Abram and his descendants. Grace is a concept that is totally unique to Judaism and Christianity. Every other religion in the world still believes in a works-retribution system. But Abram was considered righteous by God because he believed, and for no other reason. Abram was not a sinless man; just ask his wife Sarah. Nevertheless, God saw Abram as righteous because he had faith in God.

In Genesis 17:1–8 the Bible says:

> [T]he LORD appeared to him [Abram] and said, "I am God Almighty, walk before me and be blameless. I will confirm my covenant between me and you and will greatly increase your numbers." Abram fell facedown and God said to him, "As for me this is my covenant with you: You will be the father of many nations. No longer will you be called Abram; your name will be Abraham, for I have made you a father of many nations. I will make nations of you and kings will come from you. I will establish my covenant as an *everlasting covenant* between *me and you* and *your descendants after you* for the generations to come, to be your God and the God of your descendants after you. *The whole of Canaan*, where you are now an alien, I will give as an *everlasting possession* to you and to your descendants after you, and I will be their God."

There are three promises made to Abraham in this passage. The first is that God would be Abraham's God *forever*. The second is that God would be the God of Abraham's descendants *forever*, and the third is that the land of Canaan would be theirs *forever*. Did you notice a theme? The Lord used the phrase *ad-olam* in this passage (as well as using it in every other passage where the land of Canaan is promised to the children of Israel). *Olam* means "forever," but it can also mean "until something else happens." That is the argument used by critics who say Canaan does not belong to Israel. According to some, God removed Abraham's descendents from Canaan; therefore, it is no longer theirs. But *ad-olam* means "forever without end."[8] By qualifying the word *olam* with the adjective *ad*, all questions about God's promise being a temporary one are removed. It is the Hebrew way of saying this promise can never be broken. In short, God promised Abraham that he and his descendants would possess the land of Canaan forever—without any exceptions, no matter what happens.

Yet, two chapters before God's promise of eternal possession of the land, God told Abraham, "you will go to your fathers and be buried in peace at a good old age" (Genesis 15:15). So, Abraham had been told that his physical life would end before the "forever" promises of Genesis 17 were made. With that in mind, what are the implications of this new covenant with Abraham? How would this have changed Abraham's beliefs about the underworld and his future?

As I see it, there are only two options. One: Abraham believed God would bring the land of Canaan down to the underworld so he could live there. Or, two: Abraham believed God would resurrect him, and he would be brought back from the underworld to live in the land of Canaan forever.

Which option do you think Abraham believed? The evidence points to option two. Genesis 22 tells the story of Abraham obeying God by preparing to sacrifice his son, Isaac, on Mount Moriah. When he gets there, Isaac asks his father, "where is the lamb for the burnt offering?"(Genesis 22:7b). Abraham answers, "God Himself will provide the lamb for the burnt offering, my son" (Genesis 22:8). The writer of Hebrews expands upon that verse by explaining that Abraham had faith God would resurrect Isaac from the dead (Hebrews 11:17–19). Yes, after his meeting with God, Abraham had faith in a bodily resurrection. He would be brought back from the dead to live in the Land of Promise, and not the other way around.

Is there any evidence that other ancient worshippers of God had the same hope as Abraham? Yes: Job did. So what did God reveal to Job about the afterlife and the possibility of a resurrection? In Job 19, Job says:

> I know that my redeemer lives, and that in the end he will stand on the earth. And after my skin has been destroyed, yet in my flesh I will see God; I myself will see him with my own eyes—I, and not another. How my heart yearns within me!
>
> — Job 19:25–27

Job believed in an afterlife that included a bodily resurrection. This belief in a personal bodily resurrection from the dead, as well as the possession of the land of Canaan forever, has been the belief of all the true children of Abraham from 2000 BC until the present (see John 11:23–27).

As we move through the Bible, we will see the plan God laid out for the future redemption of his children and for the payback of Satan. We will trace God's plan through prophecies from Deuteronomy to Revelation. It is one never-changing plan, just like the never-changing God who laid it out in the beginning.

However, you must understand that prophecy is progressive. By that I mean each new prophet who came on the scene received a little more insight into God's never-changing eternal plan. Abraham knew more of God's plan than did Adam, Moses knew more than Abraham, David knew more than Moses, and so on.

For example, there is no prophecy in the Old Testament revealing a millennium, but there are Old Testament prophecies which speak about living conditions on earth after the Messiah returns (e.g., Isaiah 11:1–9 and 65:17–25). In the New Testament, Revelation 20:2–7 reveals a thousand-year reign of Christ on earth. Putting these together, we realize that the conditions spoken of by Isaiah will last for a thousand years. That is the result of the progress of prophecy. There is no contradiction, just expansion and explanation. We will see this time and time again through the Bible. It is our job to put the prophecies together so we can understand God's plan of redemption for his saints. Let's start with the prophecies of Moses.

ENDNOTES

1   F. Brown, S. R. Driver, and C. A. Briggs, *Hebrew and English Lexicon*, pg. 658

2   Archie T. Wright, *The Origin of Evil Spirits*, pg. 80-81

3   Abraham Cohen, *Everyman's Talmud*, pg. 30

4   Ibid.

5   Thorkild Jacobsen, *The Sumerian Kings List*, pg. 77

6   Andrew George, *The Babylonian Gilgamesh Epic*, pg. 50

7   John Gray, *Near Eastern Mythology*, pg. 16

8   F. Brown, S. R. Driver, and C. A. Briggs, *Hebrew and English Lexicon*, pg. 761

CHAPTER TWO

Moses: The Preacher of Grace

Many Christians believe Moses taught the Jews to obey the Law as their means of salvation. But Moses actually taught a gospel of grace. How quickly we forget that the first mentions of grace in the Bible were written by Moses when he recorded the promises God made to Adam and Eve, and later to Abraham.

Abraham is the father of all those who have faith, and is used as an example for us New Testament Christians repeatedly by the apostle Paul. Read Galatians 1–3, Ephesians 1–2, and Colossians 1–2 very carefully. Why does Paul stress that there is no difference between Old Testament saints and New Testament saints? Doesn't he say repeatedly that God sees no difference between us? If this is the case, then the promises of redemption made to the Old Testament saints, who believed in God by faith, apply to us as well. The saints of the Old and New Testaments are equal in God's sight and we all have the same future in store.

There are those who say that God has changed his mind over time and has dealt with people differently in different ages. They point to Moses and the Jews as an example, saying that the Jews of the Old Testament were saved by keeping the Law. This system of theology is called *dispensationalism*. Many dispensational teachers today teach that God changed his mind seven times, creating seven distinct dispensations (time periods) that each feature a different way to have a personal relationship with God. Others believe in three, five, nine, or thirteen dispensations, depending how many times they believe God changed his mind, all of which directly contradict James 1:17, which says, "the Father . . . does not change like shifting shadows."

Furthermore, dispensationalism fails to notice the purpose of the Law, repeated throughout Exodus, Leviticus, Numbers, and Deuteronomy: obeying the Law demonstrated one's faith in God, which God demanded from Abraham when he gave his promise of eternal life back in Genesis 17:1. Faith, demonstrated by obedience, resulted in temporal benefits as well as the personal assurance of salvation. There is an exact parallel between keeping the Law to demonstrate your faith in Jehovah and keeping the commands of Jesus and the apostles to demonstrate your faith in Christ. In both cases, without that demonstration of faith by obedience, it is impossible to know if one has faith, as James points out clearly, saying, "Faith without deeds is dead" (James 2:26b). Therefore, keeping the Law was not for the purpose of earning salvation; it was the demonstration that you had faith in the God of the resurrection. Furthermore, the covenant of Abraham, which promised eternal salvation to those who believed, was open to everyone, Jew and Gentile alike.

Moses makes those two points very clear in Deuteronomy 29, where he says:

> These are the terms of the covenant the LORD commanded Moses to make with the Israelites in Moab, in addition to the covenant he had made with them at Horeb.
>
> Moses summoned all the Israelites and said to them:
> Your eyes have seen all that the LORD did in Egypt to Pharaoh, to all his officials and to all his land. With

your own eyes you saw those great trials, those signs and great wonders. But to this day the Lord has not given you a mind that understands or eyes that see or ears that hear. During the forty years that I led you through the wilderness, your clothes did not wear out, nor did the sandals on your feet. You ate no bread and drank no wine or other fermented drink. I did this so that you might know that I am the Lord your God.

When you reached this place, Sihon king of Heshbon and Og king of Bashan came out to fight against us, but we defeated them. We took their land and gave it as an inheritance to the Reubenites, the Gadites and the half-tribe of Manasseh.

Carefully follow the terms of this covenant, so that you may prosper in everything you do.

— Deuteronomy 29:1–9

There was a direct tie between their faith in God, their obedience to God's Law, and their receipt of God's blessings. It is the same way with us and our relationship with the Lord, the only difference being God had set Israel aside as a nation to receive his special care and attention at that time. If they had completely obeyed, I am sure they would be the center of nations today. They would be the rulers of the earth. However, for them to obey, they would have to have changed hearts. Many of them did have a changed heart at this point in their forty-year journey, because they were the new generation, but others did not. Nevertheless, the offer to be a chosen one of God was open to all nations, as is made clear by the next few verses.

All of you are standing today in the presence of the Lord your God—your leaders and chief men, your elders and officials, and all the other men of Israel, together with your children and your wives, and the

foreigners living in your camps who chop your wood
and carry your water. You are standing here in order to
enter into a covenant with the LORD your God, a covenant the LORD is making with you this day and sealing
with an oath, to confirm you this day as his people, that
he may be your God as he promised you and as he swore
to your fathers, Abraham, Isaac and Jacob. *I am making
this covenant, with its oath, not only with you who are
standing here with us today in the presence of the LORD
our God but also with those who are not here today.*
                                    — Deuteronomy 29:10–15

Not only does Moses mention the foreigners living among the
Jews of that day, he goes on to mention all those of faith that will be
born in future generations. That's you and me!

Moses continues in chapter 30, making it very clear to all he is
not talking about receiving the blessings of God by sheer wooden
obedience to a law code. There is so much meaning in Moses'
statement for us Christians. God is not impressed by those who
obey the Law but do not have a changed heart. It is the changed
heart that makes the obedience meaningful. Moses says:

Now what I am commanding you today is not too difficult for you or beyond your reach. It is not up in heaven,
so that you have to ask, "Who will ascend into heaven to
get it and proclaim it to us so we may obey it?" Nor is it
beyond the sea, so that you have to ask, "Who will cross
the sea to get it and proclaim it to us so we may obey it?"
No, the word is very near you; it is in your mouth and in
your heart so you may obey it.

See, I set before you today life and prosperity, death
and destruction. For I command you today to love the

LORD your God, to walk in obedience to him, and to
keep his commands, decrees and laws; then you will live
and increase, and the LORD your God will bless you in
the land you are entering to possess.

— Deuteronomy 30:11–16

The Jews of Israel could not please God and receive his blessing
without a heart change. This is made clear by the next verses.

But if your heart turns away and you are not obedient,
and if you are drawn away to bow down to other gods
and worship them, I declare to you this day that you
will certainly be destroyed. You will not live long in the
land you are crossing the Jordan to enter and possess.

This day I call the heavens and the earth as witnesses against you that *I have set before you life and death,
blessings and curses. Now choose life*, so that you and
your children may live and that you may love the LORD
your God, listen to his voice, and hold fast to him. For
the LORD is your life, and he will give you many years
in the land he swore to give to your fathers, Abraham,
Isaac and Jacob.

— Deuteronomy 30:17–20

God wanted to establish a nation of born-again believers who
would shine the gospel into every corner of the earth. The choice
God offered them was between life and death, between loving him
or serving other gods. Their choice would result in either blessings
or curses. Those who had the faith of Abraham responded out of
love for God by keeping the Law. After that first generation, however,
many did not choose life, and likewise chose not to keep the Law,
which resulted in the loss of both eternal life and temporal blessings.

FAITH AND OBEDIENCE IN THE NEW TESTAMENT

This is the same gospel message found in the New Testament, originally preached to Jews by John the Baptist, and later preached to Jews and Gentiles alike by Jesus and the apostles. John the Baptist said:

> "*Produce fruit in keeping with repentance.* And do not think you can say to yourselves, 'We have Abraham as our father.' I tell you that out of these stones God can raise up children for Abraham. The ax is already at the root of the trees, and every tree that does not produce good fruit will be cut down and thrown into the fire.
>
> "*I baptize you with water for repentance.* But after me comes one who is more powerful than I, whose sandals I am not worthy to carry. *He will baptize you with the Holy Spirit and fire.* His winnowing fork is in his hand, and he will clear his threshing floor, gathering his wheat into the barn and burning up the chaff with unquenchable fire."
>
> — Matthew 3:8–12

Some argue that John the Baptist was still preaching an Old Testament message. They are right—of course he was, and that's the point. Both Testaments teach the same gospel message. Peter preached that message at the end of his life, saying:

> Peter, an apostle of Jesus Christ,
>
> To God's elect, exiles scattered throughout the provinces of Pontus, Galatia, Cappadocia, Asia and Bithynia, who have been chosen according to the foreknowledge of God the Father, through the sanctifying work of the

Spirit, *to be obedient to Jesus Christ and sprinkled with his blood*: Grace and peace be yours in abundance.

— 1 Peter 1:1–2

Peter is calling those of faith to a life of obedience to the teachings of Jesus. Why? Because obedience demonstrates our faith. The apostle John preached the same message, saying:

We know that we have come to know him if we keep his commands. Whoever says, "I know him," but does not do what he commands is a liar, and the truth is not in that person.

— 1 John 2:3–4

When the apostle Paul wrote to the church in Rome, which was a mixed church of Jews and Gentiles, he specifically tells them the purpose of his letter in his opening remarks. He said, "Through him and for his name's sake, we have received grace and apostleship to call people from among all the Gentiles to *the obedience that comes from faith*" (Romans 1:3). Paul tells them plainly their obedience to the commands of God will be the demonstration of their faith.

That is why the apostle Paul quotes from Deuteronomy 30:11–14 when he reasons with the Romans that the gospel message is one of faith, and is available to all, Jew and Gentile alike. Paul said:

Moses writes this about the righteousness that is by the law: "The person who does these things will live by them." But the righteousness that is by faith says: "Do not say in your heart, 'Who will ascend into heaven?'" (that is, to bring Christ down) "or 'Who will descend into the deep?'" (that is, to bring Christ up from the dead) But what does it say? "The word is near you; it is in your mouth and in your heart," that is, the message concerning faith that we proclaim: If you declare with your mouth, "Jesus is Lord," and believe in your heart that God raised him from the dead, you will be saved. For it is with your heart that you believe and are justified, and it is with your mouth that you profess your faith and are saved. As Scripture says, "Anyone who believes in him will never be put to shame. For there is no difference between Jew and Gentile—the same Lord is Lord of all and richly blesses all who call upon his name."

— Romans 10:5–12

GRACE IN THE OLD TESTAMENT

Many critics of Covenant theology (the idea that Old Testament saints and New Testament saints are saved in the same manner and are one body) point out that it was Moses who codified the sacrificial system for the Jews, establishing a salvation-by-works system. If those same critics would look a little more closely, they would see the sacrificial system established by Moses was not a method of salvation, but instead screams out grace.

When a worshipper took a sacrifice to the priest, the animal was roasted on the altar. Then a portion was removed by the priest and set aside as "holy unto the Lord." That set aside portion was called qadesh, which comes from the word "chop," and means "holy," "consecrated," or "sacred." (The plural form, qadeshim, is a name used for saints in the Old Testament. The writers of the Septuagint chose to translate qadeshim as hagios, which also means "holy," "sacred," or "consecrated." Likewise, hagios is used in the Greek as the name of the New Testament saints. Every epistle of Paul begins with a salute to the *hagios,* or saints, in whatever city he was writing to. In other words, we are the *qadeshim* of God.)

The *qadesh* was chosen by the priest to be the Lord's portion. It had nothing to do with the worthiness of the worshipper. Removing a portion of the sacrifice made it God's choice alone, and resulted in an acceptable sacrifice by God's grace.

In other words, the Lord's portion of the sacrifice was symbolic of those set aside by God's grace to be his chosen ones. And, because God uses that symbolism to name the people he has chosen to be set aside for him, the whole sacrificial system screams out grace. People were not saved by their righteous works, or by the action of bringing a sacrifice. Their sacrifice did not earn their salvation, it only pointed to the fact that they had been saved by God's sovereign grace. The Old Testament Jewish believers and we New Testament Gentile believers are the *qadesh* of the Lord. We, the saints of God, have been set aside as the Lord's portion by his grace alone.

But Abraham and Moses were not the only ones in the Old Testament to realize that salvation was by grace and not by works. Noah found "grace" in the eyes of God (Genesis 6:8). It's too bad the NIV has chosen to change the translation of *qhen* from "grace" to "favor." However, both words have the same meaning in the Hebrew. It means "to find acceptance" in the eyes of God. David begged for that same *qhen,* saying:

> Have mercy on me, O God, according to your unfailing love; according to your great compassion blot out my transgressions. Wash away all my iniquity and cleanse me from my sin. . . .
>
> Cleanse me with hyssop, and I will be clean; wash me, and I will be whiter than snow. . . Hide your face from my sins and blot out all my iniquity.

> Create in me a pure heart, O God, and renew a
> steadfast spirit within me. Do not cast me from your
> presence or take your Holy Spirit from me. Restore
> to me the joy of your salvation and grant me a willing
> spirit, to sustain me. . . .
> Save me from the guilt of bloodshed, O God, you
> who are God my Savior, and my tongue will sing of your
> righteousness. Open my lips, Lord, and my mouth will
> declare your praise. You do not delight in sacrifice, or I
> would bring it; you do not take pleasure in burnt offer-
> ings. My sacrifice, O God, is a broken spirit; a broken
> and contrite heart you, God, will not despise.
> — Psalm 51:1–17

When David realized God had forgiven his sins, he sang out in
praise to God, saying:

> Blessed is the man whose transgressions are forgiven,
> whose sins are covered. Blessed is the man whose sin
> the Lord does not count against him, and in whose spir-
> it is no deceit.
> — Psalm 32:1–2

Grace for salvation can also be found in Isaiah, Jeremiah,
Ezekiel, Hosea, and Zechariah, as well as numerous Psalms, but we
don't have time to look at them all. The point is, even though the
gospel of grace was preached to the saints of the Old Testament,
only a few believed. Isn't that the same way it is now with those of
us who hear the New Testament gospel? How many Western nations
consider every citizen to be a member of the "church"? Yet, how
many of those members are born-again believers?

When all is said and done, there has always been only one way
to obtain eternal life: through faith in God, demonstrated by a

changed life. There never has been an "Age of Law," when God saved people only because they kept the Law, contrasted with the "Age of Grace," when God saves people by faith alone. God is the same yesterday, today, and forever, and he has always saved people who have faith. To be more specific, he has always offered grace to those who have the faith of Abraham and who walk in obedience to his Word. As Paul said in Romans 2:28–29:

> A man is not a Jew if he is only one outwardly, nor is circumcision merely outward and physical. No, a man is a Jew if he is one inwardly; and circumcision is circumcision of the heart, by the Spirit, not by the written code. Such a man's praise is not from men, but from God.

THE ROLE OF THE HOLY SPIRIT

There is only one significant difference between the Old Testament saints and the New Testament saints; that is, the *presence* of the Holy Spirit for Old Testament saints versus the *indwelling* of the Holy Spirit for New Testament saints. In some cases, the prophets of old could not understand their own prophecies concerning Jesus because they did not have the indwelling of the Holy Spirit, as we do (see I Peter 1:10–12). None of the Old Testament prophets expected a savior to come as a meek and mild preacher, riding on a donkey! Yet this event, recorded in Matthew 21, fulfilled the prophecies written centuries earlier.

The lack of an indwelling Holy Spirit caused Peter to make some of the dumbest statements found in the New Testament (see Matthew 17:4). It seems like he had "foot-in-mouth" disease, but only from our perspective. That begs the question, at what point did Peter and the apostles stop being Old Testament saints and become New Testament saints? Wasn't it after the resurrection, when Jesus breathed on them and they received the Holy Spirit? However, they didn't start *believing* at that point; they started *understanding*. In contrast, we have the indwelling of the Holy Spirit, which is a constant source of the knowledge of spiritual truth, and Jesus promised our source of truth will stay with us forever. The Holy Spirit will not desert members of the church seven years before the end (see John 14:15–17a).

If you want some proof of this statement, other than another argument from Scripture, read the Psalms. If you are a Christian, the Holy Spirit will speak to your heart as you read. That is testimony from the Holy Spirit that those words, written by Old Testament Jews to Old Testament Jews, were written not just for them, but also for you and me. Don't you realize that God wrote those Psalms with you in mind? The reason the Psalms—and all of the Old Testament— speak to your heart is that they were written by the same Holy Spirit who lived with them, and who lives in you and me. The words of the Holy Spirit are for all of us, and that includes the prophecies of the Old Testament which have not yet been fulfilled. Therefore, the indwelling of the Holy Spirit, versus the presence of the Holy Spirit, does not constitute a separation between Old and New Testament saints that will cause us to have separate futures, but allows us to have a fuller understanding of God's Word.

The indwelling of the Holy Spirit gives us insight into the Scriptures, but it brings responsibility with it. It makes us responsible for reading, understanding, and acting upon the Word of God. We will bear a much harsher judgment if we have not obeyed the guidance that is freely offered by the Holy Spirit. If your Bible is gathering dust, get it off the shelf. Open it up and follow along as we study the prophets of both the Old and New Testaments.

With your Bible open, let's look at a very early prophecy that sets the framework for God's future plan for *all* the saints of God, whether they be Jew or Gentile.

MOSES' PROPHECY FOR THE SAINTS OF GOD

The nation of Israel did not exist before the time of the exodus. Jacob and his sons lived as migrant ranchers in the land of Canaan. But God had set in motion a plan to fulfill his promise to Abraham by saving this small group of sheepherders when he sent them to Egypt in order to save them from famine. When their numbers had grown from seventy people to well over one million, they were ready to form their own nation. This was all part of God's plan of salvation, and it would affect every believer through all the ages.

As the fledgling nation camped on the shores of the Jordan River, they listened to one of Moses' last sermons. None of the previous four hundred and thirty years had happened by chance. And, as if God was trying to emphasize that point, he gave them a prophecy through Moses concerning their future as a nation in the land of Canaan. That prophecy remains as the foundation stone of all biblical prophecy concerning the redemption and salvation of the saints of God.

In chapters 27–29 of Deuteronomy, Moses divides the children of Israel into two groups. After they entered the Promised Land, half were to stand on Mount Ebal and half on Mount Gerizim. Both mountains are in Samaria. The first group, standing on Mount Ebal, was to pronounce curses on Israel if they should ever stop following the Lord. The second group, standing on Mount Gerizim, was to pronounce blessings on Israel for following the Lord. In chapter 29, Moses explains very clearly these blessings and curses were for the prosperity of Israel as a nation, because they demonstrated the faith of the Jews in their God.

In Deuteronomy 30, God gave Moses a vision of the future of the fledgling nation. All of the curses that were to be pronounced on Mount Ebal would, in fact, come true because Israel would desert the Lord and follow other gods. However, not because they were good or righteous or deserving in any way, but because they were God's chosen people, the blessings of Mount Gerizim would also come true.

The first seven verses of Deuteronomy 30 set the foundation stone of all redemptive prophecy. They spell out God's plan, which has never changed from that day to this. The plan includes the permanent establishment of the nation of Israel and the future redemption of all of God's saints. We will see this foundation stone being built upon as we search the other prophets. There the details of the plan are further explained, but the plan remains intact. That is the nature of progressive prophecy.

In Deuteronomy 30:1–5, Moses says:

> When all these blessings and curses I have set before you come on you and you take them to heart wherever the LORD your God disperses you among the nations, and when you and your children return to the LORD your God and obey him with all your heart and with all your soul according to everything I command you today, then the LORD your God will restore your fortunes and have compassion on you and gather you again from all the nations where he scattered you. Even if you have been banished to the most distant land under the heavens, from there the LORD your God will gather you and bring you back. He will bring you to the land that belonged to your ancestors, and you will take possession of it. He will make you more prosperous and numerous than your ancestors.

The first five verses of this promise concern the repentance of Israel along with a miraculous gathering of Israel from wherever they have been scattered on earth. They will be brought back to the land that was promised to Abraham forever. Not only that, they will become more prosperous than ever before. The blessings and curses of Deuteronomy 27–29 fell upon the nation of Israel, over and over, throughout the books of Judges, Samuel, and Kings, because they fell into a cyclical pattern of backsliding and revival. However, this passage goes on to talk about more than just temporal blessings.

> The LORD your God will circumcise your hearts and the hearts of your descendants, so that you may love him with all your heart and with all your soul, and live. The LORD your God will put all these curses on your enemies who hate and persecute you.
>
> — Deuteronomy 30:6–7

Those who are miraculously gathered by God will be saved! They will be given a new heart that will love God the way we all should love God. Notice the number of events that Moses predicts will take place in the history of the nation. First, Moses says, "when all these blessings and curses I have set before you come upon you." In other words, everything Moses predicted in Genesis 27–29 has either taken place or will take place. The Jewish nation did enter and possess the Promised Land. They did fall away from following God and turn to idols. God did curse them and they scattered throughout the world. All of this began happening, and continued happening, both before and after the Babylonian captivity. This was not just a one-time event. Like so many other prophecies, there are several *typical,* or partial, fulfillments that foreshadow the final total and literal fulfillment, which is still in the future. In all of these previous punishments, there was never a miraculous gathering of the saints caused by the hand of God that involved giving a new heart to the children of Israel.

Israel fell away many times during the days of the Judges. They were punished by God, which brought about a temporary repentance. The tribe of Dan was scattered somewhere in the nations at this time, and Benjamin became a remnant living in the territory of Judah. Then the ten northern tribes fell away during the Kingdom days. They have been scattered throughout the world and have not yet been regathered.

Next, Judah fell away and was sent into seventy years of captivity. This is the scattering many people think of when they read this promise, but it was only a typical scattering, along with several others. After the resurrection of Christ, Israel was again scattered as a result of the wars of the Jews against Rome. There were three wars in all, with the last one ending in AD 135. That event began the final Diaspora (scattering) of the nation of Israel, which ceased to exist as a nation from 135 until 1948. Even now, only a portion of the worldwide population of Jews has returned to Israel, and only a small portion of them are believers in the God of the Bible. The total miraculous regathering and heart change of Israel has not been fulfilled, so that prophecy still awaits a literal fulfillment.

When it is fulfilled, several things will take place. There will be a miraculous gathering of Israel from the four corners of the earth. In other words, there will be a "rapture" of Israel. I can guarantee God is not going to wander around the world looking for Jews to offer them a bus ticket to Israel! This will be an instantaneous gathering, taking place in a moment, "in the twinkling of an eye." There is only one miraculous gathering promised to Israel, and it will happen in fulfillment of this prophecy. That final fulfillment of Israel turning back to God will happen on the day of the Lord. We will see this statement confirmed repeatedly in the prophets.

The Promised Land will be given back to the true seed of Abraham as an eternal possession. Every Jew who enters the Promised Land at that time will have a circumcised heart that will not let him stray from God ever again. In other words, they will be born again and be "complete" Jews, not just physical Jews. Furthermore, the resurrection of Abraham which was promised so long ago awaits this miraculous gathering of Israel. Finally, Abraham's eternal home will be given to him. The resurrection of the saints and the miraculous regathering of Israel will take place in nearly simultaneously (see I Corinthians 15:20–25, and I Thessalonians 4:13–18). At that time, the salvation and sanctification of the Jews will be complete and eternal.

The final event mentioned in Moses' prophecy is the destruction of the enemies of Israel. All of the curses that have fallen on Israel over the years will now fall on the enemies of God's people in one massive blow. Although we are not told in this passage who that enemy will be, we know they will be destroyed when God redeems Israel.

To summarize Deuteronomy 30:1–7 into a short list of events that will occur when this prophecy is fulfilled, and add what we know about the plan of God from Abraham's experience: There will be a resurrection of the saints, a rapture (miraculous regathering) of the Jews, a rebuilding of the nation of Israel, followed by a destruction of Israel's enemies. But the details of these events are not revealed in these verses. That is why progressive prophecy is so important.

CHAPTER THREE

Isaiah: The King of the Prophets

L et's start our survey of the Old Testament prophets with Isaiah, the king of the prophets. Isaiah was called to prophesy during the reigns of Uzziah, Jotham, Ahaz and Hezekiah, from 740 to 680 BC. During his time as a prophet of Judah, the Assyrians were the major enemy of Israel and Judah. In 722 BC, the ten northern tribes of Israel were taken captive by Assyria and dispersed throughout the Assyrian Empire.

The central theme of Isaiah is the judgment of God that will fall on all of the enemies of God at some time in the future. This judgment will happen on the day of the Lord. His theme can be easily followed through the book by tracing the passages that begin with references to "in that day," or "on the day when." As an Old Testament prophet, Isaiah had no idea when "that day" would take place, but he was certain everything he heard from the Lord would occur "in that day."

This is not a promise that everything will start and end in a twenty-four hour period "on that day"; however, everything will begin "on that day" and continue until every promise has been fulfilled. Judah and Israel will receive punishment from God for the sin of falling away from following the one true God. But the majority of Isaiah's work concentrates on the judgments of the nations around them because of their part in destroying the "children of God." Those nations were enemies of Israel then, and they are enemies of Israel now. They will play a crucial role as allies of the Antichrist, as we will see in Daniel's prophecies. Assyria is mentioned as one of those nations to be judged, along with several others, all of which are now Muslim nations. Iran now occupies the territory of ancient Assyria. This is a fact that we should not overlook.

All of the enemy nations mentioned by Isaiah are to receive their recompense from God on the day of the Lord (Isaiah 35:4), but they are not the main object of God's wrath on that day. Only one nation is singled out as the central target of God's wrath: the nation of Babylon. That fact does not make sense in the context of Isaiah's time, because during Isaiah's lifetime, Babylon was not a major threat to anyone. They were a captive nation of the Assyrian Empire and were held under yearly tribute. It would not be until seventy years after the death of Isaiah that the grandfather of Nebuchadnezzar would lead a successful revolt for independence from Assyrian domination. Nevertheless, Babylon is singled out as enemy number one in the book of Isaiah.

ISAIAH'S PROPHECY FOR JUDAH

Isaiah opens his prophecy with a message to the children of Judah concerning her rebellion against the Lord. He says:

> Why should you be beaten anymore? Why do you persist in rebellion? Your whole head is injured, your whole heart afflicted. From the sole of your foot to the top of your head there is no soundness— only wounds and welts and open sores, not cleansed or bandaged or soothed with olive oil. Your country is desolate, your cities burned with fire; your fields are being stripped

by foreigners right before you, laid waste as when overthrown by strangers. Daughter Zion is left like a shel-
ter in a vineyard, like a hut in a cucumber field, like a
city under siege. Unless the LORD Almighty had left us
some survivors, we would have become like Sodom, we
would have been like Gomorrah.

— Isaiah 1:5–9

The punishments promised by God, and pronounced on Mount
Ebal, were happening in Samaria and Judah. Assyria would be used
by God to destroy the ten northern tribes. After Isaiah's death,
Babylon would be responsible for destroying Judah. God's judgment
would fall upon the sinners in Israel through these two nations. Yet,
the central theme of Isaiah's prophecies is not the destruction that
happened in 586 BC; it is the "day of the Lord" which will happen at
the end of time. Therefore, you must not view Isaiah with a preterist
mindset and say everything has been fulfilled. Isaiah's prophecies of
the day of the Lord are yet to be fulfilled.

Even though at the present time the Jewish people have
established themselves as a nation again, a literal understanding
of Isaiah's prophecies predicts they will be scattered once more,
as God uses foreign enemies, specifically the territories that were
once Assyria and Babylon, to punish Israel for their sins. Afterward,
God's attention will turn to destroying those who are destroying his
people.

Referring to the enemies of Israel on the day of the Lord, Isaiah
says:

Go into the rocks, hide in the ground from the fearful
presence of the LORD and the splendor of his majesty!
The eyes of the arrogant will be humbled and human
pride brought low; the LORD alone will be exalted *in
that day*. The LORD Almighty has *a day in store* for all

the proud and lofty, for all that is exalted (and they will be humbled), for all the cedars of Lebanon, tall and lofty, and all the oaks of Bashan, for all the towering mountains and all the high hills, for every lofty tower and every fortified wall, for every trading ship and every stately vessel. The arrogance of man will be brought low and human pride humbled; the LORD alone will be exalted *in that day*, and the idols will totally disappear."

— Isaiah 2:10–18

THE JUDGMENT OF BABYLON

There will be a day when all sinners will be destroyed, both Jew and Gentile. No specific enemy is mentioned in this passage of Isaiah, but it doesn't take long for that situation to change. Isaiah focuses his prophecies of judgment on Babylon. For instance, he says in chapter 13:

A prophecy against **Babylon** that Isaiah son of Amoz saw: Raise a banner on a bare hilltop, shout to them; beckon to them to enter the gates of the nobles. I have commanded those I prepared for battle; I have summoned my warriors to carry out my wrath— those who rejoice in my triumph. Listen, a noise on the mountains, like that of a great multitude! Listen, an uproar among the kingdoms, like nations massing together! The LORD Almighty is mustering an army for war. *They come from faraway lands, from the ends of the heavens*— the LORD and the weapons of his wrath— to destroy the whole country. Wail, for the *day of the Lord* is near; it will come like destruction from the Almighty. Because of this, all hands will go limp, every heart will melt with fear. Terror will seize them, pain and anguish will grip them; they will writhe like a woman in labor. They will look aghast at each other, their faces aflame.

— Isaiah 13:1–6

The prophecy is directed against Babylon, the same enemy used by God to destroy Judah and destroy his temple in 586 BC. Babylon will be the object of his wrath on the day of the Lord. Isaiah says they are destroyed by the wrath of God. Notice also, there are two sources God calls upon in this prophecy to raise his army. The first source is from the distant lands of the earth: this is a human army. The second source is from the ends of the heavens: this is an angelic army. Both will be used by God "in that day" to carry out the destruction of Babylon and her allies. Isaiah continues his prophecy against Babylon, saying:

> See, the day of the Lord is coming—a cruel day, with wrath and fierce anger—to make the land desolate and destroy the sinners within it. The stars of heaven and their constellations will not show their light. The rising sun will be darkened and the moon will not give its light. I will punish the world for its evil, the wicked for their sins. I will put an end to the arrogance of the haughty and will humble the pride of the ruthless. I will make people scarcer than pure gold, more rare than the gold of Ophir. Therefore I will make the heavens tremble; and the earth will shake from its place at the wrath of the LORD Almighty, in the day of his burning anger.
>
> — Isaiah 13:9–13

This is the same day of destruction mentioned in Isaiah 2:10–18. In Isaiah chapter 13, Babylon is again named as the leader of God's enemies. Notice also, this destruction of the enemies of Israel takes place on a single day, called the "day of the Lord." We learn the sun, moon, and stars will be affected and the earth will have giant earthquakes. Jesus Christ referred to this day when warned his disciples in Matthew 24:29, saying:

> "Immediately after the distress of those days 'the sun will be darkened, and the moon will not give its light; the stars will fall from the sky, and the heavenly bodies will be shaken.'"

This is a one-time event that happens at the end of time in conjunction with the salvation of Israel.

In this same context, in order to emphasis that God's wrath will be against one nation more than any other, God says in Isaiah 13:19–20:

> Babylon, the jewel of the kingdoms, the glory of the Babylonians pride, will be overthrown by God like Sodom and Gomorrah. She will never be inhabited or lived in again through all generations: *no Arab will pitch his tent there*, no shepherd will rest his flocks there.

Do you think it is meaningless or a coincidence that Babylon has been mentioned twice so far as being destroyed by God on the day of the Lord?

The interesting thing to note about this passage is that Babylon was not the home of the Arabs in Isaiah's day. It was not until the rise of Islam in the seventh century AD that the Arabs began to dominate the land of Babylon. Furthermore, Babylonia has never yet been uninhabited. After the fall of Nebuchadnezzar's kingdom, Babylon became the capital of the Persian kingdom. When the Persians fell, Babylon became the capital of Alexander's kingdom, and when he died, Babylon became the capital of Seleucus' kingdom.

When that kingdom was overthrown by the Parthians, the territory of Babylon became the capital of the Parthians, and later of the Sassanians. They, in turn, were overthrown by the Muslim invaders, who remain in charge today. The old city of Babylon fell into ruins in the third century AD, but a new capital was built a few miles away, and the life of the nation continued. Therefore, we know this passage was not fulfilled by any event in ancient history. It awaits its fulfillment for the return of the Son of Man on the day of the Lord.

Isaiah 13 is definitely meant for the very end of times. Yet, regardless of whether this prophecy was meant for fulfillment in our near future, or at some distant future, the enemy at the center of God's predicted wrath is Babylon. The next chapter in Isaiah makes that very clear:

> *On the day* the LORD gives you relief from your suffering and turmoil and from the harsh labor forced on you, you will take up this taunt against the *king of Babylon*: How the oppressor has come to an end! How his fury has ended! The LORD has broken the rod of the wicked, the scepter of the rulers, which in anger struck down peoples with unceasing blows, and in fury subdued nations with relentless aggression.
>
> All the lands are at rest and at peace; they break into singing. Even the junipers and the cedars of Lebanon gloat over you and say, "Now that you have been laid low, no one comes to cut us down." The realm of the dead below is all astir to meet you at your coming; it rouses the spirits of the departed to greet you— all those who were leaders in the world; it makes them rise from their thrones— all those who were kings over the nations. They will all respond, they will say to you, "You also have become weak, as we are; you have become like

us." All your pomp has been brought down to the grave, along with the noise of your harps; maggots are spread out beneath you and worms cover you.

How you have fallen from heaven, morning star, son of the dawn! You have been cast down to the earth, you who once laid low the nations! You said in your heart, "I will ascend to the heavens; I will raise my throne above the stars of God; I will sit enthroned on the mount of assembly, on the utmost heights of Mount Zaphon. I will ascend above the tops of the clouds; I will make myself like the Most High." But you are brought down to the realm of the dead, to the depths of the pit.

Those who see you stare at you, they ponder your fate: "Is this the man who shook the earth and made kingdoms tremble, the man who made the world a wilderness, who overthrew its cities and would not let his captives go home?" All the kings of the nations lie in state, each in his own tomb. But you are cast out of your tomb like a rejected branch; you are covered with the slain, with those pierced by the sword, those who descend to the stones of the pit. Like a corpse trampled underfoot, you will not join them in burial, for you have destroyed your land and killed your people. Let the offspring of the wicked never be mentioned again. Prepare a place to slaughter his children for the sins of their ancestors; they are not to rise to inherit the land and cover the earth with their cities."

— Isaiah 14:3–21

For years, this passage has been the subject of allegorical interpretation, with the claim that the last king of Babylon, who is the subject of the prophecy, is actually Satan. That is based on the hyperbolic statements of verses 12–14. Yet the apostle Paul tells us that these are the very statements that will be made by the "man of lawlessness" who sits in the temple of God in the last days (II Thessalonians 2:4). Furthermore, if you read the whole passage, it is clear in the context that the passage refers to an arrogant, boastful, and cruel king. He will be the last king of Babylon at the very end of days. He will not be buried with his people because he will be destroyed by the wrath of God when God returns to redeem his saints.

THE JUDGMENT OF ASSYRIA

However, there is also a special wrath awaiting the final king of Assyria. He is destined for the lake of fire, as Isaiah tells us in chapter 30:

> The voice of the LORD will shatter **Assyria**; with his rod he will strike them down. Every stroke the LORD lays on them with his punishing club will be to the music of timbrels and harps, as he fights them in battle with the blows of his arm. **Topheth** has long been prepared; it has been made ready for the king. Its fire pit has been made deep and wide, with an abundance of fire and wood; the breath of the LORD, like a stream of burning sulfur, sets it ablaze.
>
> — Isaiah 30:31–33

A *topheth* is a burning pit that was used for burning trash and the bodies of sacrificial victims. In Revelation, God's *topheth* is called the "lake of fire." God will destroy this man at the same time he destroys the final king of Babylon. There is a definite connection between the king of Babylon and the king of Assyria which won't be explained until we get to the prophecies of Daniel. From those prophecies it will become clear that both kings are the same man.

In the meantime, notice the destruction of this man is accompanied by timbrels and harps. The saints of God are singing as God destroys Israel's enemies. That is because we are safely out of harm's way, and we have front row seats as the destruction of our enemies takes place. However, where we will be is not made clear until we get to Revelation 19.

THE RESURRECTION OF THE SAINTS

The resurrection of the saints, which was promised to Abraham, and the miraculous gathering promised by Moses, will be the source of all this music. The miraculous gathering of the saints is further described by Isaiah in chapter 27:

> In that day the LORD will thresh from the flowing Euphrates to the Wadi of Egypt, and you, Israel, will be *gathered up one by one*. And in that day a *great trumpet will sound*. Those who were perishing in Assyria and those who were exiled in Egypt will come and worship the LORD on the holy mountain in Jerusalem.
>
> — Isaiah 27:12–13

The word "thresh" in this passage, the Hebrew word *habat*, is not the word for a general harvest. It is used to indicate a very small threshing, such as that by Gideon in a wine press to keep out of sight of the Midianites. Likewise, the action of the angels is to *laqat*, to "pluck up," or to "glean," the Israelites. This is what Ruth did in the fields of Boaz. It takes place at the end of the harvest, never before. This is how God will carry out the miraculous gathering of Israel he promised through Moses in Deuteronomy 30:4–5.

The apostle Paul refers to this passage in I Thessalonians 4:13–18, and it is a passage that is often taken out of context. In the context of I Thessalonians 4, this gathering happens at the same time as the resurrection promised to Abraham, and in conjunction with the return of the Lord from heaven on the day of the Lord. Both of those events happen at the end of the "time of Jacob's trouble," according to Isaiah. Look at what Isaiah says will happen on the day of the Lord:

> A prophecy against *Babylon* that Isaiah son of Amoz saw: Raise a *banner on a bare hilltop, shout to them*; beckon to them to enter the gates of the nobles. I have commanded those I prepared for battle; I have summoned my warriors to carry out my wrath— those who rejoice in my triumph. Listen, a noise on the mountains, like that of a great multitude! Listen, an uproar among the kingdoms, like nations massing together! The LORD Almighty is mustering an army for war. *They come from faraway lands, from the ends of the heavens*— the LORD and the weapons of his wrath— to destroy the whole country.
>
> — Isaiah 13:1–5

Again, the dual source of God's army is mentioned. They come from faraway lands, and from the ends of the heavens. They are human and angelic. The purpose for these two armies will become very clear when we get to Revelation. The banner on a hill top and the sound of the shout will not be silent signals.

Listen to what Isaiah goes on to say a few chapters later:

> *All you people of the world*, you who live on the earth, when a banner is raised on the mountains, you will see it, and when a trumpet sounds, you will hear it.
>
> — Isaiah 18:3

All the people of the world will hear and see the return of the Lord from heaven on that day.

The apostle Paul links the shout of the Lord and the trumpet sound of the archangel with the resurrection of the dead saints of God and the rapture of the living saints (see II Thessalonians 4:13–18). The resurrection and miraculous gathering of the living saints will culminate in the re-establishment of the nation of Israel in a single day. As Moses promised, the land of Canaan will then become the homeland of Israel forever. That event is promised in Isaiah 66:

> Before she goes into labor, she gives birth; before the pains come upon her, she delivers a son. Who has ever heard of such things? Who has ever seen things like this? Can a country be born in a day or a nation be brought forth in a moment? Yet no sooner is Zion in labor than she gives birth to her children.
>
> — Isaiah 66:7–8

In other words, there will be a miraculous re-creation of the homeland of the Jews on the day the Messiah returns to gather them from the nations.

APPROPRIATING THE PROMISES

The irony of all ironies is that the Christian church has appropriated these promises of a rapture for the saints of Israel and claimed them as their own, while excluding the children of Israel from them. The arrogance of this theology makes a mockery of the word of God. We members of the Gentile church are included in the promises made to the saints of Israel only because we are sons of Abraham by faith. For us to include ourselves while excluding those to whom the promises were made is outrageous. We have been grafted into their olive tree, and we remain as branches of that tree by faith alone. When God decides to fulfill these promises, he will do so in a literal way, just as it was written. We Gentile Christians will be included in those promises only by faith in the God of Abraham who made these promises to Israel in the first place. We have not replaced Israel in the eyes of God! If we do not claim to be a part of the children of Israel by faith alone, then we have no part in these promises.

There is another irony involved with this teaching of a rapture for the Gentile church: the belief that the rapture of the Gentile church will occur seven years before the day of the Lord. There are thousands of Christian preachers and millions of Christians who believe they can appropriate the promises God made to Israel and rewrite them according to their own desires. The context of the day of the Lord is ignored, and a new teaching has replaced the correct context with "stories they have made up" (II Peter 2:3b). Instead, the Gentile church is being told they will receive Israel's rapture seven years before the day of the Lord, and the Jewish saints, to whom the promises were made, will remain here on earth. Just remember, God will not judge lightly the teachers of his Word.

PROPHECIES REGARDING OTHER NATIONS

Even though Babylon is the object of God's wrath on the day of the Lord, it is not the only nation mentioned by Isaiah as being punished on Judgment Day. Assyria is mentioned in chapter 14, Moab in 15 and 16, Syria in 17, Sudan in 18, Egypt in 19 and 20, and Lebanon in chapter 23. Every country mentioned was an enemy of Judah in Isaiah's day and is an enemy of Israel today. Furthermore, every nation mentioned in Isaiah is now an Islamic nation and will be a part of the empire of the Antichrist. They will all meet their end on the day of the Lord.

The same thing is true of the prophecies we find in the Minor Prophets. The majority of them speak about the need for reform and revival in Judah and Israel. They predict the same two nations, Babylon and Assyria, will be the instrument of God's punishment for the sins of the Jews. Nahum, in particular, focuses on Assyria more than the need for reform in Israel or Judah.

However, Obadiah mentions a special destruction for Saudi Arabia (Edom), the homeland of Mohammad and Islam, the religion of the Antichrist. For those who doubt this, I would ask one question: Can anyone name a nation that is the subject of God's wrath on the day of the Lord that is not Islamic today? Search the prophets to find the answer to this question. Who is going to be destroyed when Christ returns?

CHAPTER FOUR

Jeremiah: The Weeping Prophet

Jeremiah was a prophet to Judah and Jerusalem, just like Isaiah. He began his ministry in the thirteenth year of the reign of Josiah, around 626 BC, approximately fifty-four years after the death of Isaiah. At that time, Babylon was the major enemy threatening Israel, and Assyria was dominated by Babylon. Jeremiah lived through Nebuchadnezzar's siege of Jerusalem and the burning of the temple in 587–6 BC. He wanted to stay in Jerusalem after Nebuchadnezzar returned to Babylon with his booty, but he was taken captive by a group of Jewish rebels and carried off to Egypt, where he died.

A large portion of Jeremiah's prophecy concerns his personal struggle to carry out his ministry as he preaches of the need for the people of Jerusalem to repent. The priests of Jerusalem are preaching a syncretized religion of Jehovah/Baal worship that considers Jehovah to be the Baal of Judah. The king and the high priest consider Jeremiah to be a traitor because he preaches a message of surrender to Nebuchadnezzar. Jeremiah faces a daunting plight, which includes being held prisoner in Jerusalem and later being thrown into a well where he barely survives. His prophecies are burned by King Jehoiakim; however, he writes another copy and sends it out by his servant Baruch. Jeremiah gives private council to

Jehoiakim's successor, King Zedekiah, but that council is rejected. If we were to measure Jeremiah's ministry by the number of converts he made, we would consider him a failure. But that is not how God measures his servants.

The unique aspect of Jeremiah's prophecy is that he reveals more of the time span involved for the completion of God's promises. For instance, Jeremiah reveals that Judah's exile to Babylon will last for seventy years (chapter 25). But more than that, Jeremiah reveals more about the events that begin with the trumpet call of God on the day of the Lord and culminate with the destruction of Babylon.

Most conservative Christians believe that when the trumpet blows, everything will happen in the "twinkling of an eye." They believe we will be raptured to heaven and that will be it; everything will be finished for us at that time. Meanwhile, the Jews are to be punished for their sins here on earth for another seven years. Then the Antichrist will be thrown into the lake of fire, and the tribulation period will be over without a Christian receiving a single scratch. Then there will be another trumpet call of God, one not mentioned in Scripture, along with a second coming of Jesus Christ in the clouds of heaven, also not mentioned in Scripture, which will fulfill God's promises to Israel. We will then have a thousand years of life as kings of the world, ruling with Christ. That is the scenario presented in hundreds of conservative churches every Sunday.

But in truth, there is only one trumpet call of God, and it comes at the end of the tribulation period, not at the beginning. Furthermore, it will be the signal that sets off a chain of events, some of which will happen in the twinkling of an eye, and some of which will take time to complete. One of the events that happens instantly is the rapture of Israel. Jeremiah is in agreement with Moses and Isaiah concerning the regathering of the Jews at the end of time. In chapter 32 he says:

"You are saying about this city, 'By the sword, famine and plague it will be given into the hands of the *king of Babylon*'; but this is what the LORD, the God of Israel, says: I will surely gather them from all the lands where I banish them in my furious anger and great wrath; I will bring them back to this place and let them live in safety."

— Jeremiah 32:36–37

The regathering of the Jews mentioned in these verses did not take place in 539 BC. It will take place after the saints of God have suffered at the hands of the last king of Babylon, as prophesied by Isaiah in chapter 14. The trumpet call of God will be the signal for the angels to start the regathering. When the angels have completed their job, something even more miraculous will take place in the hearts of those who have been gathered. Jeremiah goes on to explain:

They will be my people, and I will be their God. I will give them singleness of heart and action, so that they will always fear me and that all will then go well for them and for their children after them. I will make an everlasting covenant with them: I will never stop doing good to them, and I will inspire them to fear me, so that they will never turn away from me. I will rejoice in doing them good and will assuredly plant them in this land with all my heart and soul.

This is what the LORD says: As I have brought all this great calamity on this people, so I will give them all the prosperity I have promised them. Once more fields will be bought in this land of which you say, 'It is a desolate waste, without people or animals, for it has been given into the hands of the Babylonians.' *Fields will be bought*

for silver, and deeds will be signed, sealed and witnessed
in the territory of Benjamin, in the villages around Jeru-
salem, in the towns of Judah and in the towns of the hill
country, of the western foothills and of the Negev, because
I will restore their fortunes, declares the LORD.

— Jeremiah 32:38-44

It is obvious that Jeremiah believed that when the Babylonian captivity ended, God would regather Israel, as he promised earlier through Moses and Isaiah. Surely all the Jews would see the hand of God in all of this and repent, as Jeremiah had been preaching they should. Jeremiah bought a field in Anathoth, about one-half mile north of Jerusalem (Jeremiah 32:6-9), believing he would live there in peace and prosperity after the Babylonians had been dealt with by God. He did not have the advantage of 2,500 years of history and the indwelling of the Holy Spirit, which would have allowed him to see God's promise does not refer to the first Babylonian captivity, but to a second Babylonian captivity which had not yet taken place. Isaiah spoke of this second captivity in Isaiah 6:11-13. That passage says:

Then I said, "For how long, Lord?" And he answered:
"Until the cities lie ruined and without inhabitant, until
the houses are left deserted and the fields ruined and
ravaged, until the LORD has sent everyone far away and
the land is utterly forsaken. *And though a tenth remains*
in the land, it will again be laid waste. But as the ter-
ebinth and oak leave stumps when they are cut down,
so the holy seed will be the stump in the land."

And then in 11:10-11, Isaiah says:

In that day the Root of Jesse will stand as a banner
for the peoples; the nations will rally to him, and his

resting place will be glorious. *In that day the Lord will reach out his hand a second time to reclaim the surviving remnant of his people* from Assyria, from Lower Egypt, from Upper Egypt, from Cush, from Elam, from Babylonia, from Hamath and from the islands of the Mediterranean.

Even with all the limitations of the Old Testament prophets, there is nothing in Isaiah's or Jeremiah's prophecies that needs to be corrected. Everything that Jeremiah has said so far is nearly a word-for-word repetition of what Moses said in Deuteronomy 30:1–7. Jeremiah's own understanding of what he wrote does not change the meaning of the prophecy. As we have seen from Moses, Isaiah, and now from Jeremiah, the Jews would be banished from the land because of their sins. But then God will forgive their sins and miraculously regather them, giving them back the land forever. The church has named this miraculous regathering "the rapture," claiming it was meant for Gentile Christians. But remember, it was promised to Israel, and it will take place after the Antichrist has done his best to kill the Jews. This event was not accomplished in the days of Ezra, or Nehemiah, or Esther, or the apostles, or Bar Kokhba, or Golda Meier. It awaits a future fulfillment.

The Punishment of Babylon

As for Babylon, their punishment will begin on the day of the Lord. That is the day the trumpet sounds and the angels appear in the sky to redeem the saints of God. Jeremiah repeats his predictions against Babylon in chapters 50, 51, and 52. For example, he says:

This is the word the LORD spoke through Jeremiah the prophet concerning **Babylon** and the land of the Babylonians: "Announce and proclaim among the

nations, lift up a banner and proclaim it; keep nothing
back, but say, 'Babylon will be captured; Bel will be put
to shame, Marduk filled with terror. Her images will be
put to shame and her idols filled with terror.' *A nation
from the north* will attack her and lay waste her land.
No one will live in it; both people and animals will flee
away.

— Jeremiah 50:1–3

In this passage a nation from the north will be used by God
to carry out his vengeance against Babylon. This will be a very
short war that will conclude with the everlasting punishment of
Babylon, as predicted by Isaiah and Jeremiah. God will use a human
army to carry out his mission, which means there will be a time
period involved in accomplishing this mission. The length of the
time period is not stated, but the beginning date coincides with the
conversion of Israel, as Jeremiah goes on to say:

"In those days, at that time," declares the LORD, "the
people of Israel and the people of Judah together will
go in tears to seek the LORD their God. They will ask
the way to Zion and turn their faces toward it. They will
come and bind themselves to the LORD in an everlasting covenant that will not be forgotten. "My people have
been lost sheep; their shepherds have led them astray
and caused them to roam on the mountains. They wandered over mountain and hill and forgot their own resting place. Whoever found them devoured them; their
enemies said, 'We are not guilty, for they sinned against
the LORD, their verdant pasture, the LORD, the hope of
their ancestors.'"

— Jeremiah 50:4–7

Then a command to flee out of Babylon is given in order to protect the saints of God from the wrath that is already on the way. The saints of God are asked many times in Scripture to flee from the sins of the world. In this case, anyone who does not heed the warning will be destroyed along with the city that epitomizes the sins of the world.

> *"Flee out of **Babylon**; leave the land of the **Babylonians**,* and be like the goats that lead the flock. For I will stir up and bring against **Babylon** an *alliance of great nations from the land of the north.* They will take up their positions against her, and from the north she will be captured. Their arrows will be like skilled warriors who do not return empty-handed. So **Babylonia** will be plundered; all who plunder her will have their fill," declares the LORD.
>
> "Because you rejoice and are glad, you who pillage my inheritance, because you frolic like a heifer threshing grain and neigh like stallions, your mother will be greatly ashamed; she who gave you birth will be disgraced. *She will be the least of the nations— a wilderness, a dry land, a desert. Because of the LORD's anger she will not be inhabited but will be completely desolate.* All who pass **Babylon** will be appalled; they will scoff because of all her wounds."
>
> — Jeremiah 50:8–13

The nation from the north in this passage is now expanded to an alliance. Babylon's punishment will be to become a dry, uninhabited desert forever. This is something that was not accomplished by any of the invasions from past history. Even though we think of Iraq as being a desert land, it is far from uninhabited. This punishment awaits a future invasion.

Jeremiah concludes this prophecy with a description of the total devastation of Babylon that will leave the place uninhabited forever:

"Take up your positions around **Babylon,** all you who draw the bow. Shoot at her! Spare no arrows, for she has sinned against the LORD. Shout against her on every side! She surrenders, her towers fall, her walls are torn down. Since this is the vengeance of the LORD, take vengeance on her; do to her as she has done to others. Cut off from **Babylon** the sower, and the reaper with his sickle at harvest. Because of the sword of the oppressor let everyone return to their own people, let everyone flee to their own land.

"Israel is a scattered flock that lions have chased away. The first to devour them was the king of Assyria; the last to crush their bones was Nebuchadnezzar king of **Babylon.**" Therefore this is what the LORD Almighty, the God of Israel, says: "*I will punish the king of Babylon and his land as I punished the king of Assyria.*"

— Jeremiah 50:14–18

The prophecies against Babylon go on in chapter 51 to name a few of the nations in the "alliance of great nations from the land north," who will destroy Babylon. Jeremiah says:

"Lift up a banner in the land! Blow the trumpet among the nations! Prepare the nations for battle against her; summon against her these kingdoms: *Ararat, Minni and Ashkenaz.* Appoint a commander against her; send up horses like a swarm of locusts. Prepare the nations for battle against her— *the kings of the Medes,* their governors and all their officials, and all the countries they rule. The land trembles and writhes, for the Lord's purposes against Babylon stand— to lay waste the land of Babylon so that no one will live there.

— Jeremiah 51:27–29

The destruction of Babylon by a coalition army on the day of the Lord is a recurring theme in Old Testament prophecy. Yet it is completely ignored by the modern church for two different reasons. The liberals have chosen to see the word of God as mythology, and the conservatives have chosen to ignore the Old Testament prophecies because they are meaningless to those with a pretribulational view. However, if we interpret Scripture literally, there will be an army raised from among the nations who rebel against the rule of the Antichrist. Jeremiah gives us specifics as to who will be a part of that army.

The homeland of the Medes was in the area of the Caucasus, which includes Georgia, Azerbaijan, and southern Russia today. Ararat is Turkey; Minni was the land of the Kurds, where the Armenian Christians used to live; and Ashkenaz was the Jewish name for Europe. These areas will be emboldened to revolt and strike Babylon. This begs the question: Will these be the only nations in the coalition? Will America be a part of this great alliance? That is my hope, but we will have to wait and see.

The apostle John predicts this same event in Revelation 17:15– 18, which says:

Then the angel said to me, "The waters you saw, where the prostitute sits, are peoples, multitudes, nations and languages. The beast and the ten horns you saw will hate the prostitute. They will bring her to ruin and leave her naked; they will eat her flesh and burn her with fire. For God has put it into their hearts to accomplish his

purpose by agreeing to hand over to the beast their royal authority, until God's words are fulfilled. The woman
you saw is the great city that rules over the kings of the
earth."

The city of Babylon will be devastated by a coalition army that
had been supporting her. This is a human army raised up by God
to accomplish his wrath against Babylon in fulfillment of Isaiah
13. Because of that, you must remember this event will not be
accomplished in a moment, "in the twinkling of an eye." It will take
an unknown number of days to accomplish—possibly even weeks.
Therefore, even though this event begins to be accomplished on the
day of the Lord, it will take more than the twinkling of an eye for
everything to be finished. We will understand the reason for God's
use of a human army and an undetermined period of time when we
get to Ezekiel.

The connection between the destruction of the kings of Assyria
and Babylon is repeated by Jeremiah, even though Jeremiah wrote
more than fifty years after Isaiah's death. Some believe all of this has
been fulfilled because of the mention of a great army from the north,
whom they claim was ancient Media, a part of the Persian Empire
in 539 BC. The problem with that theory is that Media was not the
leader of the army that invaded Babylon. Yes, the Medes were part
of a coalition, but Cyrus, King of Persia, led the coalition and the
Medes were only a small part of the Persian Empire. Furthermore,
the city of Babylon fell without a single arrow being fired. There was
no destruction, no death, and no oppression of the fallen. But the
most telling difference between the 539 BC invasion and the literal
fulfillment is the fact that after 539 BC, Babylon continued to be
the capital of the Persian Empire for a number of years until a new
capital was built for them at Susa. Even then, Babylon remained a
major city with a very large population.

For those who believe this was all fulfilled when Persia captured Babylon in 539 BC, I have to ask: When did Babylon ever become a permanent wasteland? The answer is never. It is still a flourishing area today. There is a glaring contrast between the literal interpretation of this passage and the allegorical interpretation as expressed by the preterists, or any of the other millennial views that routinely substitute symbolic interpretation. Those who turn to symbolic interpretation disrespect the word of God. Who are we to change it or give it a symbolic meaning? Notice very carefully the words of Jeremiah 50:1, "This is the word the Lord spoke through Jeremiah the Prophet. . ."

It is interesting to note the pretribulational-premillennial view claims to always interpret Scripture literally. Yet they are very quick to switch to a symbolic interpretation when faced with passages like Jeremiah 51. The real question concerning this passage is: Will present-day Baghdad, fifty-five miles from the ruins of the city of Babylon, be destroyed on the day of the Lord? Or will the old ruins of Babylon be rebuilt and then destroyed? I believe either scenario will fulfill this prophecy because Babylon was a territory as well as a city.

Meanwhile, as Babylon is being destroyed, God takes a special vengeance on the nation of Saudi Arabia. That vengeance is carried out by Jesus Christ without the aid of any human allies. The passage describing that vengeance is found in Isaiah 63, which says:

> Who is this coming from Edom, from Bozrah, with his garments stained crimson? Who is this, robed in splendor, striding forward in the greatness of his strength? "It is I, proclaiming victory, mighty to save." Why are your garments red, like those of one treading the winepress? *"I have trodden the winepress alone; from the nations no one was with me. I trampled them in my anger and trod*

them down in my wrath; their blood spattered my gar-
ments, and I stained all my clothing. It was for me the
day of vengeance; the year for me to redeem had come. I
looked, but there was no one to help, I was appalled that
no one gave support; so my own arm achieved salvation
for me, and my own wrath sustained me. I trampled the
nations in my anger; in my wrath I made them drunk
and poured their blood on the ground."

— Isaiah 63:1-6

Jeremiah goes on to say:

How broken and shattered is the hammer of the whole
earth! How desolate is **Babylon** among the nations! I
set a trap for you, **Babylon**, and you were caught before you knew it; you were found and captured because
you opposed the LORD. The LORD has opened his arse-
nal and brought out the weapons of his wrath, for the
Sovereign LORD Almighty has work to do in the land
of the **Babylonians**. Come against her from afar. Break
open her granaries; pile her up like heaps of grain.
Completely destroy her and leave her no remnant. Kill
all her young bulls; let them go down to the slaughter!
Woe to them! For their day has come, the time for them
to be punished. Listen to the fugitives and refugees
from **Babylon** declaring in Zion how the LORD our God
has taken vengeance, vengeance for his temple.

— Jeremiah 50:23-28

There was no destruction in 539 BC, but there will be when
Christ returns. All the prophecies mentioned await the day of the
Lord for fulfillment. Six things will happen at that time: the Messiah
will return, Babylon will be destroyed, the army of Antichrist will

be destroyed, Israel and Jerusalem will be rebuilt, the dead saints will be resurrected, and the living saints of God will be raptured. Some of these events will happen immediately, and some will take an undetermined amount of time to accomplish, but all will be fulfilled just as they were spoken by the prophets.

THE REGATHERING OF ISRAEL

Now let's look a little closer at the regathering and spiritual renewal of the Jews of Israel on that day. Jeremiah 30:3 says:

> "The days are coming," declares the LORD, "when I will bring my people Israel and Judah back from captivity and restore them to the land I gave their ancestors to possess," says the LORD.

Jeremiah continues with the same theme in chapter 31, saying:

> This is what the LORD says: "Sing with joy for Jacob; shout for the foremost of the nations. Make your praises heard, and say, 'LORD, save your people, the remnant of Israel.' See, I will bring them from the land of the north and gather them from the ends of the earth. Among them will be the blind and the lame, expectant mothers and women in labor; a great throng will return. They will come with weeping; they will pray as I bring them back. I will lead them beside streams of water on a level path where they will not stumble [Psalm 23], because I am Israel's father, and Ephraim is my firstborn son.
> — Jeremiah 31:7–9

Those who could not make it on their own will be brought back to the land of Judah with a first class ticket on Angelic Air. As Isaiah said, they will be plucked up by the angels of God, one by one. But there will be no time to serve meals! When that happens, the New Covenant will find its final fulfillment.

"The days are coming," declares the LORD, "when I will make a new covenant with the people of Israel and with the people of Judah. It will not be like the covenant I made with their ancestors when I took them by the hand to lead them out of Egypt, because they broke my covenant, though I was a husband to them," declares the LORD. "This is the covenant I will make with the people of Israel after that time," declares the LORD. *"I will put my law in their minds and write it on their hearts. I will be their God, and they will be my people. No longer will they teach their neighbor, or say to one another, 'Know the LORD,' because they will all know me, from the least of them to the greatest," declares the LORD. "For I will forgive their wickedness and will remember their sins no more."*

— Jeremiah 31:31–34

In summary, Jeremiah, just like Isaiah, restates everything that was said by Moses in Deuteronomy 30:1–7. God will gather his people from the four corners of the globe and give them a new heart: a heart that will not allow us to wander ever again. At the same time, Babylon will be destroyed because it has been the enemy of God and his people from the days of the Tower of Babel. Furthermore, these events will all begin with the trumpet call of the Archangel and the return of the Lord in the sky at the end of the tribulation period. Praise the Lord, I can hardly wait!

CHAPTER FIVE

EZEKIEL: THE CAPTIVE PRIEST

Ezekiel was a priest of the Lord in Jerusalem. He was taken captive in Nebuchadnezzar's second raid of Jerusalem in 597 BC. Ezekiel and Daniel probably knew each other, but Ezekiel might have been too young to have been taken in the first raid in 601 BC. His earliest messages can be dated to 593 BC as he wrote from captivity in Babylon, and later from Susa, in southern Mesopotamia.

Ezekiel does not single out Babylon as the main bad character of the tribulation, as do Isaiah and Jeremiah. However, like Isaiah and Jeremiah, Ezekiel mentions the same long list of enemies of Israel who will be judged on the day of the Lord. They were enemies of Israel then, and they are enemies of Israel now. All were pagan idol worshipers then; all are Muslim now. And, like Jeremiah, a large part of Ezekiel's message is directed against his own people for their refusal to repent from their idol worship.

THE JUDGMENT OF THE SAINTS

Even with all their sin, God still gives Ezekiel a promise of restoration for the nation of Israel and for Jerusalem. But that restoration will not come without first judging the children of Israel for their sins.

> As surely as I live, declares the Sovereign LORD, *I will reign over you with a mighty hand and an outstretched arm and with outpoured wrath. I will bring you from the nations and gather you from the countries where you have been scattered*—with a mighty hand and an outstretched arm and with outpoured wrath. I will bring you into the wilderness of the nations and there, face to face, I will execute judgment upon you. As I judged your ancestors in the wilderness of the land of Egypt, *so I will judge you, declares the Sovereign LORD. I will take note of you as you pass under my rod, and I will bring you into the bond of the covenant.* I will purge you of those who revolt and rebel against me. Although I will bring them out of the land where they are living, yet they will not enter the land of Israel. Then you will know that I am the LORD.
>
> — Ezekiel 20:33–38

We now learn the miraculous regathering of Israel, as promised by Moses, Isaiah, and Jeremiah, will not be completed in "a moment, in the twinkling of an eye," even though the "rapture" portion of the gathering will be completed almost instantly, according to Paul. The redemption of the saints will not be complete until the gathered saints reach their destination. That will involve a trip through the wilderness for the children of Israel. During the trip, the children of Israel will go through a mini-exodus experience where they will be judged by God and the rebels among them will be purged, just as in the first exodus.

This may be a surprise to many Christians. The Gentile church has been taught we will be raptured and that will be the end of it; we will end up in heaven with Jesus, never having faced the judgment of God. But Paul tells us plainly in the New Testament we will all face the judgment seat of God (Romans 14:9–11), and this is where that will happen. The entire nation of Jews will be raptured along with the Gentile church, and together we will face the judgment of God as we pass under the rod of the Great Shepherd in the wilderness. The sinners will be purged, and the saints will enter the Promised Land. We won't be in heaven. We will be in our eternal homeland, Israel.

This sequence of events is also described in the book of Isaiah, where Isaiah repeats the promises of God for a highway in the wilderness, traveled only by the people of God (see Isaiah 11:16, 19:23, and 35:8). One of the most beautiful and often-quoted passages in Isaiah is Isaiah 40:1–5. It is also one of the least understood prophecies in Isaiah. In these verses, he says:

> Comfort, comfort my people, says your God. Speak tenderly to Jerusalem, and proclaim to her that her hard service has been completed, that her sin has been paid for, that she has received from the LORD's hand double for all her sins.
>
> A voice of one calling: "In the wilderness prepare the way for the LORD; make straight in the desert a highway for our God. Every valley shall be raised up, every mountain and hill made low; the rough ground shall become level, the rugged places a plain. And the glory of the LORD will be revealed, and all people will see it together. For the mouth of the LORD has spoken."

After the Jews have experienced the suffering of the tribulation period, having received double payment for all their sins, the command goes out to prepare a highway for the return of the Lord. Every mountain and hill are shaken to the ground; every valley is filled in. This is the day of the Lord and the command that was shouted is the voice of the Archangel shaking the heavens and the earth. But for those who love God this is not a day of fear and trembling, it is a day of joy and rest.

David writes of this promised day in Psalm 23, saying:

> The LORD is my shepherd, I lack nothing. He makes me lie down in green pastures, he leads me beside quiet waters, he refreshes my soul. He guides me along the right paths for his name's sake. Even though I walk through the darkest valley, I will fear no evil, for you are with me; your rod and your staff, they comfort me.
>
> You prepare a table before me in the presence of my enemies. You anoint my head with oil; my cup overflows. Surely your goodness and love will follow me all the days of my life, and I will dwell in the house of the LORD forever.

David knows what is at the end of this trip through the valley of the shadow of death: it is everlasting life in the presence of the Lord.

Returning to the prophecies of Ezekiel, the principle of progressive revelation is again evident as he reveals more details about the resurrection of the dead and the rapture of the living than any of the prophets before him. He says:

> Then he said to me: "Son of man, these bones are the people of Israel. They say, 'Our bones are dried up and our hope is gone; we are cut off.' Therefore prophesy and say to them: 'This is what the Sovereign LORD says: *My people, I am going to open your graves and bring you up from them; I will bring you back to the land of Israel.* Then you, my people, will know that I am the LORD, when I open your graves and bring you up from them.

I will put my Spirit in you and you will live, and I will settle you in your own land. Then you will know that I the LORD have spoken, and I have done it, declares the LORD.'"

— Ezekiel 37:11–14

From the first line of this passage, it seems the ones who are resurrected are those who were expecting a Messiah to rescue them. No mention is made of those who had deserted the Lord and turned to idol worship. It is only the believing saints who died before the day of the Lord who are resurrected. That message is repeated by the apostle Paul in I Thessalonians 4:13–17, saying:

Brothers and sisters, we do not want you to be uninformed about those who sleep in death, so that you do not grieve like the rest of mankind, who have no hope. *For we believe that Jesus died and rose again, and so we believe that God will bring with Jesus those who have fallen asleep in him. According to the Lord's word, we tell you that we who are still alive, who are left until the coming of the Lord, will certainly not precede those who have fallen asleep.* For the Lord himself will come down from heaven, with a loud command, with the voice of the archangel and with the trumpet call of God, and the dead in Christ will rise first. After that, we who are still alive and are left will be caught up together with them in the clouds to meet the Lord in the air. And so we will be with the Lord forever.

In other words, Paul is quoting from the promises made to the children of Israel by the prophets Isaiah, Jeremiah, and Ezekiel, and Paul is including the Thessalonian Gentiles as children of Israel. Ezekiel says:

"For I will take you out of the nations; I will gather you
from all the countries and bring you back into your
own land. I will sprinkle clean water on you, and you
will be clean; I will cleanse you from all your impurities
and from all your idols. I will give you a new heart and
put a new spirit in you; I will remove from you your
heart of stone and give you a heart of flesh. And I will
put my Spirit in you and move you to follow my decrees
and be careful to keep my laws. Then you will live in the
land I gave your ancestors; you will be my people, and I
will be your God.

— Ezekiel 36:24–28

So the resurrection and rapture of the children of Israel will be
in conjunction with a national turning to faith in God by the Jewish
people. For many Jews, their repentance and acceptance of Jesus as
the Messiah will take place when they see him "in the air." This is a
reference to Daniel 7:13 and the Son of Man prophecy. Daniel 7:13
says, "In my vision at night I looked, and there before me was one
like a son of man, *coming with the clouds of heaven*. He approached
the Ancient of Days and was led into his presence."

Let's review what we have learned of the promises of God for
the redemption of his saints. If we combine the prophecies of Moses,
Isaiah, Jeremiah, Ezekiel, and Paul, we find that on the day of the
Lord, the Jewish people will all be gathered from the nations, both
those who believe and those who are sinners. At the same time, all
the saints who did believe, but died, will be resurrected, and the
living Gentile saints who have joined the family of Abraham by
faith will be "plucked up one by one" to join the resurrected saints
in the air (I Thessalonians 4:17).

The resurrection and rapture will be accomplished in an instant,
"in the twinkling of an eye." However, those who are "caught up" will
be taken to the wilderness of Judah to be cleansed of sin before they

are allowed to enter Jerusalem. They will be brought into the bond of Abraham's covenant, "and so all Israel will be saved" (Romans 11:26). In other words, for a short period of time, Israel, including *all* of Abraham's children (Jews and Gentiles), will reenact the exodus. But the unbelieving Jewish rebels who are brought back to Israel with the believing children of Israel will die in the wilderness.

This is the reason all living Jews will go through the tribulation. The promises of God spoken by Moses were made to the nation of Israel. Those promises in Deuteronomy 30 included believers and non-believers alike. Therefore, all Jews, believers and non-believers, will experience the purging that takes place through the tribulation and the miraculous regathering at the end of the tribulation. During the regathering, we children of Abraham, both Jews and Christians, will receive our crowns and rewards as promised in Revelation.

Furthermore, there is a parallel between the Old Testament nation of Israel and the Gentile church today. The church, which is also a mixed bag of believers and non-believers, will experience that same purging by going through the same tribulation. There are millions of church members today that have never experienced what it means to be born again. That number includes those who only attend church on Christmas and Easter. It also includes all those who are seen in church three times in their lives: once when they are baptized as an infant, once when they married, and once when they are carried in feet first in their coffin. That is why John gives such strong warnings in Revelation: only those who remain faithful to the end will be saved.

The parallel between Israel and the church is too close to separate. Just as the saints of God, both Old Testament and New Testament, are the same in God's eyes, so Israel and the church are the same in God's eyes. Both will be purged through the tribulation, and judged or rewarded at the end of the tribulation.

Ezekiel tells us that on the day the saints are saved, the nation of Israel will be re-established and Jerusalem will be rebuilt.

"'This is what the Sovereign LORD says: *On the day I cleanse you from all your sins, I will resettle your towns, and the ruins will be rebuilt.* The desolate land will be cultivated instead of lying desolate in the sight of all who pass through it. They will say, "This land that was laid waste has become like the garden of Eden; the cities that were lying in ruins, desolate and destroyed, are now fortified and inhabited." Then the nations around you that remain will know that I the LORD have rebuilt what was destroyed and have replanted what was desolate. I the LORD have spoken, and I will do it.'

"This is what the Sovereign LORD says: Once again I will yield to Israel's plea and do this for them: I will make their people as numerous as sheep, as numerous as the flocks for offerings at Jerusalem during her appointed festivals. So will the ruined cities be filled with flocks of people. Then they will know that I am the LORD."

— Ezekiel 36:33–38

From these quotes, and from dozens of others I have not mentioned, it is obvious the plan of God for redeeming his saints will begin with a tribulation to punish the nation of Israel for turning away from God, which they have done today. The leaders of the nations that will be the instruments of God's punishment are Assyria and Babylon. Then, on the day of the Lord, Jesus will return to earth with great power and fury to destroy those nations. This event will be accompanied by dramatic signs in the sky and earth, and accompanied by a trumpet blast from an archangel that could never be called "secret." In the blink of an eye, the dead saints will rise and the living saints will be gathered up one by one, and brought back to Israel. After the sinners of Israel are purged, the saints will enter Jerusalem by way of a desert road; that is, "through the valley of the shadow of death." They will be given new hearts and never stray from God again. This has been God's plan for redeeming Israel from the beginning. And since we, "like Isaac" (Galatians 4:28), are a part of true Israel, we Gentile born-again believers will be a part of those who enter Jerusalem, wearing white robes and crowns of gold.

The Trumpet Call of God

In I Thessalonians 4:16, the apostle Paul tells us these events will begin with the "trumpet call of God," but few Christians have any idea what that refers to. The reference is to the Feast of Trumpets which is held every fall to mark the harvest time for Israel. Since the time of Ezra, it has been Jewish tradition that when the last trumpet is blown at the end of the Feast of Trumpets, the Messiah will return to save Israel from her enemies and to re-establish the nation of Israel. The Feasts of Trumpets is followed ten days later by the Day of Atonement and the cleansing of Israel's sins. Could it be that Israel's second exodus on the desert road mentioned above will last for ten days, and the sinners will fall in the wilderness, just as the children of Israel died in the wilderness the first time? Will the cleansed saints of God then re-enter Jerusalem on the Day of Atonement with their Savior at their head? That is something to think about.

The association between the last trumpet, mentioned so many times by the prophets, and the resurrection is most clearly indicated in I Corinthians 15:51–56, which says:

> Listen, I tell you a mystery: We will not all sleep, but we will all be changed—in a flash, in the twinkling of an eye, *at the last trumpet.* For the trumpet will sound, the dead will be raised imperishable, and we will be changed. For the perishable must clothe itself with the

imperishable, and the mortal with immortality. When the perishable has been clothed with the imperishable, and the mortal with immortality, then the saying that is written will come true: "Death has been swallowed up in victory." "Where, O death, is your victory? Where, O death, is your sting?" The sting of death is sin, and the power of sin is the law.

Paul emphasizes the resurrection of the dead and the rapture of the living saints will happen in conjunction with the last trumpet. The trumpet and the miraculous gathering of the saints can be found in the passage quoted earlier from Isaiah 27:12–13. This is what Paul is referring to in I Thessalonians 4:16. The trumpet that is sounded by the archangel of God on the day of the Lord is meant for every nation on earth to hear. Listen to what Isaiah says about that trumpet: "All you people of the world, you who live on the earth, when a banner is raised on the mountains, you will see it, and when a trumpet sounds you will hear it" (Isaiah 18:3).

This is the same trumpet that was referred to earlier in Jeremiah chapter 51.

"Lift up a banner in the land! Blow the trumpet among the nations! Prepare the nations for battle against her; summon against her these kingdoms: Ararat, Minni and Ashkenaz. Appoint a commander against her; send up horses like a swarm of locusts. Prepare the nations for battle against her— the kings of the Medes, their governors and all their officials, and all the countries they rule. The land trembles and writhes, for the LORD's purposes against Babylon stand— to lay waste the land of Babylon so that no one will live there."

— Jeremiah 51:27–29

When the trumpet is heard around the world, signaling the return of the Messiah, the armies of those who have resisted the Antichrist will arise and attack Babylon. The destruction of Babylon will happen at the hands of a human army who revolt against the Antichrist and follow the commands of God. However, I do not believe these are the only nations that will be involved; we will just have to wait and see if I am right about that.

This same last trumpet which is heard among the nations is also referred to by Joel, Amos, Zephaniah, and Zechariah. I will only quote the last two. Zephaniah says:

> "The great day of the LORD is near— near and coming quickly. The cry on the day of the LORD is bitter; the Mighty Warrior shouts his battle cry. That day will be a day of wrath— a day of distress and anguish, a day of trouble and ruin, a day of darkness and gloom, a day of clouds and blackness—a *day of trumpet and battle cry* against the fortified cities and against the corner towers. I will bring such distress on all people that they will grope about like those who are blind, because they have sinned against the LORD. Their blood will be poured out like dust and their entrails like dung. Neither their silver nor their gold will be able to save them on the day of the LORD's wrath. In the fire of his jealousy the whole earth will be consumed, for he will make a sudden end of all who live on the earth."
>
> — Zephaniah 1:14–18

Zechariah says:

> Then the LORD will appear over them; his arrow will flash like lightning. *The Sovereign LORD will sound the*

trumpet; he will march in the storms of the south, and the LORD Almighty will shield them. They will destroy and overcome with slingstones. They will drink and roar as with wine; they will be full like a bowl used for sprinkling the corners of the altar. The LORD their God will save his people on that day as a shepherd saves his flock. They will sparkle in his land like jewels in a crown.

— Zechariah 9:14–16

Whether or not the last trumpet will sound on the last day of the Feast of Trumpets is not for us to say. That day is known only to the Father. In any event, it will signal the beginning of several events that will all be accomplished in a short period of time; I believe no more than ten days. Regardless of the time frame, there will be a banquet waiting for them when they get there. And, because Christ is with the saints, except for his excursion into Arabia, the battle of Armageddon will occur after everyone has eaten and is satisfied.

THE BATTLES

There are two prophecies in Ezekiel that seem to refer to a single battle. In reality, they refer to two battles separated by a thousand years, and their order in time is reversed from their order in Ezekiel. The Ezekiel 38 battle will take place at the end of the millennium, and the Ezekiel 39 battle will end the tribulation. We know this to be true because the apostle John quotes from Ezekiel 39:17–18 in Revelation 19:17b–18. This is clearly demonstrates that the Old Testament prophets did not fully understand their own prophecies because the later one is listed first.

In Ezekiel 39, Ezekiel records the event that will trigger the return of Christ. The Antichrist will gather an army of his followers for a final assault on Israel. His goal will be to kill every Jew on earth. From the size of his army, it would seem his goal is within easy reach. We discover that the main fighting force of the army of the Antichrist will come from Gog and Magog. Some commentators say this refers to Russia; others say it refers to Turkey. There are issues with both interpretations. Whoever those nations are, the battle will pit the human army of the Antichrist against the heavenly army of God, with Jesus Christ leading the way. Listen to what Ezekiel says:

> "Son of man, prophesy against Gog and say: 'This is what the Sovereign LORD says: I am against you, Gog, chief prince of Meshek and Tubal. I will turn you around and drag you along. I will bring you from the far north and send you against the mountains of Israel. Then I will strike your bow from your left hand and make your arrows drop from your right hand. On the mountains of Israel you will fall, you and all your troops and the nations with you. I will give you as food to all kinds of carrion birds and to the wild animals. You will fall in the open field, for I have spoken, declares the Sovereign LORD. I will send fire on Magog and on those who live in safety in the coastlands, and they will know that I am the LORD.
>
> "'I will make known my holy name among my people Israel. I will no longer let my holy name be profaned, and the nations will know that I the LORD am the Holy One in Israel. It is coming! It will surely take place, declares the Sovereign LORD. This is the day I have spoken of.
>
> "'Then those who live in the towns of Israel will go out and use the weapons for fuel and burn them up— the small and large shields, the bows and arrows, the war clubs and spears. For seven years they will use them for fuel. They will not need to gather wood from the

fields or cut it from the forests, because they will use the weapons for fuel. And they will plunder those who plundered them and loot those who looted them, declares the Sovereign LORD.

"'On that day I will give Gog a burial place in Israel, in the valley of those who travel east of the Sea. It will block the way of travelers, because Gog and all his hordes will be buried there. *So it will be called the Valley of Hamon Gog.*"

— Ezekiel 39:1–11

The name Hamon Gog means "the multitude of Gog." It will take the first seven years of the millennium to get rid of the remains of that battle. More than likely, it will take at least that long to complete the building project that will begin with the trumpet call of God and the shout of the archangel on the day of the Lord. This prophecy depicts the fulfillment of Deuteronomy 30:7. As Moses said, the Lord will pour out on Israel's enemies all the wrath and trouble they had poured out on Israel.

The battle prophesied in Ezekiel 38 must have been very confusing to the Old Testament Jews. How could they understand a prophecy that will be fulfilled at the end of what they believed would be eternity? They had no concept of the millennium. Nor did they realize Isaiah 11 and Isaiah 66 would come to an end and culminate in another battle designed to destroy the Jews. Yet that is what John would prophesy 680 years after Ezekiel 38 was written, thanks to the progress of prophecy.

THE RETURN OF JESUS

There is one more prophecy in Ezekiel that we cannot overlook. Let's look at what Ezekiel says about how Jesus will return on the day of the Lord. Turn to Ezekiel 43.

Then the man brought me to the gate facing east, and I saw the glory of the God of Israel coming from the east. His voice was like the roar of rushing waters, and the land was radiant with his glory. The vision I saw was like the vision I had seen when he came to destroy the city and like the visions I had seen by the Kebar River, and I fell facedown. *The glory of the LORD entered the temple through the gate facing east.* Then the Spirit lifted me up and brought me into the inner court, and *the glory of the LORD filled the temple.*

— Ezekiel 43:1–5

Ezekiel goes on to say the Lord God will cleanse the Temple for the last time on that same day (Ezekiel 43:6–7).

Zechariah also gives a prophecy about this same event. In Zechariah 14 he says:

I will gather all the nations to Jerusalem to fight against it; the city will be captured, the houses ransacked, and the women raped. Half of the city will go into exile, but the rest of the people will not be taken from the city.

Then the LORD will go out and fight against those nations, as he fights on a day of battle. *On that day his feet will stand on the Mount of Olives,* east of Jerusalem, and the Mount of Olives will be split in two from east to west, forming a great valley, with half of the mountain moving north and half moving south. You will flee by my mountain valley, for it will extend to Azel. You will flee as you fled from the earthquake in the days of Uzziah king of Judah. Then the LORD my God will come, and all the holy ones with him.

— Zechariah 14:2–5

Zechariah starts his prophecy at the halfway point of the tribulation. This invasion of Jerusalem is the same one predicted by Islamic prophecy, when al-Mahdi will invade and rule Jerusalem. The invasion will reveal the true identity of al-Mahdi as the man of lawlessness. The city is ransacked, half the people killed and the rest enslaved. Then, three and a half years later, Christ will appear over the Mount of Olives. There will be a massive earthquake, and the Jews who remain will be able to escape to the other side of the Mount of Olives.

But why weren't these Jews of Jerusalem "raptured" with all the other Jews when the earthquake happens at the return of Christ? The answer should be obvious: they were already in Jerusalem, where Christ was heading. When they flee out of the city by way of the newly created valley, they will end up on the other side of the Mount of Olives with the rest of the saints of God. And so, as Zechariah says, "the LORD my God will come, *and all the holy ones with him*" (Zechariah 14:5).

Now let's look at the "triumphal entry" of Jesus into Jerusalem, as recorded by Matthew.

> "As they approached Jerusalem and came to Bethphage on the Mount of Olives, Jesus sent two disciples, saying to them, "Go to the village ahead of you, and at once you will find a donkey tied there, with her colt by her. Untie them and bring them to me. If anyone says anything to you, say that the Lord needs them, and he will send them right away." This took place to fulfill what was spoken through the prophet:
>
> "Say to Daughter Zion, 'See, your king comes to you, gentle and riding on a donkey, and on a colt, the foal of a donkey.' "

The disciples went and did as Jesus had instructed them. They brought the donkey and the colt and placed their cloaks on them for Jesus to sit on. A very large crowd spread their cloaks on the road, while others cut branches from the trees and spread them on the road. The crowds that went ahead of him and those that followed shouted,

"Hosanna to the Son of David!" "Blessed is he who comes in the name of the Lord!" "Hosanna in the highest heaven!"

When Jesus entered Jerusalem, the whole city was stirred and asked, "Who is this?"

The crowds answered, "This is Jesus, the prophet from Nazareth in Galilee. Jesus entered the temple courts and drove out all who were buying and selling there. He overturned the tables of the money changers and the benches of those selling doves. 'It is written,' he said to them, 'My house will be called a house of prayer,' but you are making it 'a den of robbers.'"

— Matthew 21:1–13

The cleansing of the temple recorded by Matthew was a foreshadowing of the final cleansing prophesied by Ezekiel. We know this because Luke continues the story of the final cleansing in Acts 1:9–13:

After he said this, he was taken up before their very eyes, and a cloud hid him from their sight.

They were looking intently up into the sky as he was going, when suddenly two men dressed in white stood beside them. "Men of Galilee," they said, "why do you stand here looking into the sky? *This same Jesus, who has been taken from you into heaven, will come back in the same way you have seen him go into heaven."*

Then the apostles returned to Jerusalem from the hill called the Mount of Olives, a Sabbath day's walk from the city. When they arrived, they went upstairs to the room where they were staying. Those present were Peter, John, James and Andrew; Philip and Thomas, Bartholomew and Matthew; James son of Alphaeus and Simon the Zealot, and Judas son of James.

In other words, when Jesus entered Jerusalem as a king riding on a donkey, he came to Jerusalem from beyond Bethphage on the Mount of Olives. His probable starting point was the Garden of Gethsemane. That means he had to enter Jerusalem by the eastern gate of the city. The eastern gate opens up to the Kidron Valley, which divides Jerusalem from the Mount of Olives. The village of Bethphage was on the western side of the Mount of Olives and the Garden of Gethsemane was just across the crest of the hill on the eastern side. On the day of his ascension, Jesus retraced his steps out of Jerusalem by the eastern gate across the Kidron Valley, then up and over the Mount of Olives to the Garden of Gethsemane. The final fulfillment of Ezekiel's prophecy will take place on the day of the Lord when Christ returns through the eastern gate in judgment to remove sinners from the earth.

If we put these facts from Ezekiel and Zechariah together with what we learn from Matthew and Luke, it becomes apparent why it is necessary for Jesus to lead the saints to Jerusalem by way of a road in the wilderness, and why he will lead that multitude of saints across the Mount of Olives and into Jerusalem. It will be to fulfill God's promise to Abraham, who will be among those resurrected saints on the day of the Lord. He is taking the saints to Jerusalem, their eternal home.

The imams of Islam also know about these verses and have tried to prevent this from ever happening. In 1514, Suleiman the Magnificent, in response to Ezekiel's and Luke's prophecies, blocked the eastern gate to prevent the return of the Jewish Messiah. The original gate had collapsed before Suleiman's time, and a replacement gate was built over the ruins of the original gate. It is known as the Golden Gate. In order to insure that Christ could not return through this gate, Suleiman bricked up the gate and placed a graveyard in front of it. Walking on graves makes a person unclean and disqualifies them for service to the Lord. But Suleiman didn't realize those graves will be empty as soon as the trumpet sounds to mark of the return of Christ!

Looking back on Moses and the first three major prophets, we can see the foundation stone of redemptive prophecy laid down by Moses is confirmed in chapter after chapter of the writings of Isaiah, Jeremiah, and Ezekiel. There will be a day at the end of the tribulation period when a great trumpet call will be heard throughout the heavens and the earth. The Messiah will appear in the sky for every eye to see, and the saints of God will be raptured. They will be brought back to Israel, where they will be judged on the desert road before they re-enter Jerusalem. Along with them will be the multitude of resurrected saints who will receive the reward they thought they had lost. This is what a literal, historical, grammatical, and contextual reading of Scripture says will happen.

However, there is one more major prophet left to read, and that one is extraordinary. Daniel will reveal details that none of the other Old Testament prophets dreamed of.

CHAPTER SIX

Daniel: The Forerunner of John

Daniel was taken captive along with several other good-looking and bright youths from Jerusalem in 601 BC. He wrote all of his prophecies from Babylon and Persia. He died as a very old man sometime during the reign of Darius Hystaspes (521–486 BC) after the Jews were released from Babylon.

The theme of Daniel centers on the rulers of the nation of Babylon. If you will recall, Babylon was the homeland of idolatry. We learned from the first three major prophets that Babylon is the nation God used, and will use again, to punish Israel. Daniel concentrates his prophecies on the rulers of Babylon from Nebuchadnezzar to the Antichrist. The final ruler of Babylon will be destroyed by the Messiah when he returns to earth on the day of the Lord. This fact is stated three times in Daniel's visions, leaving no room for doubt as to God's sovereign use of the nations to carry out his will, regardless of their intent.

The reason Daniel is not well understood is that it is based on a cyclical-progressive theme that builds and expands from one vision to the next. Each new vision Daniel receives from the angel of the Lord is related to the previous vision, while giving us new information which explains both. New metaphors are used from vision to vision, which can be confusing and frightening, but they are all related to the rulership of Babylon. Each ruler that follows Nebuchadnezzar makes Babylon his capital, and Babylon will be the homeland of the Antichrist, the final enemy of the saints of God.

THE VISION OF THE STATUE

In Daniel 2, King Nebuchadnezzar has a dream that is interpreted for him by Daniel. Here is that dream:

> "Your Majesty looked, and there before you stood a large statue—an enormous, dazzling statue, awesome in appearance. *The head of the statue was made of pure gold, its chest and arms of silver, its belly and thighs of bronze, its legs of iron, its feet partly of iron and partly of baked clay.* While you were watching, a rock was cut out, but not by human hands. It struck the statue on its feet of iron and clay and smashed them. Then the iron, the clay, the bronze, the silver and the gold were all broken to pieces and became like chaff on a threshing floor in the summer. The wind swept them away without leaving a trace. But the rock that struck the statue became a huge mountain and filled the whole earth."
>
> "This was the dream, and now we will interpret it to the king. Your Majesty, you are the king of kings. The God of heaven has given you dominion and power and might and glory; in your hands he has placed all mankind and the beasts of the field and the birds in the sky. Wherever they live, he has made you ruler over them all. *You are that head of gold.*
>
> "*After you, another kingdom will arise*, inferior to yours. Next, *a third kingdom, one of bronze*, will rule

over the whole earth. Finally, *there will be a fourth kingdom, strong as iron*—for iron breaks and smashes everything—and as iron breaks things to pieces, so it will crush and break all the others. *Just as you saw that the feet and toes were partly of baked clay and partly of iron, so this will be a divided kingdom*; yet it will have some of the strength of iron in it, even as you saw iron mixed with clay. As the toes were partly iron and partly clay, so this kingdom will be partly strong and partly brittle. And just as you saw the iron mixed with baked clay, so the people will be a mixture and will not remain united, any more than iron mixes with clay."

"*In the time of those kings, the God of heaven will set up a kingdom that will never be destroyed*, nor will it be left to another people. It will crush all those kingdoms and bring them to an end, but it will itself endure forever. This is the meaning of the vision of the rock cut out of a mountain, but not by human hands—a rock that broke the iron, the bronze, the clay, the silver and the gold to pieces.

"The great God has shown the king what will take place in the future. The dream is true and its interpretation is trustworthy."

— Daniel 2:31–45

Most readers of Daniel conclude that the angel is predicting there will be four world empires from the time of Nebuchadnezzar until the return of Christ at the end of time. The common interpretation is the fourth kingdom is Rome. But the power of Rome was never centered in Babylon. This distortion of the text was invented by the followers of John Nelson Darby in order to support their view of a pretribulational rapture, but that is not what this passage says.

In the first place, you must remember there are several visions in Daniel, and they are progressive in nature. You cannot read the first vision and think you know the whole story. Furthermore, the very first verse of this passage breaks the empires down into five parts, not four. Notice the statue has a head of gold (one), chest and arms of silver (two), belly and thighs of bronze (three), legs of iron (four), and feet and toes of mixed iron and clay (five). In other words, this statue vision is far more complex than most people think, and it will get even more complex as the explanation is given in Daniel's later revelations.

Even more importantly, this vision has nothing to do with the number of empires that will rule the world. There are only two nations at the center of Daniel's prophecies: Israel and Babylon. Daniel's visions are all about the future of those two kingdoms. All other kingdoms of the world and their future rulers are ignored. The Caesars of Rome don't matter. The Xis and Mings of China don't matter. The Khans of Central Asia don't matter. The Merovingians and Franks of Europe don't matter. The Czars of Russia don't matter. The Hanovers of England (even though their empire was four times the size of Nebuchadnezzar's Babylonian Empire at its peak) don't matter. The nationality and religion of the rulers of Babylonia will change through time; that too doesn't matter. The only nations that matters in Daniel's visions are Babylon and Israel, because Babylon is the enemy of both God and Israel.

Israel ceased to be a nation in AD 135 and didn't become a nation again until May 18, 1948. This time frame marks the Diaspora (scattering) of the Jews. Everything that happened in the world during that time period had no effect on the nation of Israel because it did not exist and is therefore not important to Daniel's visions. This is also the "gap period" which we will see when we look deeper into Daniel. Now that the nation of Israel has been re-established, the final prophecy of Daniel concerning the revival of the Kingdom of the North (the homeland of Antichrist) can be fulfilled.

Now let's look at Daniel's vision again. Starting with the first ruler, the head represents Nebuchadnezzar and his Babylonian Empire. We are not told who the several other rulers will be at this point. However, we are told that the last kingdom will be in power when the kingdom of God comes to earth. From our point in history, that means there must be a very large time gap that ignores everything from the time of the rulers of the legs of iron until the appearance of the final ruler of Babylon. He will be the last King of the North, which will be the kingdom of feet and toes. Furthermore, we know the last kingdom will be divided into ten parts, some of which are strong and some weak.

The Vision of the Beasts

The statue of Daniel 2 is only the beginning of Daniel's visions of the future. In Daniel 7, he has another vision that gives more detail about Nebuchadnezzar's vision of a statue. Daniel's vision is cyclical and progressive and builds on the previous vision, giving us more detail about those kingdoms with each new vision. But in Daniel 7, the metaphor has changes from a statue to beasts, the first three of which are composed of various parts of earthly creatures. The last one is not, and challenges Daniel's ability to describe it.

> Daniel said: "In my vision at night I looked, and there before me were the four winds of heaven churning up the great sea. *Four great beasts, each different from the others, came up out of the sea.*
>
> "The first was like *a lion,* and it had the wings of an eagle. I watched until its wings were torn off and it was

lifted from the ground so that it stood on two feet like a human being, and the mind of a human was given to it.

"And there before me was a second beast, which looked like *a bear*. It was raised up on one of its sides, and it had three ribs in its mouth between its teeth. It was told, 'Get up and eat your fill of flesh!'

"After that, I looked, and there before me was another beast, one that looked like *a leopard*. And on its back it had four wings like those of a bird. This beast had four heads, and it was given authority to rule.

"After that, in my vision at night I looked, and there before me was *a fourth beast—terrifying and frightening* and very powerful. It had large iron teeth; it crushed and devoured its victims and trampled underfoot whatever was left. It was different from all the former beasts, and *it had ten horns*.

"While I was thinking about the horns, there before me was *another horn*, a little one, which came up among them; *and three of the first horns were uprooted before it*. This horn had eyes like the eyes of a human being and a mouth that spoke boastfully."

— Daniel 7:2–8

The four beasts seen by Daniel resemble a lion, a bear, a leopard, and something else that defies description. It is different from any of the other earthly beasts and much more vicious. We will see these same beasts later, brought back to life in Revelation. These beasts coincide with the head of gold, the chest and arms of silver, the belly and thighs of bronze, and the feet and toes of mixed iron and clay. However, no mention is made of the two legs of iron. That should be a signal to us that the number of those kingdoms is not the significant point of this passage. The point is that the final beast with ten horns is the final enemy of God's people, and it will be destroyed by the return of the Messiah at the end of time.

Notice the fourth beast (kingdom) is not described as an animal that we would be familiar with, because it will be unlike any other kingdom the world has seen. It is made up of ten kings. It will actually be a coalition of ten nations, which will eventually be ruled by one man. He takes control of that ten-nation coalition after it is established by defeating three of the kings and taking their authority away from them. This final kingdom of Babylon matches Daniel's first vision of chapter 2; being ten toes, some of which are weak and some of which are strong. We will be given more detail about this ten-nation coalition in Daniel's final vision located in chapters 11–12. But for now it is important that we know these kings will be united by a common desire to destroy Israel.

THE VISION OF THE SON OF MAN

Daniel, like Jeremiah and Ezekiel, did not fully understand his visions. In order to explain what he didn't fully understand himself, Daniel makes uses of a *parenthesis* (a change in the story line) to introduce another vision related to what he sees here on earth but is unrelated to the beasts of Babylon. This is the same method John uses to give warnings and encouragement to the church in his Book of Revelation. That fact, along with John's cyclical-progressive structure and his multiple quotes and allusions from Daniel, are the reasons I believe Revelation is based solidly on Daniel.

What follows is one of the most quoted passages of the Bible in relation to Jesus Christ. It is the source of the name "Son of Man" which Jesus consistently uses of himself in the four gospels. Jesus never calls himself the son of Mary and Joseph, nor does he ever say he is the son of David. In fact, he openly challenges those who call him the son of David (Matthew 22:41–45). Instead, Jesus refers to himself over seventy times in the four gospels as the Son of Man. Here's why:

> "As I looked, "thrones were set in place, and the Ancient of Days took his seat. His clothing was as white as snow; the hair of his head was white like wool. His throne was flaming with fire, and its wheels were all ablaze. A river of fire was flowing, coming out from before him. Thousands upon thousands attended him; ten thousand times ten thousand stood before him. The court was seated, and the books were opened.
>
> "Then I continued to watch because of the boastful words the horn was speaking. I kept looking until the beast was slain and its body destroyed and *thrown into the blazing fire.* (The other beasts had been stripped of their authority, but were allowed to live for a period of time.)
>
> "In my vision at night I looked, and there before me was one like a son of man, coming with the clouds of heaven. He approached the Ancient of Days and was led into his presence. He was given authority, glory and sovereign power; all nations and peoples of every language worshiped him. His dominion is an everlasting dominion that will not pass away, and his kingdom is one that will never be destroyed."
>
> — Daniel 7:9–14

The phrase "a son of man" refers to being the finest example of humanity. This is a clear indication that the one who takes the authority from the hand of God to judge the earth will be a human being, but not just any human being. He will be the finest example of humanity ever known. Therefore, he can empathize with our weaknesses and intercede for us. At the same time, he is fully God, as indicated by Isaiah 45:22–25, which says:

> "Turn to me and be saved, all you ends of the earth; *for I am God, and there is no other.* By myself I have sworn, my mouth has uttered in all integrity a word that will not be revoked: Before me every knee will bow; by me every tongue will swear. They will say of me, 'In the LORD alone are deliverance and strength.'" All who have raged against him will come to him and be put to shame. But all the descendants of Israel will find deliverance in the LORD and will make their boast in him.

That is why Jesus Christ chose to use this name exclusively when referring to himself in the gospels. Jesus calls himself the Son of Man because he is both fully God and fully man.

The Son of Man takes authority from the hands of God the Father and begins his reign on earth. This event is predicted by Paul in I Corinthians 15:20–28, and we see it happening in Revelation 4–5. Jesus does that by stripping power away from the four beasts Daniel has seen in the vision of chapter 7. The boastful little horn that defies description, the last ruler of Babylon, is destroyed by the Son of Man, and thrown into the blazing fire. This is in perfect harmony with what Isaiah has to say about the last king of Babylon.

There is no question that the fourth beast of Daniel 7 is the Kingdom of Babylon at the end of time, and its final ruler will be the Antichrist. The fact that Jesus destroys this ruler by his triumphal return to earth makes it plain this cannot take place at any time except the very end of the age. It certainly did not happen in 164 BC!

The Rulers of Babylon

At this point, the only problem we have is not having the names of the rulers of Babylon who will follow Nebuchadnezzar. Finally, in Daniel's next vision, we are given those names. That vision is found in chapter 8.

In the third year of King Belshazzar's reign, I, Daniel, had a vision, after the one that had already appeared to me. In my vision I saw myself in the citadel of Susa in the province of Elam; in the vision I was beside the Ulai Canal. I looked up, and there before me was *a ram with two horns,* standing beside the canal, and the horns were long. One of the horns was longer than the other but grew up later. I watched the ram as it charged toward the west and the north and the south. No animal could stand against it, and none could rescue from its power. It did as it pleased and became great.

As I was thinking about this, suddenly *a goat with a prominent horn* between its eyes came from the west, crossing the whole earth without touching the ground. It came toward the two-horned ram I had seen standing beside the canal and charged at it in great rage. I saw it attack the ram furiously, striking the ram and shattering its two horns. The ram was powerless to stand against it; the goat knocked it to the ground and trampled on it, and none could rescue the ram from its power. The goat became very great, but at the height of its power the large horn was broken off, *and in its place four prominent horns grew up* toward the four winds of heaven.

Out of one of them came another horn, which started small but grew in power to the south and to the east and toward the Beautiful Land. It grew until it reached the host of the heavens, and it threw some of the starry host down to the earth and trampled on them. It set itself up to be as great as the commander of the army of the Lord; it took away the daily sacrifice from the Lord, and his sanctuary was thrown down. Because of rebellion, the Lord's people and the daily sacrifice were given over to it. It prospered in everything it did, and truth was thrown to the ground.

Then I heard a holy one speaking, and another holy one said to him, "How long will it take for the vision to be fulfilled—the vision concerning the daily sacrifice, the rebellion that causes desolation, the surrender of the sanctuary and the trampling underfoot of the Lord's people?"

He said to me, "It will take 2,300 evenings and mornings; then the sanctuary will be reconsecrated."

"While I, Daniel, was watching the vision and trying to understand it, there before me stood one who looked like a man. And I heard a man's voice from the Ulai calling, "Gabriel, tell this man the meaning of the vision."

As he came near the place where I was standing, I was terrified and fell prostrate. "Son of man," he said to me, "understand that the vision concerns the time of the end."

"While he was speaking to me, I was in a deep sleep, with my face to the ground. Then he touched me and raised me to my feet.

 He said: "I am going to tell you what will happen later in the time of wrath, because the vision concerns the appointed time of the end. The two-horned ram that you saw represents the kings of *Media and Persia*. The shaggy goat is the king of *Greece*, and the large horn between its eyes is the first king. The four horns that replaced the one that was broken off represent *four king-doms* that will emerge from his nation but will not have the same power.

"*In the latter part of their reign*, when rebels have become completely wicked, a *fierce-looking king, a master of intrigue, will arise.* He will become very strong, but not by his own power. He will cause astounding devastation and will succeed in whatever he does. He will destroy those who are mighty, the holy people. He will cause deceit to prosper, and he will consider himself superior. When they feel secure, he will destroy many and take his stand against the Prince of princes. Yet he will be destroyed, but not by human power.

"The vision of the evenings and mornings that has been given you is true, *but seal up the vision, for it concerns the distant future.*"

— Daniel 8:1–26

From this vision, we learn that the second ruler of Babylon will be the dual kingdom of Media-Persia (the kingdom of the chest and arms of silver), which will become the kingdom of Persia, as Media fades into the background. Then Persia will be overthrown by the king of Greece.

Now we are given much more information about the third kingdom destined to rule from Babylon. It will not be one simple dynasty, nor will it appear and then just as quickly disappear, as did Nebuchadnezzar's kingdom. Instead, the kingdom of the belly and thighs of bronze from Daniel 2 will be shattered into four separate kingdoms, which will for a short time become their own bronze kingdom.

As if that did not complicate matters enough, we learn that after an unspecified gap in time, the final ruler, "a master of intrigue," will appear out of the territory of one of those four rulers. That kingdom will later morph into the kingdom of the feet and toes of iron and clay. This vision seems to skip over the legs of iron that appear in the earlier vision of Daniel 2. The significance of this fact is not clear now, but it will become apparent when the angel gets to the visions of the Kings of the North and South.

We know from history the first king of Greece was Alexander the Great; he was part one of the kingdom of the belly and thighs of bronze. In 331 BC, Alexander's army overthrew Darius III of Persia. Alexander then set up his capital in Babylon and married a Persian princess. However, Alexander died young in 322 BC, and his kingdom was divided by four generals, just as this prophecy predicts; they are part two of the kingdom of the belly and thighs of bronze. In the later part of the reign of one of the four generals, the final beast will appear. He will be a fierce-looking man who is a master of intrigue. This man will appear at the end of time as the Antichrist.

We know the four generals who divided up the kingdom of Alexander were Cassander, Lysimachus, Ptolemy, and Seleucus. None of these men died from divine intervention at the end of time, so none of them are a fulfillment of this prophecy. The answer to this problem is found in Daniel 8:23, where we are told it will happen in the "later part of their reign." Daniel 8:26 says the vision concerns the "distant future." In other words, at the end of time, a master of intrigue will establish his rule in the remnants of the kingdom of one of these four generals. But which one? That part of the message has not been revealed to Daniel at this point; it will come later. Up to this point, we only know the statue vision of Daniel 2 should be understood to mean the kingdom of the belly and thighs represents two separate kingdoms which will rule over Babylon. Then the feet and ten toes will be the last kingdom at the very end of time. However, we have again skipped over the legs of iron.

Daniel's next vision predicts the first coming of Jesus Christ as the Anointed One. Daniel writes in chapter 9:

> While I was speaking and praying, confessing my sin and the sin of my people Israel and making my request to the Lord my God for his holy hill—while I was still in prayer, Gabriel, the man I had seen in the earlier vision, came to me in swift flight about the time of the evening sacrifice. He instructed me and said to me, "Daniel, I have now come to give you insight and understanding. As soon as you began to pray, a word went out, which I have come to tell you, for you are highly esteemed. Therefore, consider the word and understand the vision:
>
> "Seventy 'sevens' are decreed for your people and your holy city to finish transgression, to put an end to sin, to atone for wickedness, to bring in everlasting righteousness, to seal up vision and prophecy and to anoint the Most Holy Place.
>
> "Know and understand this: From the time the word goes out to restore and rebuild Jerusalem until the Anointed One, the ruler, comes, there will be seven 'sevens,' and sixty-two 'sevens.' It will be rebuilt with streets and a trench, but in times of trouble."
>
> "After the sixty-two 'sevens,' the Anointed One will be put to death and will have nothing. The people of the ruler who will come will destroy the city and the sanctuary. The end will come like a flood: War will continue until the end, and desolations have been decreed. *He will confirm a covenant with many for one 'seven.' In the middle of the 'seven' he will put an end to sacrifice and offering.* And at the temple he will set up an *abomination*

that causes desolation, until the end that is decreed is
poured out on him."

— Daniel 9:20–27

In this vision, Daniel predicts the first coming of Jesus. Some
have calculated his birth to have been in 3 BC. But Daniel goes on
to say the Messiah will be cut off by the people of the final ruler. In
other words, the people who crucified Jesus—the high priest and the
Sanhedrin— did so at the behest of the ultimate ruler of Babylon.
That begs the question: Did the spirit of the Antichrist control the
Sanhedrin?

There is an obvious gap between the sixty-ninth week (AD 30)
of Daniel's prophecy, and the final seventieth week (the return of
Christ). Jesus Christ is the "Anointed One" who was cut off. But the
last verse of this promise has not been fulfilled. I don't know of a
single Christian commentator who does not recognize this fact.
This passage also shows that the final ruler will make a covenant
with the people of Israel, as stated in Daniel 9:27. The signing of this
covenant will signal the beginning of the tribulation period, which
is the final seventieth week of Daniel's prophecy.

At first, the Antichrist will be hailed as a great peacemaker, and
he will probably allow the Jews to finish rebuilding their temple
next to the Dome of the Rock. This will be the final proof that he
wants peace between Judaism and Islam, and he will make everyone
believe there is no danger. However, after three and a half years, the
Antichrist will break this covenant and set up the abomination of
desolation in the temple of God. This is the same temple that was
measured by Ezekiel in 40–47, and by John in Revelation 11. It is
where the Two Witnesses of Revelation 11 will minister for the first
three and a half years of the tribulation.

The breaking of the covenant will be the point in the tribulation
when Jesus' words in Matthew 24:15–22 will be fulfilled:

"So when you see standing in the holy place 'the abomination that causes desolation' *spoken of through the
prophet Daniel*—let the reader understand—then let
those who are in Judea flee to the mountains. Let no
one on the housetop go down to take anything out of
the house. Let no one in the field go back to get their
cloak. How dreadful it will be in those days for pregnant women and nursing mothers! Pray that your flight
will not take place in winter or on the Sabbath. For then
there will be great distress, unequaled from the beginning of the world until now—and never to be equaled
again. If those days had not been cut short, no one
would survive, *but for the sake of the elect those days
will be shortened.*"

The final scattering of Israel will take place at this time. The
Diaspora of Israel ended in 1948. But as predicted in Isaiah 6:13 and
11:10–11, the oak tree of Israel will be cut down again. The breaking
of the covenant by the Antichrist will signal this last scattering.
Many Jews will be killed, many will be captured and put in prison,
and the Antichrist will have his way for three and a half years. Those
who are able to escape will flee into the desert, where they will be
protected by God until the day they are rescued by their promised
Redeemer. That Redeemer will be Jesus Christ, who will fulfill the
prophecy of Moses in Deuteronomy 30:1–7 by rapturing Israel from
all corners of the earth. This very basic fact of prophecy is missed
by the modern church because so many have believed there is a
difference between Jews and Christians in the eyes of God.

Notice also, after Jesus warns his disciples in Matthew 24
about the suffering they will go through, and the abomination
of desolation, he tells them about his coming again as the Son of
Man in 24:27–28, fulfilling the prophecy of Daniel's vision in 7:13.

Then, without giving a date, Jesus gives the timing of his return in relationship to the other events of the tribulation.

He says in Matthew 24:29–31:

> "*Immediately after the distress* of those days 'the sun will be darkened, and the moon will not give its light [Isaiah 24:23]; the stars will fall from the sky [Isaiah 34:4], and the heavenly bodies will be shaken.'
>
> "Then will appear the sign of the Son of Man in heaven [Daniel 7:13]. And then all the peoples of the earth will mourn when they see the Son of Man coming on the clouds of heaven, with power and great glory. *And he will send his angels with a loud trumpet call, and they will gather his elect from the four winds, from one end of the heavens to the other*" [Isaiah 27:12–13].

The word "distress" in this passage is actually the word "tribulation." Look at the timing of this event: it will happen, not before, not during, but *after* the distress of those days. That means the events of the tribulation he was just speaking about will happen prior to his appearing, when the Son of Man returns with the loud trumpet call and the army of heaven to rapture his saints from the four corners of heaven.

The apostle Paul writes to the Thessalonian church to tell them they have not missed the rapture of the church, because the man of lawlessness must appear in the temple of God and claim to be God before the church is raptured and redeemed by Christ (see II Thessalonians 2:1–12). Daniel tells us the event will take place halfway through the reign of the Antichrist, the last king of Babylon. That means there will be seven years of rule by this evil man.

The start of the reign of the Antichrist, and therefore the start of the tribulation, is marked by the signing of a peace treaty with Israel.

The halfway point is marked by the breaking of that treaty, which will expose his true nature. The prophecies of Jesus and the apostle Paul fit hand in glove with the prophecies of Isaiah and Daniel. It is as if they are speaking with one voice—the voice of the Holy Spirit!

Now let's return to Daniel.

THE VISIONS OF THE KINGS OF THE NORTH AND SOUTH

After this, Daniel has another series of visions concerning the Kings of the North and the Kings of the South. Finally, this is where the kingdom of the legs of iron from Daniel 2 is explained. Those visions are important to our understanding of prophecy. They explain Daniel 2, and they provide a typical fulfillment of what the final ruler of Babylon will be like.

The King of the North is the Seleucid dynasty of Babylonia, and the King of the South is the Ptolemaic Empire of North Africa. This is historic fact: they are the two legs of iron who ruled the world. The kingdom of Seleucus controlled all the territory from Turkey to India, with the exception of Israel, which they wanted. The kingdom of Ptolemy controlled Egypt, Libya, and Cush (or Northern Sudan). The early portion of these visions as written by Daniel has been fulfilled. However, it is important to remember that we have been told in Daniel 7 that the Antichrist will arise out of the territory of the kingdom of the King of the North, the Seleucids. That means the final Babylonian kingdom of the Antichrist will arise in the area that was once ruled by the Seleucids.

Now this is where most people get very confused. The third kingdom (the kingdom of the belly and the thighs) has two parts: the kingdom of Alexander the Great, followed by the divided kingdom of the four generals (Seleucus, Ptolomy, Cassander, and Lysimachus).

This third kingdom is followed by the kingdom of the legs of iron, which consists of the King of the North (the Seleucid dynasty) and the King of the South (the Ptolomic dynasty). Suddenly, the King of the North morphs into the Antichrist, but he is not Seleucus. How did that happen?

Most people miss the indicator in Daniel 11:29 that shows that a jump in time is occurring. This is the same gap in time that we know exists between the sixty-ninth and seventieth weeks of Daniel 9:26–27. We are now going from the kingdom of the legs of iron, ignored in earlier visions, to the final kingdom of the feet and toes.

The Final Kingdom

In this last vision of Daniel, the angel gets much more specific about the final ruler of Babylon. We are told where he will come from, who he will defeat in his rise to power, and what he will do once he gets in power. He is the one who is called the Antichrist by the church. Here is Daniel's final vision:

> "*At the appointed time* he will invade the South again, but this time the outcome will be different from what it was before. Ships of the western coastlands will oppose him, and he will lose heart. Then he will turn back and vent his fury against the holy covenant. He will return and show favor to those who forsake the holy covenant.
>
> "His armed forces will rise up to desecrate the temple fortress and will abolish the daily sacrifice. Then they will set up the abomination that causes desolation. With flattery he will corrupt those who have violated the covenant, but the people who know their God will firmly resist him.

"Those who are wise will instruct many, though for a time they will fall by the sword or be burned or captured or plundered. When they fall, they will receive a little help, and many who are not sincere will join them. Some of the wise will stumble, so that they may be refined, purified and made spotless until the time of the end, for it will still come at the appointed time.

"The king will do as he pleases. He will exalt and magnify himself above every god and will say unheard-of things against the God of gods. He will be successful until the time of wrath is completed, for what has been determined must take place. He will show no regard for the gods of his ancestors or for the one desired by women, nor will he regard any god, but will exalt himself above them all. Instead of them, he will honor a god of fortresses; a god unknown to his ancestors he will honor with gold and silver, with precious stones and costly gifts. He will attack the mightiest fortresses with the help of a foreign god and will greatly honor those who acknowledge him. He will make them rulers over many people and will distribute the land at a price.

"At the time of the end the king of the South will engage him in battle, and the king of the North will storm out against him with chariots and cavalry and a great fleet of ships. He will invade many countries and sweep through them like a flood. He will also invade the Beautiful Land. Many countries will fall, but *Edom, Moab* and the leaders of *Ammon* will be delivered from his hand. He will extend his power over many countries; *Egypt* will not escape. He will gain control of the treasures of gold and silver and all the riches of Egypt, with the *Libyans* and *Cushites* in submission. But reports from the east and the north will alarm him, and he will set out in a great rage to destroy and annihilate many. He will pitch his royal tents between the seas at the beautiful holy mountain. Yet he will come to his end, and no one will help him.

"At that time Michael, the great prince who protects your people, will arise. There will be a time of distress such as has not happened from the beginning of nations until then. But at that time your people—everyone whose name is found written in the book—will be delivered. Multitudes who sleep in the dust of the earth will awake: some to everlasting life, others to shame and everlasting contempt. Those who are wise will shine like the brightness of the heavens, and those who lead many to righteousness, like the stars for ever and ever. But you, *Daniel, roll up and seal the words of the scroll until the time of the end.* Many will go here and there to increase knowledge."

— Daniel 11:29–12:4

The verses in Daniel 11:1–28 talk about all the kings of the North and South who were from the kingdom of the legs of iron (the kings of the Seleucid and Ptolomic dynasties). The secular history of those kings matches what is said by Daniel's prophecy so closely that most skeptics believe Daniel 11 and 12 were written after the fact by another author, whom they call Daniel-Two.

However, verse 29 marks a jump in time in Daniel's prophecy, from the Seleucid and Ptolomic dynasties to the Antichrist's kingdom at the end of time. Everyone clearly sees the gap in time that exists in Daniel's previous prophecy of Christ's first coming. Yet the majority of conservative commentators do not seem to see the very obvious gap that exists in chapter 11 between the ancient

Seleucid kingdom and the future revived Seleucid kingdom ruled by the Antichrist. Instead, they look to Rome to fulfill this prophecy and try to make the seventeen nations of the European Union fit into the prophecy of the ten horns that will form a coalition to rule the world.

The preterists argue the ruler of Seleucia's kingdom mentioned in Daniel 11 was Antiochus IV. But in doing so they ignore Daniel 8:17, 8:19, 8:26, 10:14, 11:40, and 12:4. All of these verses are directly relevant to the context, and all tell us that the vision will happen at the very end of time at the return of the Son of Man. Furthermore, we know the final ruler of Babylon will be killed by the second coming of the Anointed One; Daniel 2, 7, and 9 are very clear about that. Yet Antiochus IV died in 164 BC while doing battle against the Parthians. There was nothing divine about his death. The arrow that pierced his chest was not fired by Jesus Christ.

Therefore, we must conclude this final ruler will come from the *territory* of the ancient Seleucid kingdom, but he will not be a member of that dynasty. By conquering the Kingdom of the South, the Antichrist will unite the two legs of iron into one final kingdom of the feet and toes of iron and clay. He will appear at the end of time as the ruler of a coalition of ten nations from the combined territories of Seleucus and Ptolemy. The Antichrist and his kingdom make up the fourth beast of Daniel's vision as seen in Daniel 7. In other words, the fourth beast of Daniel's vision in Daniel 7 is both a man and a coalition of ten nations; the two are very hard to separate. This problem of separating the man from the coalition of nations will arise again when we get to Revelation 17, where the man and the coalition are divided by the angel who spoke to John.

There is a very specific reason why the kingdom that rules Babylon during the gap is not mentioned in Daniel: There was no kingdom of Israel during most of that gap! The first five kingdoms were gone by the time of John's writing. Furthermore, John was present during the reign of the ruler of the gap period, which turns out to be Parthia. The Diaspora began approximately forty years after the writing of Revelation. That means there was no nation of Israel to be invaded and destroyed by the Antichrist. So nothing counts as a threat to Israel from 135 to 1948.

With all that being said, we know from this prophecy the final king of Babylon will come to power from the territory of the Seleucid Empire, which is made up of modern day Iran, Iraq, Syria, Turkey, Afghanistan, and Pakistan. He will take over the leadership of a ten-nation coalition. We know at least six of the names of those nations from this prophecy. Three of them will not be overthrown but will side with the Antichrist. They will be Edom, Moab, and Ammon (Daniel 11:41), which are Saudi Arabia, Jordan and Syria. Three others will oppose him and be defeated. Those three nations are named for us in Daniel 11:42–43: Egypt, Libya, and Cush (or Northern Sudan). Is it a coincidence that the three kingdoms which were ruled by Ptolemy, the King of the South, were Egypt, Libya, and Cush (or Northern Sudan)?

We are not told how long the ten-nation coalition will rule over the nations of the world. We are only told the Antichrist will rule this coalition for the final seven years of this age. The Antichrist will make a covenant with Israel which he will break after three and one-half years (Daniel 9:27a). Then he will set up the abomination of desolation in the temple of God and claim to be God (Daniel 9:27b). At the end of his rule he will be defeated and his kingdom destroyed by the second coming of Jesus Christ. We now can see the connection between Isaiah 14, Isaiah 30, and Daniel 7. The final king of Babylon will be a Satan-indwelt man from Babylonia who will rule both Assyria and Babylon and is destined for the lake of fire. The final kingdom of Babylon, the archenemy of God's people, will be made up of ten nations which will be the target of God's overpowering wrath.

However, the church today seems to believe that these prophecies are irrelevant. The area that was called Babylon then has not been

known by that name for more than 1,700 years. We are blind to the
fact that it is still the number-one enemy of Israel, and therefore
the enemy of all God's children. Likewise, the religion that tried to
destroy Israel in the past is gone, and now there is a new religion
in that area. However, both religions serve the same god and both
religions have the same ultimate purpose of destroying the children
of God.

This should be a wake-up call to America. As the United States
wanes from a position of world power, a new threat rises on the
horizon, waiting for a chance to fulfill its own prophecies about
Israel and Jerusalem. Those prophecies concern the other Redeemer
of prophecy, the Muslim redeemer known in Arabic as al-Mahdi.
When that happens, the Muslim threat of anti-Semitic genocide will
turn out to be the fulfillment of all prophecy, biblical and Islamic.

Section Two

Islamic History, Theology, and the Twelver Tradition

CHAPTER SEVEN

ISLAMIC HISTORY, THEOLOGY,
AND THE TWELVER TRADITION

Now it is time to take a look at Islam to see if the Word of God conflicts or agrees with what the Muslims believe. There will be no attempt to distort Islamic prophecy. The references to the Qur'an are their own scriptures in their own words. (The Qur'an can also be spelled Koran or Quran; we have chosen to use Qur'an.) I will simply let them speak for themselves. The history of Islam section can be verified by numerous sources, and will make no judgments as to right or wrong.[1]

ISLAMIC HISTORY

Mohammad lived from AD 570 to 632. His father abandoned his mother while she was still pregnant, and he was orphaned at the age of six. He was raised by his uncle Abu Talib and his aunt Khadija. After Abu Talib died, Mohammad married Khadija. Mohammad was a very spiritually minded man who sought to know God. His chief source of information about God came from his wife's cousin Nawfal ibn Waraqah, who was a Christian and familiar with the Hebrew and Greek writings of the Christian faith. Nawfal tutored Mohammad in religion as he grew up,[2] but when he became an adult,

Mohammad sought his own religious truth. At the age of 40, in the year 610, Mohammad went into a cave near Mecca to meditate.

Muhammad ibn Ishaq gives the details of the event in his biography of Mohammad:

> Whilst I was asleep, with a coverlet of silk brocade whereon was some writing, the angel Gabriel appeared to me and said, "Read!" I said, "I do not read." He pressed me with the coverlet so tightly that me thought 'twas death. Then he let me go and said, "Read!". . . So I read aloud, and he departed from me at last. And I awoke from my sleep, and it was as though these words were written on my heart. I went forth until when I was midway on the mountain I heard a voice from heaven saying, "O Mohammad, thou art the messenger of Allah, and I am Gabriel." I raised my head toward heaven to see, and lo, Gabriel in the form of a man, with feet set evenly on the rim of the sky, saying, "O Mohammad, thou art the messenger of Allah, and I am Gabriel."[3]

This was the first indication that Mohammad intended to start his own religion. He did not write down his visions because he was illiterate all his life. Instead, he communicated his visions to his followers through sermons. These sermons were not recorded at the time but were remembered by his followers. Various believers contributed their remembrances to Abu Bekr (the leader of the Sunni division of Islam) for the sake of a written record after the death of Mohammad.

Mohammad's visions continued until his death in the year 632. There is one major difference that must be noted between the visions that came to Mohammad and the visions of the prophets of the Bible. Nothing that was said by the prophets of the Bible was ever negated by a later prophecy. When God speaks, he speaks only the truth. The message may be further explained through the process of progressive revelation, but it is never wrong.

That is not true of the messages given to Mohammad from the angel Gabriel. The earlier messages are *abrogated*, or superseded, by later visions. This is especially true of Mohammad's earliest messages concerning relations with Jews and Christians. The early sayings are peaceful and conciliatory towards Jews and Christians. The later sayings are harsh and unforgiving, and promise death for anyone who does not convert. When Muslims are challenged concerning the passages that prescribe death for non-believers, they usually point to the earlier abrogated verses as proof of their peaceful intentions. Yet these abrogated verses are not to be followed by orthodox Muslims.

The harsh and unforgiving statements of the Qur'an derive from Mohammad's fight to establish his religion in the Arabian Peninsula. He was rejected in Mecca, his hometown, and driven north to a small village called Medina. There he and his small band of followers were able to live and gradually gain control of the town. He was able to support himself and his followers by robbing caravans as they travelled from Syria to Mecca. His followers saw his numerous victories over the much larger forces of the caravan guards as proof that God was on his side.[4] This made him a wealthy and powerful man in Medina. Once he gained the authority to become supreme judge in Medina, he turned from a conciliator to a murderer. The five hundred Jewish men from the area who refused to convert were beheaded. The women and girls were taken alive and forced to be concubines and slaves.[5]

As an incentive to gather more warriors to his cause, Mohammad divided the female captives from the caravans among his fighters.[6] Some fighters complained that if they died in battle, they would not get such a reward. Mohammad's reply was to promise that those who died for the cause of Islam would go directly to Paradise, where their reward would be an eternity of being serviced by *houris,* or eternal virgins, who were far more skilled in sex than any earthly woman.[7] *Houris* were masters of every sexual act, and their sex organs remained forever in the same virginal state, even after they became the prize of an Islamic warrior. This promise is found in numerous *suras,* including Sura 38:51, 44:54, 55:55-74, 56:22, 34-36.[8, 9] For instance:

> This is a monition: and verily, the pious shall have a goodly retreat: Gardens of Eden, whose portals shall stand open to them: Therein reclining, they shall there call for many a fruit and drink: And with them shall be virgins [*houris*] of their own age, with modest retiring glances: this is what ye were promised at the day of reckoning: Yes! This is your provision: It will never fail.
>
> — Sura 38:50-51

> In Gardens of Bliss: a number of people from those of old, and a few from those of later times. They will be on thrones covered with gold and precious jewels, reclining on them, facing each other round about them will serve youths of perpetual freshness, with goblets, shining beakers and cups filled out of clear flowing fountains; No after-ache will they receive therefrom, nor will they suffer intoxication, and with fruits, any that they select; and the flesh of fowls, any that they desire. And there will be virgins [*houris*] with big lustrous eyes like unto pearls well-guarded, a reward for the deeds of their past lives.
>
> — Sura 56:12-24 (Compare to Matthew 22:29-30)

Don Richardson says, "In the Qur'an, he [Mohammad] repeatedly redefines Judeo-Christianity's heaven as an enormous God-owned bordello in the sky."[10] The task of constantly servicing *houris* day and night will not be a problem for the faithful Muslim. Noted Islamic author and journalist Muhammad Galal Al-Kushk said, "In Paradise a believer's penis will be eternally erect."[11] These promises of eternal sex with beautiful masters of the art, as well as with boys who are "eternally fresh," while being waited on hand and foot by ordinary women, swelled the ranks of Muhammad's fighters. But these promises were made only to those who died in the fight to make Islam the sole religion in Arabia.

The struggle to conquer the other pagan tribes of Arabia was called *jihad*, which means "to struggle." Many fighters lost their lives in the battles, expecting to be ushered in to Allah's bordello. The total number of *houris* who would service each fallen fighter was never set in the Qur'an. However, it has grown through the years by the continual process of new *hadiths* (sayings) from one *houri* for each fighter to seventy-two *houris* for each fighter. The reward has also increased to include seventy-two relatives of the fallen fighter, who will be allowed to enter Paradise with him.

These seventy-three Muslims are guaranteed an entrance to Paradise, but there is no guarantee of Paradise for anyone who does not die in the cause of *jihad*. Those who die apart from the "struggle" to glorify Allah must hope their lives are good enough to please Allah on the Day of Judgment, but they have no guarantee. It will depend solely on their good works.

With rapidly growing numbers of converts, Mohammad was able to return to Mecca in the year 630 and overwhelm the city with followers. Those who refused to convert were executed. The Kaaba (a holy shrine in Mecca) was purged of its 360 idols, and only four were allowed to remain: Allah and his three fertility goddess daughters.

The concept of Allah and three fertility goddesses was taken by the Arabs directly from Greek story of Zeus and his daughters.[12]

Salman Rushdie's book, *The Satanic Verses*, is about the early worship of these three daughters of Allah who were allowed to remain in the Kaaba until the Middle Ages. At that time, all mention of these fertility goddesses was purged from Islamic beliefs and their idols were removed from the Kaaba. Only at that point did Islam become purely monotheistic.[13] Now, true Muslims pray five times per day, "Allah is the greatest God, and he has no son," but no mention is ever made of his daughters.

If we were to summarize the driving forces that allowed Mohammad to conquer Arabia and then the Middle East, we would have to say they are sex and murder. Sex was the reward for murder, but that reward was true only for Muslim males. The discrimination against females would continue even in Paradise. Don Richardson looks at Islamic society today and concludes:

> Consider what must have been the social effect of Mohammad's constant bandying of the promise of increased sex with extra wives and slaves in this life plus even more and better sex with bevies of virgins in paradise. Understandably, pagan Arab men, snagged into Islam by this almost irresistible lure of sex, had sex on their minds even more than before their conversion. This presents a dilemma. No Muslim man wanted his own wives and daughters to become objects of so much increased male sexual desire in the general community. So Muslim men felt obligated to cover and even hide their wives and daughters from view even more than pagan Arab culture required. What began as a safeguard soon became an entrenched cultural imperative. Islam's widespread practice of amputating the clitoris and sometimes part or even all of the vulva from the

genitalia of Muslim women, affirmed in a hadith by Mohammad himself, most likely also traces back to the founder's deliberate abuse of the male sex drive to lure pagan men into his cult.[14]

When Mohammad died in 632, the two major tribes of Mecca fought for the right to name the next leader of Islam. The split was between the followers of Abu Bekr of the Umayya tribe and Ali of the Hashim tribe, who was the cousin and son-in-law of Mohammad. After a series of bloody battles, the larger Umayya tribe drove out the Hashim tribe, who then migrated from Arabia to the Mesopotamian Valley.

This formed the two major divisions of Islam: the Sunni, who followed Abu Bekr, and the Shi'a, who followed Ali, the son-in-law of Mohammad. The word *Shi'a* is actually a contraction from *Shi Atu Ali*, which means "the followers of Ali." *Sunni* means "traditions." The Sunni derive their name from the fact that they were the first to follow the "traditions" of the Qur'an as it was composed by Abu Bekr.

Islamic tradition says the Qur'an was compiled in Cairo by Abu Bekr around the year 634. The Qur'an is divided into 114 *suras*, or sermons. All statements in this text referring to the Qur'an have been verified by cross-checking four editions of the Qur'an. References to passages in the Qur'an list the number of the *sura* first, then the verse number in the *sura*. There is no standard edition of the Qur'an and no standard way to number the verses in each *sura*. This can be overcome by checking the verses within five numbers each way of the reference listed.

Since the writing of the Qur'an, about 25,000 other *hadiths*, or "sayings," of Mohammad have been collected over the centuries. Along with the Qur'an, these sayings are accepted by Muslims as scripture. Some of these *hadiths* are remembrances from contemporaries of Abu Bekr and Mohammad. However, most *hadiths* are visions that came to various imams over the centuries concerning Mohammad and his future replacement, al-Mahdi. Visions of imams continue even to this day, and, as a result, the Muslim scriptures continue to grow. Today there are five major volumes of *hadiths* and several minor ones. The collections of *hadiths* which are universally accepted as scripture are Sahih Muslim, Sahih Bukhari, Sunan Abu Dawud, Sunan al-Sughra, and Sunan al-Tirmidhi. Others are accepted by many, but not all, Muslims. The *hadiths* referred to in this text can be found online at www.thejerusalemfund.org and at www.jihadwatch.org. A version that is designed for Western eyes can be found at www.hadithcollection.com. Several other sites offer a variety of *hadiths* as well.

ISLAMIC THEOLOGY

The practice of Islam is based on the "five pillars" that every Muslim must follow. They are:

- *Shahadah:* The declaration: "There is no god but Allah and Mohammad is his Messenger."
- *Salat:* Prayer five times per day declaring, "Allah is the Greatest God and he has no son."
- *Sawn:* The forty-day fast of Ramadan
- *Zakat:* The giving of alms
- *Hajj:* A pilgrimage at least once in your lifetime to Mecca

Anyone who does these five things is considered a *Muslim*, or "one who is submitted to God."

Mohammad taught that God created Adam and Eve as perfect creatures in the Garden of Eden, which was located in heaven, not on earth. When they sinned, God made them come down to earth, but when Adam repented of his sin, God forgave him. Therefore, when Adam and Eve had children, they had no sin nature to pass along to their children. That means everyone is basically good but occasionally does things wrong. On Judgment Day, God will weigh your good deeds against your mistakes. If your acts of charity outweigh your bad deeds, you will be admitted into Paradise (Sura 23:102-103). That is why doing acts of charity is one of the five pillars of Islam. Muslims reject the idea of needing a Savior to redeem them from their sins. You can save yourself, no matter how bad your sins are, by putting a little more money in the offering on Friday night. Charity, or doing good deeds, erases your sins.

Second, Mohammad taught that all of the patriarchs of the Bible were apostles of Allah and true Muslims; that includes Abraham, Isaac, Ishmael, Jacob, Joseph, and Jesus. They all taught the message of the Qur'an to their followers, but that message was confused and distorted by those who actually wrote the Old and New Testaments. Therefore, Mohammad wrote his own version of what really happened in the Old and New Testaments. Mohammad believed if people knew what really happened, we would all be Muslims today.

Much of the Qur'an consists of messages spoken in the first person plural (we), indicating Mohammad was speaking for God and from God. Sura 4, section 23 says:

> We have sent thee inspiration, as we sent it to Noah and the Messengers after him: We sent inspiration to Abraham, Ishmael, Isaac, Jacob and the tribes, to Jesus, Job, Jonah, Aaron, and Solomon, and We gave the Psalms to David.
>
> Of some apostles We have already told thee the story; of others We have not. And to Moses God spoke directly.
>
> Apostles who gave good news as well as warning, that mankind, after the coming of the apostles should

have no plea against God [Allah]: For God is Exalted in Power, Wise.

But God beareth witness that what he hath sent unto thee from his own knowledge, and the angels bear witness: But enough is God for a witness.

Those who reject the faith and keep men from the way of God have verily strayed far, far away from the Path.

Those who reject faith and do wrong—God will not forgive them, nor guide them to any way, except the way of Hell, to dwell therein forever. And this to God is easy.

O Mankind! The Apostle [Mohammad} hath come to you in truth from God: believe in him: It is best for you. But if ye reject faith, to God belong all things in the heavens and on earth: and God is All-Knowing, All-Wise.

O People of the Book! Commit no excesses in your religion: nor say of God aught but the truth.

Christ Jesus, the son of Mary, was no more than an apostle of God, and his word, which he bestowed on Mary, and a spirit proceeding from him: so believe in God and his apostles. Say not "Trinity": desist: It will be better for you: For God is One God: Glory be to Him. Far exalted is He above having a son. To him belong all things in the heavens and on earth. And enough is God as a disposer of affairs.[15]

Let's compare Mohammad's version of the story of Isaac and Ishmael with the Bible. To whom did God promise to give the land of Canaan? As we saw in Genesis 12-17, the promise is made to Abraham repeatedly. However, Abraham had more than one son. To whom was the promise passed along? In Genesis 16, Sarai gets fed up with being barren and gives her servant girl Hagar to Abram in order to have a child (Genesis 16:1-2). All children born in the master's house, including the children of slaves, belonged to the master of the house. It was up to the master to decide if he would adopt the child as his own, or give it back to the birth-parents to keep as their own.

The child born to Hagar was named Ishmael. He would have been adopted by Abram, if Abram had his way, and the promise of God could have been fulfilled in that way. But that was not God's plan. In Genesis 17:4-8, God gives Abraham this promise:

> "As for me, this is my covenant with you: You will be the father of many nations. No longer will you be called Abram; your name will be Abraham, for I have made you a father of many nations. I will make you very fruitful; I will make nations of you, and kings will come from you. I will establish my covenant as an everlasting covenant between me and you and your descendants after you for the generations to come, to be your God and the God of your descendants after you. The whole land of Canaan, where you now reside as a foreigner, I will give as an everlasting possession to you and your descendants after you; and I will be their God."

At the age of ninety-nine, Abraham doubts his ability to keep up his end of the bargain, and he complains that Sarah is barren. Abraham tries to bargain with God by asking God to make Ishmael his child of promise. Genesis 17:19-21 gives God's reply:

> Then God said, "Yes, but your wife Sarah will bear you a son, and you will call him *Isaac. I will establish my covenant with him* as an everlasting covenant for his descendants after him. *And as for Ishmael, I have heard you: I will surely bless him; I will make him fruitful and*

will greatly increase his numbers. He will be the father of
twelve rulers, and I will make him into a great nation.
But my covenant I will establish with Isaac, whom Sarah
will bear to you by this time next year."

One year later, Sarah gave birth to Isaac, but Ishmael, who is
thirteen years old, makes fun of the baby. So Sarah demands that
Abraham get rid of Ishmael. Genesis 21:11-13 says:

The matter distressed Abraham greatly because it con-
cerned his son. But God said to him, "Do not be so distressed about the boy and your slave woman. Listen to
whatever Sarah tells you, *because it is through Isaac that
your offspring will be reckoned.* I will make the son of the
slave into a nation also, because he is your offspring."

Abraham followed the will of God even though he was distressed
about the matter. Genesis 21:14-21 says:

Early the next morning Abraham took some food and
a skin of water and gave them to Hagar. He set them
on her shoulders and then sent her off with the boy.
She went on her way and wandered in the Desert of
Beersheba.

When the water in the skin was gone, she put the
boy under one of the bushes. Then she went off and sat
down about a bowshot away, for she thought, "I cannot
watch the boy die." And as she sat there, she began to
sob.

God heard the boy crying, and the angel of God
called to Hagar from heaven and said to her, "What is
the matter, Hagar? Do not be afraid; God has heard the

> boy crying as he lies there. Lift the boy up and take him
> by the hand, for I will make him into a great nation."
>
> Then God opened her eyes and she saw a well of
> water. So she went and filled the skin with water and
> gave the boy a drink.
>
> God was with the boy as he grew up. He lived in
> the desert and became an archer. While he was living
> in the Desert of Paran, his mother got a wife for him
> from Egypt.

If you continue reading in Genesis 21, you find that it was
Abraham who dug the well at Beersheba (Genesis 21:22-34). In
the days of the kings of Judah, Beersheba was considered to be the
southern border of Judah. It is 27.4 miles south of Hebron. The
wilderness of Paran is the area south of Beersheba in the Negev. It is
an easy one day or two day walk from Hebron.

When Isaac was a little older, God demanded that Abraham
take Isaac to Mount Moriah and offer him as a sacrifice. Even
though Abraham was distressed by the idea, he decides to trust God
and obey. Just as Abraham raises the knife to sacrifice Isaac, God
intercedes.

> The angel of the LORD called to Abraham from heaven
> a second time and said, "I swear by myself, declares the
> LORD, that because you have done this and have not
> withheld your son, *your only son*, I will surely bless you
> and make your descendants as numerous as the stars in
> the sky and as the sand on the seashore. Your descen-
> dants will take possession of the cities of their enemies,
> and through your offspring all nations on earth will be
> blessed, because you have obeyed me."
>
> — Genesis 22:15–18

So Isaac was taken to Mount Moriah, seventeen miles north of Hebron, to be offered as a sacrifice. At this point, Ishmael is no longer considered to be a son of Abraham. He has been given to Hagar and let go from Abraham's household. He no longer has any claim to the promises of Abraham, nor to any of his wealth. Isaac is considered the firstborn of Abraham and has the birthright.

But what does the Qur'an teach about this matter? According to Sura 2:122-141, it was Ishmael who was nearly sacrificed on Mount Moriah, and it was Ishmael who inherited the birthright. The Qur'an says Abraham left Sarah in Hebron and took his wife Hagar and first-born son Ishmael to Mecca in Saudi Arabia, which is 793 miles to the south of Hebron. The story continues in the Qur'an:

> And remember that Abraham was tried by his Lord with certain commands, which he fulfilled: He said: "I will make thee an Imam to the nations." He pleaded: "And also Imams from my offspring!" He answered: "But my Promise is not within reach of evil doers."
>
> Remember we made the House [Kaaba] a place of assembly for men and a place of safety; and take ye the station of Abraham as a place of prayer; and we covenanted with Abraham and Ishmael, that they should sanctify My House for those who compass it as a retreat, or bow, or prostrate themselves therein in prayer.
>
> And remember Abraham said: "My Lord, make this a City of Peace, and feed its people with fruits such of them as believe in God and the Last Day." He said, "Yea, and such as reject faith [Islam] for a while I will grant them their pleasure, but will soon drive them to the torment of Fire: an evil destination indeed."
>
> And remember Abraham and Ishmael raised the foundations of the House with this prayer, "Our Lord,

Accept this service from us; for thou art the All-Hearing
and the All-Knowing."[16]

— Sura 11:124-127

According to the Qur'an, Abraham and Ishmael built the Kaaba
in Mecca four hundred years before Moses built the tabernacle in
the wilderness. Furthermore, according to the Qur'an, Isaac and
Ishmael are both prophets, but Ishmael is also an apostle because he
is superior to Isaac as the first-born of Abraham.

This raises a few questions that need answers. The Kaaba
encompassed the pantheon of Arab gods. There were 360 idols in the
Kaaba when Mohammad was born, one for each day of the year.[17]
The idols at the cardinal points of the compass (N, S, E, and W)
were Allah and his three daughters, who were the fertility god and
goddesses of Arabia. The question that must be answered is: Why
would Abraham and Ishmael build a pantheon for 360 idols? Why
would someone who had just met God face-to-face and received the
promise of eternal life in the Promised Land then desert that God
and go off to an arid wilderness to build a pantheon for idols? Does
that make sense?

Furthermore, the Qur'an says, "And commemorate Ishmael in
the 'Book;' for he [Allah] was true to his promise, and he [Ishmael]
was an Apostle and a Prophet" (Sura 19:55). The Qur'an says the
Promised Land was given to Ishmael, not to Isaac. In other words,
the Qur'an makes birth order the deciding factor in receiving the
promises of God, which is exactly the opposite of what Genesis says.

What does the New Testament say about this? John 1:12-13 says:

Yet to all who did receive him, to those who believed
in his name, he gave the right to become children of
God—children born not of natural descent, nor of
human decision or a husband's will, but born of God.

Birthright has nothing to do with the choice of God, yet it means everything to Islam.

Now let's look at Romans 9:6-13:

> It is not as though God's word had failed. For not all who are descended from Israel are Israel. Nor because they are his descendants are they all Abraham's children. On the contrary, *"It is through Isaac that your offspring will be reckoned."* In other words, it is not the children by physical descent who are God's children, but it is the children of the promise who are regarded as Abraham's offspring. For this was how the promise was stated: *"At the appointed time I will return, and Sarah will have a son."*
>
> Not only that, but Rebekah's children were conceived at the same time by our father Isaac. Yet, before the twins were born or had done anything good or bad—in order that God's purpose in election might stand: not by works but by him who calls—she was told, "The older will serve the younger." Just as it is written: *"Jacob I loved, but Esau I hated."*

Esau became a co-founder of the Arab tribes along with Ishmael, his uncle. But God re-affirmed his covenant with the line of Isaac by choosing Jacob.

The issue is: Who do you believe is telling the truth? Is the Bible true or is the Qur'an true? Make up your mind, and follow the God of that book! Which God do you have a personal relationship with? Has Allah ever spoken to your heart or answered your prayers? Has he given you hope and comforted you in times of need? That is not Allah's style.

The truth is, Allah is a god of fear, and every true Muslim lives his life in fear of Allah. No Muslim will tell you he has a loving, personal relationship with Allah, because Allah demands that you give your physical life to please him. If you should utter something that could be interpreted as dishonoring to Allah or Mohammad, you will be executed in any of the fifty-seven Islamic states of the world. The average Muslim lives in fear of the day some imam will tell him it is time for him to give his life as an act of *jihad*.[18]

According to Mohammad, those who believe the Bible are sinners because they have not accepted the true message from God revealed by him. Because this is an early *sura*, he is willing to forgive them. However, he offers those who have not yet converted this warning:

> "Oh people of the Book: Now hath come to you, making things clear unto you, our Apostle, after the break in the series of Apostles [the time between the writing of the New Testament and the preaching of Mohammad]; lest ye say: 'There came unto us no bringer of glad tidings and no warner from evil. But now hath come to you a bringer of glad tidings, a warner from evil and God hath power over all evil.. . . O my people: enter the Holy Land which God hath assigned to you, and turn not back ignominiously, for then you will be overthrown to your own ruin!"[19]
>
> — Sura 5:21 and 23

The ruin spoken of by Mohammad in this passage refers to the slaughter of Christians and Jews by the followers of Islam when al-Mahdi appears. There is a distinction made in the Qur'an between converted Jews and non-converted Jews. Those who have converted to Islam are called "Children of Israel" (Sura 2:47). Those who don't convert are called *yahudis*, or Jews, and are said to be descended from pigs and apes (Sura 5:60). Along with all Christians, they are considered *kuffar*, or infidels (Sura 41:83).

Mohammad allowed for Jews and Christians who lived in Muslim controlled lands to keep their faith as long as they were punished by paying a very large tax. He said:

> Make war upon such of those to whom the Scriptures have been given as believe not in God [Allah], or in the last day [Al-Mahdi's victory], and who forbid not that which God and his Apostle [Isa, son of Mary] have forbidden, and who profess not the profession of the truth [Allah Akbar], *until they pay tribute out of hand, and they are humbled.*
>
> — Sura 9:29

Those who paid this tax were called *dhimmis,* and the tax is known as *jizya.* Any unconverted Christian or Jew who refused this offer to live in submission and pay the tax was executed.

The apostle referred to in Sura 9 is Isa, the son of Mary, which means Jesus in Arabic. He is not to be confused with the biblical Jesus. According to Mohammad, Jesus was an apostle like him. He never claimed to be the son of God, because saying Jesus is the son of God means you believe Allah had sex with Mary. They do not believe in a Holy Spirit, and therefore immaculate conception is impossible. That is why Mohammad said, "In blasphemy indeed are those that say that God is Christ the son of Mary" (Sura 5:13-19a). Later, in Sura 5, a conversation between Jesus, son of Mary, and Allah is relayed by Mohammad, which says:

> And behold, Allah will say: Oh Jesus, son of Mary, didst thou say unto men, "Worship me and my mother as Gods;" in derogation of Allah? He will say: "Glory to thee! *Never could I say what I had no right to say.* Had I said such a thing, thou wouldst indeed have known it.

Thou knowest what is in my heart, though I know not is in thine. For thou knowest all things that are hidden. Never said I to them aught except what thou didst command me to say, to wit: "Worship Allah, my Lord and your Lord." And I was witness over them whilst I dwelt amongst them; *when thou didst take me up* thou wast the watcher over them, and thou art a witness to all things.[20]

— Sura 5:119-120

The reference to Jesus being "taken up" by Allah refers to the belief that Allah substituted Judas Iscariot for Jesus, who died in his place on the cross, while Jesus was "raptured" by Allah so he can return to earth at the appropriate time, to become the helper of al-Mahdi. However, the theology of slaughter did not die out with Mohammad. In 1994, Ayatollah Komeni said:

If one allows the infidels to continue playing their role of corrupters on earth, their moral punishment will be all the stronger. Thus, if we kill the infidels in order to put a stop to their activities, we have indeed done them a service. . . . To kill them is a surgical operation commanded by Allah the creator. . . . Those who follow the rules of the Qur'an are aware that we have to apply the laws of retribution and that we have to kill. . . . War is a blessing for the world and for every nation. It is Allah himself who commands men to wage war and to kill. The Qur'an commands: "Wage war until all corruption and all disobedience are wiped out."[21]

The last of the five basic tenets of Islam is *jihad*, which means "struggle," but the true meaning of *jihad* is more complicated than that. It actually refers to the struggle to see the world worship God as *Allah Akbar* (the Greatest God). That struggle can be through peaceful means, such as Muslim evangelism in the prisons, which will not guarantee your entrance into Paradise. It can be the legal struggle to get Shariah law accepted in the court system of the United States through organizations like the Council on American-Islamic Relations (CAIR). However, that too, will not guarantee your entrance into Paradise. The most prized form of *jihad* is violent terrorism resulting in many deaths.

The reason is simple: Muslims who do not kill non-believers and die in the process run the risk of not being good enough to get into Paradise. That is because Islam is a works-retribution religion, and Allah must be pleased with you for you to earn your way into Paradise. No one can know if he is good enough to enter Paradise through good works alone. Did you put enough money in the offering? Does Allah know about this sin or that one? There is no way to know, and there are no guidelines in the Qur'an. There is only one way to be sure of your acceptance into Paradise: by violent *jihad* that concludes with your own death.

At the present time, experts from the Department of Homeland Security estimate that approximately seven percent of Muslims are dedicated enough to Islam to carry out acts of violent *jihad* that most people would label as murder and terrorism. Add to that number another thirty percent who give their total support to the actions of the terrorists. That means thirty-seven percent of Muslims today give their total support to terrorism.[22] It is the only world religion based on the premise that true believers must kill all those who do not believe. There are 1.5 billion Muslims on earth today. Thirty-seven percent of that number is a huge fighting force. How much higher will that thirty-seven percent go when al-Mahdi makes his appearance?

Walid Shoebat tells a story of a dinner party he had at a Middle Eastern restaurant in New York. At his table were a pastor and a rabbi. When the waiter came to their table, Walid recognized that the waiter was an Arab like himself. As Shoebat recounts:

> I asked him [the waiter] in Arabic, "Do you believe this; I am sitting here with a Christian pastor and a rabbi. "So, what do you think?" I asked him. "Is it valid then to kill Jews?"
> "No," he replied, "the time is not ripe." Then he added, "We need to wait for the Mahdi!"[23]

The most crucial factor required for Islam to carry out this plan is for Muslims to sell the idea that Islam is a peaceful religion. The Qur'an makes it easy for the followers of Islam to continue that lie. Allah is the liar who leads infidels astray (Sura 16:104). In fact, in the Qur'an, Allah is called *al Khayrul-Makireen* (Sura 3:54), which means "the Greatest Deceiver." He is also called *al-Makr*, which means "the deceiver" (Sura 30:27; 50:13; 42:10; 21:14, 46; 43:79; 86:15). Likewise, Muslims are commanded to follow his example and deceive non-believers (Sura 2:6, 2:9, 4:142, 5:19, 5:41, 5:101, 8:18, 8:30, 8:32, 8:49, 8:58, 9:3, 33:1, 40:32, 61:5, 74:38, 89:5, 92:8).

ISLAMIC PROPHECY

According to Mohammad, the true message of Jesus, son of Mary, was there would be a redeemer of mankind who would come to earth sometime in the future. This redeemer would come not to save mankind, but to lead Islam to world domination. When Jesus, son of Mary, returns, he will come to act as the prophet of al-Mahdi and to clarify the distortions of the original twelve apostles of Jesus.

Muslims believe God will make war against all Christians in the last days. His chosen instrument of punishment will be the followers of Islam. For example:

They surely are Infidels who say, "God is the third of three" for there is no God but one God: and if they refrain not from what they say, a grievous chastisement shall light on such of them as are Infidels.

— Sura 113:78

This belief is demonstrated by the prophecy of Ibrahim M. Kunna, who said in Hadith Qudsi, "On the day of Resurrection Allah will take all the sins committed by Muslims and place them on the backs of the Jews and Christians, who will be thrown into the fire of Hell."

There are at least 109 verses in the later non-abrogated verses of the Qur'an that instruct Muslims to kill unbelievers.[24] The armies who follow Allah will be his instrument of punishment for nonbelievers. The Qur'an says:

- "So make war on them: By your hands will God chastise them, and will put them to shame, and will give you victory over them, and will heal the bosoms of a people who believe" (Sura 9:14).

- "March ye forth the light and heavily armed, and contend with your substance and your persons on the Way of God [jihad]. This, if ye know it, will be better for you" (Sura 9:43).

- "Kill the disbelievers wherever you find them" (Sura 2:191).

- "Strike off the heads of the disbelievers, and after making a great slaughter among them, carefully tie up the remaining captives [the women]" (Sura 47:4). I wonder why he wants the women?

According to Islamic prophecy, on the day of Armageddon,

a massive Muslim army will assemble from all over the world to kill every Jew on earth and wipe out those Christians who will not convert to Islam. This is in direct contrast to the prophecies of the Bible that say the army of God will fight against this massive Islamic army. But God's army will not be made up of Christians and Jews; instead, it will be the hosts of heaven with Jesus Christ at the head (Revelation 19:14). Christ does not ask Christians to violate our Christian beliefs by committing murder in his name. He will rid the world of this violent religion by the sword of his mouth. The same power that created the universe with a word will also destroy his enemies by a single utterance (Revelation 19:15).

THE TWELVER TRADITION

Without doubt, the most disturbing prophecies of Islam have to do with the "Twelver" tradition. Both Sunnis and Shi'as agree a Redeemer will arise in the last days who will lead Islam to world domination. However, they disagree on how it will happen. The "Twelver" is a Shi'a tradition found in many hadiths.

During the first hundred years after the death of Mohammad and the split into Sunni and Shi'a factions, there was constant warfare between these two groups. The *imams* (spiritual leaders) of both groups led campaigns of *jihad* against each other. Muhammad ibn Mansur, (al-Mahdi) (744-785), was the Twelfth Imam of the Shi'as. He became the *caliph* (political leader) of the Abbasid State (Iraq) in 775. The title al-Mahdi is not his last name, but means "the Redeemer." He went to battle in 785 against the forces of the Sunnis who were revolting in Syria.

There are two versions of what happened during the battle. The Sunnis believe he was either killed in battle or he was poisoned by one of his concubines the night before the battle. Sunnis believe the Messiah of Islam has not been born yet. However, they do acknowledge that Islam's Redeemer will be a descendant of

Mohammad and come from Khorasan, which is the Middle-Persian name for Babylonia.

Shi'as have kept the "Twelver" tradition as a part of Shi'a faith since the eighth century. They believe God "raptured" Muhammad ibn Mansur in order to prevent him from being killed. He is currently being kept in a suspended state called *occultation* by the Muslims. They believe that at the appropriate time, God will sent al-Mahdi back to earth to unite all the Muslims into one force to conquer the world. But before al-Mahdi makes his appearance, the Islamic nations will establish a caliphate which will rule over all Muslims and unite them in their attempt to make Islam the sole religion of the world. There are currently fifty-severn Islamic states scattered around the globe. If they were to unite today, there is no nation capable of defeating such a force.

This caliphate will be a council made up of ten representatives from ten nations. It is the standard practice of Muslims to establish councils with ten representatives. Walid Shoebat says:

> In 2002 a plan for the reestablishment of the Caliphate was written by Abu Qanit al-Sharif al-Hasani of the Guiding Helper Foundation entitled, "*The Plan for the Return of the Caliphate.*" According to this plan, the Caliph would be assisted in his rule by a ten-member council of "Assistant Caliphs." These assistants, or council members, are similar to Ministers in many of today's governments.[25]

Once this caliphate has been established, al-Mahdi will go on a pilgrimage to Mecca, where he will be recognized by most Muslims as their new leader. However, the *hadiths* tell us three Islamic states will rebel against al-Mahdi. Just by coincidence, it will be the three Islamic nations that made up the Ptolemaic Empire: Egypt, Libya, and Sudan. Also, just as a coincidence, it will be the same Islamic states that made up the Seleucid Empire who will support him. After a bloody conflict, al-Mahdi will win, take control of the caliphate, and unite the entire Muslim world behind him. His next step will be to establish a *hudna* with Israel, which is an Arabic term for a peace treaty which is "meant to produce a period of calm with an enemy in order to gain concessions, regroup, rearm, and re-attack at the appropriate time."[26] It is a part of the plan of Islam to win by deception, following the example of Allah, the greatest deceiver. This *hudna* is predicted in the *hadith* Sunan Abu Dawud 36:4273-4274.

The first *hudna* was established by Mohammad with the Jews of the Bani Quraithah tribe in Medina. They voluntarily laid down their weapons after the peace treaty was signed. When the time was right, Mohammad had his men (the only ones with weapons) round up the Jews and slaughter them. The number of Jews who were killed has been estimated anywhere from four hundred to nine hundred, with six hundred being the most often used estimate.[27] Mohammad's excuse for the slaughter was that a Jewish goldsmith had insulted a Muslim woman.

This type of false peace treaty is exactly what Daniel says will happen when the Antichrist appears. He says:

> "He will confirm a covenant with many for one 'seven.' In the middle of the 'seven' he will put an end to sacrifice and offering. And at the temple he will set up an abomination that causes desolation, until the end that is decreed is poured out on him."
>
> — Daniel 9:27

Since 1948, Israel has been in a constant struggle with the Islamic states that surround it. Israel has been willing to sign a peace treaty ever since, so the peace treaty offered them by Muhammad ibn Mansur will be welcome news, and they will lay down their arms. It is more than likely the supporters of Israel will lay down their arms as well, since they will be deceived into thinking that there is "peace, when there is no peace" (Ezekiel 13:10).

The breaking of this covenant will mark the midway point of the tribulation period. Then al-Mahdi will subdue Israel, make war against the West, and eventually rule the world. There are numerous prophecies about Islam conquering Rome throughout the Qur'an and *hadiths*. Byzantine Rome was the enemy in Mohammad's day, and today, anything having to do with Europe or the Americas is considered by the Muslims to be Rome. Therefore, we in the United States will be singled out as one of the worst enemies of Islam, right behind the number-one enemy: Israel.

Every Muslim on earth will be dedicated to *jihad* at that time. The current number of Muslims stands a 1.5 billion, which means there will be a lot of potential army members for al-Mahdi. The following is a quote from a work done by Joel Richardson on the history of *jihad*. It demonstrates what we can expect in the future. I have added this quote to help explain what is meant by the black flags of Islam. Richardson says:

> In Islam there are two flags. One is white and one is black. Written across both flags in Arabic are the words, "There is no God but Allah and Muhammud is his messenger." The white flag is called Al-Liwaa and serves as the sign for the leader of the Muslim army and is the flag of the Islamic State. The black flag is called Ar-Raya, and is used by the Muslim army. It is also called the flag of jihad, and is carried into battle. When Muhammud returned to his home city of Mecca after eight years of exile, he returned as a conqueror. With him were ten thousand Muslim soldiers. They carried with them

black flags. On them was one word written in Arabic: "Punishment."[28]

The primary goal of al-Mahdi will be to kill every Jew on earth, putting an end to God's plan of redeeming his chosen people and fulfilling his promise to Abraham. By doing so, Satan would be able to replace Isaac, the "child of promise," with Ishmael, the child who was rejected, but who eventually became the father of the Arab people. Besides the Jewish people, the number-one enemy of Islam is the United States, which is the only nation that supports Israel today.

Al-Mahdi will rule from Jerusalem where he will make his new home. However, he will not do this on his own: he will have help from Isa (Jesus), the son of Mary, who Muslims believe will arise from the earth to perform miracles and convince millions to convert to Islam. Isa will mark the foreheads of those who convert and kill all those who refuse his mark.

According to Islam, al-Mahdi and Isa will fight against the real Antichrist, known as ad-Dajjal (the deceiver). Ad-Dajjal will be a Jew who rallies the nations to revolt against al-Mahdi. He is called the Jewish Redeemer. The two will meet in battle at Armageddon and, according to Islam, al-Mahdi will win. Then al-Mahdi and Isa will rule the world together for the next forty years until Allah comes to earth to take over. Draw your own conclusions as to the parallels between al-Mahdi and Isa, and the biblical Antichrist and False Prophet of Revelation 13 as we explore Islamic prophecy.

Verses from the Qur'an and Hadiths Concerning al-Mahdi

- "He [al-Mahdi] will come from Khorasan" (Sunan Abu Dawud 36:4277). Khorasan was the Middle-Persian name for the province of Babylonia. Compare with Daniel 11-12.

- "The Prophet [Mohammad], peace be upon him, said: 'If only one day of this world remained, Allah would lengthen that day, till He raise up in it a man who belongs to me or to my family whose father's name is the same as my father's, who will fill the earth with equity and justice as it has been filled with oppression and tyranny. The world will not pass away until the Arabs are ruled by a man of my family whose name will be the same as mine'" (Sunan Abu Dawud 36:4269).

- "There will be many armies after me. You must join that army which will come from Khorasan [Babylon]" (Sahih Bukhari).

- "[Muslim] [a]rmies carrying black flags will come from Khorasan [Babylon]. No power will be able to stop them and they will finally reach Eela [Holy House; the Arabic name for the temple in Jerusalem], where they will erect their flags" (Sunan al-Tirmidhi). Compare with Daniel 11:31, and 11:41.

- "He will make his capital in Jerusalem" (Sahih Tirmidhi 2:86). Compare with Daniel 11:31.

- "An expeditionary force will then be sent against him [al-Mahdi] from Syria but will be swallowed-up in the desert between Mecca and Medina. When the people see that, the eminent saints of Syria and the best people of Iraq will come to him and swear allegiance to him between the Corner and the Maqam" (Sunan Abu Dawud 36:4273). Compare with Daniel 11:40-43.

- "Three [Muslim] nations will oppose him. He will defeat them and unite all Islam into a kingdom that shall rule the world" (Sahih Muslim 41:6930). Compare with Daniel 11:41.

- "He will bring forth the Ark of the Covenant from the cave of Antakya." And, "He will bring forth the Ark of the Covenant from a cave near Lake Tiberias [Sea of Galilee]" (Alamat al-Mahdi al-Muntadhur). *Explanation:* Antioch in central Syria was the summer home of Seleucus, not far from the Sea of Galilee. Muslims believe the Ark of the Covenant was buried there. They believe the Ark of the Covenant carried by Moses in the wilderness will be found, and inside the Ark will not be the Law of Moses but the Qur'an and Shariah Law. This "miracle" will be the evidence that Mohammad was telling the truth about the distortions of the Bible, and that al-Mahdi has been sent by God. Millions will be convinced by this miracle, and Shariah will be declared the only law on earth. Everyone will be forced to obey the new law. According to the *hadiths*, this Ark will be placed in the temple in Jerusalem, replacing the Torah. This will be the abomination that causes desolation! Compare with Daniel 11:31.

- "I repeat on the fingers of my hand, that he said: 'You will attack Arabia and Allah will enable you to conquer it, then you will attack Persia and He will make you to conquer it. Then you will attack Rome and Allah will enable you to conquer it, then you will attack al-Dajjal [the Jewish Messiah] and Allah will enable you to conquer him'" (Sahih Muslim 41:69). Compare with Revelation 19:19-21.

VERSES FROM THE QUR'AN AND HADITHS CONCERNING ISA

- "And when the word is fulfilled concerning them, we shall bring forth a beast of the earth to speak unto them because mankind hath not faith in our revelations" (Sura 27:82). Compare with Revelation 13:11.

- "As the animal emerges from the ground, it will be dusting the sand off its head. It will proceed towards the area between Hajrul and Maqaamul Ibraheem [in Mecca]. The people on seeing it will flee in all directions, except for one group of people [Muslims]. It will approach this group and illuminate their faces like shining stars. Thereafter it will set out and travel throughout the whole world. It will mark the faces of the Kuffar [infidels] and none will be able to escape it" (Hadrat Talha bin Umar, the general of Mohammad's army).

- "He said: 'Isa, son of Mary, would descend and their commander will invite him to come and lead them in prayer, but he will say, 'No, some amongst you are commanders over others.' This is the honor from Allah for his Imam [showing Isa's subservience to al-Mahdi]'" (Sahih Muslim 1:293)

- "How will you [Jews and Christians] be when the son of Mary descends amongst you and he will judge people by the Law of the Qur'an and not by the law of the Gospel?" (Sunan Bukhari 4:55).

- "By Him in whose hand is my life, the son of Mary, may peace be upon him, will soon descend among you as a just judge. He will break crosses, kill swine, and abolish

Jizya" (Sahih Muslim 1:287). *Explanation: Jizya* is the tax that allowed non-Muslims to live in Muslim lands and still worship as they pleased. As the Muslims conquered Christian lands, the Christians were given three choices: they could convert to Islam and not pay any tax; they could continue as Christians and pay the *jizya* tax; or, if they refused to pay the tax or convert, they would be killed as an infidel. When the *jizya* tax option is removed, the only options are to convert or die.

- "A great false prophet, king of the Jews, will come with his army. He will be accompanied by 70,000 Jews from Isfahan wrapped in their robes and armed with polished sabers; their heads covered with a sort of veil. When ad-Dajjal [the Jewish Messiah] is defeated his Jewish companions will be slaughtered—everything will deliver them up except for the *Gharkad* tree" (Sahih Muslim 40:6985). *Explanation:* The Gharkad tree is a very small shrub or tree that grows in the desert, and it would be very hard for a man to hide behind one. This is a cynical way of saying that they intend to kill every Jew on earth. According to the hadiths, after the battle of Armageddon, al-Mahdi and Isa will rule the earth for forty years until Allah comes to reign on earth.

Let me summarize what we know from Islamic prophecy concerning its final ruler. He will come from Khorasan/Babylon. He will defeat three of the Islamic nations of a ten-nation coalition ruling the Middle East. At that point, he will be named supreme ruler of the coalition and unite all Muslims into a massive fighting force. He will come with a huge and overpowering army and take Jerusalem, setting up residence in the temple. He will "find" the Ark of the Covenant and inside it will be a Qur'an. He will place the Ark in the temple.

His helper will be called Isa, the Arabic form of Jesus. Isa will perform miracles and cause people to worship al-Mahdi. The faces of those who believe will be easy to identify because they will shine. Those who will not worship al-Mahdi will be killed by Isa.

You decide. Does this coincide with the prophecies of Daniel and Revelation, or is it all a coincidence? Will the final kingdom of Babylonia be a coalition of Islamic nations whose ruler will originate from the territory of the Seleucid Empire? Will all the forces of Islam unite and rise up to invade Israel again as they have in the past? Will they kill a large percentage of the Jewish population of Israel and scatter the remnants throughout the nations, as Isaiah and Revelation predict? Will their final leader sit on his throne in the temple of God in Jerusalem, calling himself God, as II Thessalonians and Revelation predict? Or could all of this be just nonsense and coincidence? Is Islam truly a religion of world peace, or will Islam and Babylon be the instruments used by God to fulfill all prophecy?

The most important question is this: Which God is God? Will the forces of Allah and Islam be the final victors? Or will Jesus Christ, the Son of Man, come back on the day of the Lord and destroy them all?

So far, you have seen the prophecies of the Old Testament and Islam. Both predict the Redeemer of the saints and the Redeemer of Islam are headed for a final showdown at Armageddon. You must decide for yourself which God to worship, Allah or Jehovah. There will be no fence to sit on. In the meantime, Revelation predicts millions of followers of Jehovah will be killed by the forces of Allah. Will that be a defeat for them or a crown of victory?

We cannot prevent this final showdown from happening. God is sovereign, and this plan has been in place since the Tower of Babel. Babylon, the first center of idolatry on earth, is destined for one final showdown with God. The outcome of that showdown will affect the whole earth and every inhabitant on it.

ENDNOTES

1 Sources include Reza Aslan. *No God but God*; Bernard Lewis, *Islam in History*; Adil Salahi, *Muhammad, Man and Prophet*; and Will Durant, *The Age of Faith*

2 Will Durant, *The Age of Faith*, pg. 163

3 R. A. Nicholson, R. A., *Translations of Eastern Poetry and Prose*, pg. 38-40

4 Will Durant, *The Age of Faith*, pg. 166-167

5 Adil Salahi, *Muhammad: Man and Prophet*, pg. 429-430

6 Donald Richardson, *Secrets of the Koran*, pg. 38

7 Ibid., pg. 38

8 *The Holy Qur'an: Text, Translation, and Commentary*

9 The first number indicates the Sura, or sermon number; the second number indicates the verse number. All references to the Qur'an will be given a Sura and verse reference.

10 Donald Richardson, *Secrets of the Koran*, pg. 38

11 Walid Shoebat and Joel Richardson, *God's War on Terror*, pg. 108

12 Herodotus, *The Histories*, trans. by John M. Marincola & Aubrey DeSelincourt, Book 3, pg. 8

13 Will Durant, *The Age of Faith*, pg. 161

14 Donald Richardson, *Secrets of the Koran*, pg. 42

15 *The Holy Qur'an*, Sura 4, section 23, Ahmadiyya Anjuman Isha'at Islam Lahore Inc, trans. by A. Yusuf Ali, pg. 233-234

16 Ibid, pg. 546-547

17 Will Durant, *The Age of Faith*, pg. 161

18 This is the personal testimony of Shahram Hadian, a native Iranian. He was raised as a Muslim in Iran and converted to Christianity in America. He is now a pastor in Bothell, WA.

19 Ibid, pg. 248

20 Ibid, pg. 280

21 T. Davis Bunn, *Riders of the Pale Horse*, pg. iv

22 This statement comes from statistics supplied by the Department of Homeland Security

23 Walid Shoebat and Joel Richardson, *God's War on Terror*, pg. 46

24 Donald Richardson, *Secrets of the Koran*, pg. 28

25 Walid Shoebat and Joel Richardson, *God's War on Terror*, pg. 108

26 Ibid., pg. 108

27 Adil Salahi, *Muhammad: Man and Prophet*, pg. 431

28 Joel Richardson, *Antichrist, Islam's Awaited Messiah*, pg. 42

Section Three

Prophecy in the Gospels
and the Epistles

CHAPTER EIGHT

Jesus' Prophecies in the Gospels

This is where the question of the rapture becomes the focus of our attention. Most conservative Christians today believe the rapture is strictly a New Testament teaching which was revealed by Paul for the first time in I Thessalonians 4:13–18. But is that true? Is the rapture a New Testament teaching, or did Jesus—and every one of the apostles—base their teaching on Moses and the Old Testament prophets? If, indeed, the rapture is a New Testament teaching, why do Jesus and the apostles keep referring to Old Testament passages?

We must also ask ourselves, why did Jesus spend so much time preaching on the kingdom of heaven? What kingdom was he speaking of? Was it a kingdom he intended to establish at his first appearance, or was it a future kingdom? Was his teaching about the kingdom consistent with Old Testament teaching, or was it a new revelation?

With these questions in mind, let's look at Jesus' teaching on the kingdom of heaven in the parables of Matthew 13. There Jesus gives five parables describing what will happen on earth at the end of the age. The first parable is the "wheat and the tares." Matthew says:

> Jesus told them another parable: "*The kingdom of heaven* is like a man who sowed good seed in his field.

But while everyone was sleeping, his enemy came and sowed weeds among the wheat, and went away. When the wheat sprouted and formed heads, then the weeds also appeared.

"The owner's servants came to him and said, 'Sir, didn't you sow good seed in your field? Where then did the weeds come from?'

"'An enemy did this,' he replied. "The servants asked him, 'Do you want us to go and pull them up?'

"'No,' he answered, 'because while you are pulling the weeds, you may uproot the wheat with them. Let both grow together until the harvest. At that time I will tell the harvesters: *First collect the weeds and tie them in bundles to be burned; then gather the wheat and bring it into my barn.*'"

— Matthew 13:24–30

It seems the disciples were very confused by this parable, which is understandable since the Holy Spirit had not come to them yet. Their understanding of Scripture was still at the level of the Old Testament saints. They ask Jesus to give them a private lesson to clear things up. That explanation is found a few verses later, where Matthew says:

Then he left the crowd and went into the house. His disciples came to him and said, "Explain to us the parable of the weeds in the field."

He answered, "The one who sowed the good seed is the Son of Man. The field is the world, and the good seed stands for the people of the kingdom. The weeds are the people of the evil one, and the enemy who sows them is the devil. The harvest is the end of the age, and the harvesters are angels.

"As the weeds are pulled up and burned in the fire, so it will be at the end of the age. The Son of Man will send out his angels, and they will weed out of his kingdom everything that causes sin and all who do evil. They will throw them into the blazing furnace, where there will be weeping and gnashing of teeth. Then the righteous will shine like the sun in the kingdom of their Father. Whoever has ears, let them hear."

— Matthew 13:36–43

Jesus points out several truths that we pass over without notice. First, the world is the kingdom. When Jesus comes again, it will be to establish his millennial kingdom here on earth, not seven years before. Next, he comes as judge, to remove sinners from his kingdom. The weeds are gathered and burned, but the wheat never leaves the farm. Instead, it is gathered into the barn. Notice also, the weeds are gathered first. Is this a picture of a pretribulational rapture? Why isn't the wheat gathered first and taken away to the kingdom of heaven seven years before the weeds are gathered? After all, the parable is about the kingdom of heaven, as stated in verse 31. That means the kingdom of heaven Jesus referred to is the "barn" right here on earth. Therefore, what Moses and the Old Testament prophets referred to as a gathering from the four corners of the earth, and we Gentile Christians refer to as the rapture, will be the gathering of the living saints into the barn of Christ, right here on earth. And the barn will be located in Israel.

Let's look at the parable of the "net," also in Matthew 13. Again, this is Jesus' explanation of the kingdom of heaven.

"Once again, *the kingdom of heaven* is like a net that was let down into the lake and caught all kinds of fish. When it was full, the fishermen pulled it up on the shore. Then they sat down and collected the good fish in baskets, but threw the bad away. *This is how it will be at the end of the age. The angels will come and separate the wicked from the righteous and throw them into the blazing furnace, where there will be weeping and gnashing of teeth.*

"Have you understood all these things?" Jesus asked.

"Yes," they replied.

— Matthew 13:47–51

It seems now the disciples are getting the message. It is at this point in history the historical premillennial truth begins to gel in the minds of the apostles. To be a member of the kingdom of heaven means you are kept here by God, but the evil ones are removed from the kingdom of heaven and thrown into the fire. There is no mention of the faithful being removed from the earth in either parable. This is the same message proclaimed to Abraham 2,000 years earlier. The saints of God will inherit the Land of Canaan forever. That is our "heaven."

There is another prophecy mentioned by Jesus in Matthew 8 that will be fulfilled after the saints enter Jerusalem. In Revelation 19, the Apostle John calls it the Wedding Supper of the Lamb. However, Jesus calls it by another name. In Matthew 8:11–12, Jesus said:

"I say to you that many will come from the east and the west, *and will take their places at the feast with Abraham, Isaac and Jacob in the kingdom of heaven.* But the subjects of the kingdom will be thrown outside, into the darkness, where there will be weeping and gnashing of teeth."

According to Revelation 19, the Wedding Supper of the Lamb— or the feast of Abraham, Isaac, and Jacob—will happen after the Temple is cleansed and before the battle of Armageddon.

Once again we are reminded that the last trumpet will be the signal to begin the events associated with the day of the Lord. Some of those events will be accomplished immediately, but for others the trumpet will mark the beginning of a process that will take an unspecified amount of time to complete. My personal belief is that they will last for ten days, until the Day of Atonement.

The last trumpet will start the following chain of events: the resurrection of the dead saints, the rapture (gathering) of the living saints, Jesus' trip through the wilderness with the saints, the uprising against Babylon, Jesus entering Jerusalem and cleansing the Temple, and the Wedding Supper of the Lamb. Another event that I believe will fall into this category will be the rebuilding of Jerusalem and the towns of Israel. Unless Jesus uses better contractors than the ones I know, this will not happen in one day!

Now let's turn to Luke 17 for another parable concerning the day of the Lord.

> Once, on being asked by the Pharisees when the kingdom of God would come, Jesus replied, "The coming of the kingdom of God is not something that can be observed, nor will people say, 'Here it is,' or 'There it is,' because the kingdom of God is in your midst."
>
> Then he said to his disciples, "The time is coming when you will long to see one of the days of the Son of Man, but you will not see it. People will tell you, 'There he is!' or 'Here he is!' Do not go running off after them. *For the Son of Man in his day will be like the lightning, which flashes and lights up the sky from one end to the other.* But first he must suffer many things and be rejected by this generation.
>
> "Just as it was in the days of Noah, so also will it be in the days of the Son of Man. People were eating, drinking, marrying and being given in marriage up to

the day Noah entered the ark. Then the flood came and destroyed them all.

"It was the same in the days of Lot. People were eating and drinking, buying and selling, planting and building. But the day Lot left Sodom, fire and sulfur rained down from heaven and destroyed them all.

"It will be just like this on the day the Son of Man is revealed. On that day no one who is on the housetop, with possessions inside, should go down to get them. Likewise, no one in the field should go back for anything. Remember Lot's wife! Whoever tries to keep their life will lose it, and whoever loses their life will preserve it. *I tell you, on that night two people will be in one bed; one will be taken and the other left. Two women will be grinding grain together; one will be taken and the other left."*

"Where, Lord?" they asked.

He replied, "Where there is a dead body, there the vultures will gather."

— Luke 17:20–37

Where will we find the ones who are taken? The last sentence of this passage tells us they are taken to where dead bodies are found; where birds of prey eat dead bodies. In the two previous parables, this place was described as a "blazing furnace where there is weeping and gnashing of teeth." In this parable, the birds of prey gather to eat carrion at the *topheth*, or fire pit, located at the city trash dump. The trash dump for Jerusalem was located in the Valley of Hinnom on the southwest side of the city. The *topheth* there was often used as a metaphor to describe what Gehenna would be like. For too long now, this parable has been misunderstood by the church. It is the ones who are left who are saved, not the ones who are taken to the *topheth*. Being taken away on the day of the Lord is not a good thing. You want to be left in Jerusalem.

What happens to the ones who are left? The three parables listed above beg the question: where is heaven? What was Abraham, the father of our faith, promised in Genesis 17:8? What did Moses promise the children of Israel in Deuteronomy 30:4–5? What did Isaiah promise the saints in Isaiah 27:12–13? What did Jeremiah promise the saints in Jeremiah 32:36–37? And what did Ezekiel promise the saints in Ezekiel 37:11–12? Israel is the Promised Land, and Jerusalem is its capital. Look at Hebrews 11:8–10:

> By faith Abraham, when called to go to a place he would later receive as his inheritance, obeyed and went, even though he did not know where he was going. By faith he made his home in *the promised land* like a stranger in a foreign country; he lived in tents, as did Isaac and Jacob, who were heirs with him of the same promise. For he was looking forward to *the city with foundations, whose architect and builder is God.*

What city is that? Jerusalem, of course! What city will the saints of God live in during the millennium? Jerusalem. In fact, once Jesus Christ returns from the battle of Armageddon to Jerusalem, he will never leave that city again.

I want to stretch your mind a little further. Is the term "heaven" the New Testament word for the upper reaches of the underworld? In the Old Testament, when someone died, they were said to go down to the grave, or to the pit, meaning the underworld. Is that where the "bosom of Abraham" was located? Is it a temporary holding place until Jerusalem is ready for the saints to inherit forever? Look at Luke 16:19–26:

"There was a rich man who was dressed in purple and fine linen and lived in luxury every day. At his gate was laid a beggar named Lazarus, covered with sores and longing to eat what fell from the rich man's table. Even the dogs came and licked his sores.

"The time came when the beggar died and the angels carried him to Abraham's side. The rich man also died and was buried. In Hades, where he was in torment, he looked up and saw Abraham far away, with Lazarus by his side. So he called to him, 'Father Abraham, have pity on me and send Lazarus to dip the tip of his finger in water and cool my tongue, because I am in agony in this fire.'

"But Abraham replied, 'Son, remember that in your lifetime you received your good things, while Lazarus received bad things, but now he is comforted here and you are in agony. *And besides all this, between us and you a great chasm has been set in place, so that those who want to go from here to you cannot, nor can anyone cross over from there to us.*'"

It would seem, then, that heaven and hell are within sight of each other, but crossing over is impossible. I think it is safe to say these parables teach the wicked will be removed from the earth on the day of the Lord and thrown into hell, while the righteous stay here on earth and are brought back to the kingdom of heaven, which is synonymous with Jerusalem. That is why heaven and earth are joined into one city in Revelation 21 and become the New Jerusalem. And what does the angel of Jesus say is just outside the city walls of the New Jerusalem? It is the fires of hell! (Revelation 22:15).

Now let's look at the Olivet Discourse. This speech is mentioned in Matthew 24:1–26:46, Mark 13:1–37, and Luke 21:5–36. Many believe this passage was spoken publicly to the nation of Israel. They also say it has no bearing on the church, but is meant strictly for unconverted Jews. The fact that Jesus was in the temple court in Jerusalem at the beginning of the passage has caused many to come to that conclusion. However, the passage says clearly the only thing Jesus responded to in the courtyard was the apostles' request to look at the beautiful buildings. Matthew records:

> Jesus left the temple and was walking away when his disciples came up to him to call his attention to its buildings. "Do you see all these things?" he asked. "Truly I tell you, not one stone here will be left on another; every one will be thrown down."
>
> — Matthew 24:1–2

Jesus gives only one response at this time, and it is unrelated to when he will come again. In fact, he gives a prophecy that was literally fulfilled in AD 135. But it is the next verse that gives the true setting for the Olivet Discourse. Matthew continues:

> *As Jesus was sitting on the Mount of Olives, the disciples came to him **privately.*** "Tell us," they said, "when will this happen, and what will be the sign of your coming and of the end of the age?"
>
> — Matthew 24:3

Jesus and his disciples had left the temple courtyard and journeyed out of the Eastern Gate as they had so many times before. They traveled across the Kidron Valley to the Mount of Olives. That is where the Garden of Gethsemane was located, and that is probably where this dialogue took place. Second, notice his disciples came to him privately. If we check Mark 13:3, we see it wasn't even the twelve disciples who came to him; it was only four: Peter, James, John, and Andrew.

Furthermore, the entire purpose of this lesson is found in the question the disciples ask Jesus in the same verse, which says, "'Tell us,' they said, 'When will this happen, and *what will be the sign of your coming at the end of the age?'"*

Everything Jesus says, from Matthew 24:4 to 26:46, is directly related to that question. The apostles asked Jesus about his coming, or *parousia*. *Parousia* is a Greek compound word made up of the prefix *para-*, which means "to be beside," and *ousa,* which is the feminine form of the word "to be." In other words, *parousia* means "to be present with someone, or to appear publicly." According to Arndt, Bauer, and Gingrich, when *parousia* is used in the New Testament it speaks "of Christ, and nearly always of his Messianic Advent in glory to judge the world at the end of this age."[1] And that is exactly the case in Matthew 24:3. The disciples asked about his *parousia* in relation to the end of the age.

Therefore, there cannot be anything secret about this coming; it will be a public appearance. The few times in the New Testament *parousia* does not refer to the public appearance of Christ at the end of the age, it refers to some other person making a public appearance. It can never be used in connection with a "secret" return of Christ. Those two thoughts—secret return and public appearance—are diametrically opposed.

Jesus continues with his explanation of his appearance:

> Jesus answered: "Watch out that no one deceives you. For many will come in my name, claiming, 'I am the Messiah,' and will deceive many. You will hear of wars and rumors of wars, but see to it that you are not alarmed. Such things must happen, but the end is still to come. Nation will rise against nation, and kingdom

against kingdom. There will be famines and earthquakes in various places. All these are the beginning of
birth pains.

— Matthew 24:4–8

Wars, famines, and earthquakes have happened since the first
recordings of history. They are nothing new and do not give an
accurate indication of time. Jesus mentions them as a forerunner
of the tribulation for a very specific reason. We know from John's
Revelation, the Two Witnesses will be given three and a half years
to preach in the temple courtyard, and the Antichrist will be given
three and a half years to rule the governments of the world. That
means the length of the tribulation will be seven years, which agrees
with Daniel 7:27.

Those seven years will begin with the signing of a peace treaty
between Israel and the ten-nation coalition run by the Antichrist.
However, the ten-nation coalition will come to power through
a series of wars, and will be a world power *before* the Antichrist
replaces the head of the coalition. This is the reason Jesus starts his
discourse with a very non-specific reference to wars and rumors of
wars, earthquakes, and famines. These are the first series of God's
wrath which is poured out in Revelation 6:1–11. The actual seven-
year period will begin with the next events mentioned by Jesus as he
continues his discourse:

"Then you will be handed over to be persecuted and put
to death, and you will be hated by all nations because
of me. At that time many will turn away from the faith
and will betray and hate each other, and many false
prophets will appear and deceive many people. Because
of the increase of wickedness, the love of most will grow
cold, but the one who stands firm to the end will be

saved. And this gospel of the kingdom will be preached
in the whole world as a testimony to all nations, and
then the end will come."

— Matthew 24:9–12

Church history records the execution of only three apostles in
the first century. James the brother of Jesus was executed by the
Sanhedrin in about AD 45, and Peter and Paul were executed by Nero
in AD 65. As for the deaths of the other apostles, we have traditions
but no facts. Regardless, Christianity was not hated by all nations.
There were thriving Christian communities in Syria, India, China,
and Africa in the first six centuries. Furthermore, not all of the
Roman Empire was hostile to the church in the first three centuries;
James the Younger founded the church in Spain, and Mark founded
the church in Egypt. Furthermore, church membership grew at an
enormous rate rather than most falling away and betraying each
other, as this prophecy predicts. It is therefore obvious that Jesus
is speaking to a future generation of disciples who will experience
these problems.

There is a parallel passage to this message found in Matthew
10:5–23. This is a message given by Jesus before he sent out the
twelve disciples to the villages of Israel to spread the gospel. Again,
it is a private lesson given only to his selected disciples; no one else
was present. After giving them instructions on where to go, what
to take, and how to respond if they are not welcomed, Jesus gives a
warning that sounds very much like Matthew 24:9–12. Starting in
verse 17, Jesus says:

"Be on your guard; you will be handed over to the local
councils and be flogged in the synagogues. On my account you will be brought before governors and kings
as witnesses to them and to the Gentiles. But when they
arrest you, do not worry about what to say or how to

say it. At that time you will be given what to say, for it will not be you speaking, but the Spirit of your Father speaking through you.

"Brother will betray brother to death, and a father his child; children will rebel against their parents and have them put to death. You will be hated by everyone because of me, but the one who stands firm to the end will be saved. When you are persecuted in one place, flee to another. Truly I tell you, you will not finish going through the towns of Israel before the Son of Man comes."

— Matthew 10:17–23

None of this happened when the twelve disciples were sent out in AD 28. They were not arrested, or betrayed, or executed. In fact, Jesus went on to send out seventy-two more disciples, as recorded by Luke. When they returned, they were filled with joy, and reported that even the demons were obedient to them in his name (Luke 10:12). It is obvious the message of Matthew 10:17–23 is meant for the disciples who will be present at his coming on the day of the Lord at the end of the age. And that is the same situation we find in the Matthew 24 passage.

Furthermore, Jesus tells the disciples plainly and clearly which generation of evangelists he is speaking of. He says:

"So when you see standing in the holy place '*the abomination that causes desolation,*' spoken of through the prophet Daniel—*let the reader understand*—then let those who are in Judea flee to the mountains. Let no one on the housetop go down to take anything out of the house. Let no one in the field go back to get their cloak. How dreadful it will be in those days for pregnant women and nursing mothers! Pray that your flight will not take place in winter or on the Sabbath. For then there will be great distress, unequaled from the beginning of the world until now—and never to be equaled again. If those days had not been cut short, no one would survive, but for the sake of the elect those days will be shortened."

— Matthew 24:15–22

Did you notice that Matthew added the phrase "let the reader understand"? This is a clear indication the Matthew wrote this passage to be understood by a future generation. We know from our study of Daniel the signing of the peace treaty between the Antichrist and Israel will be the beginning of the tribulation's seven-year period (Daniel 9:27). Furthermore, we know the "abomination of desolation" will occur at the halfway point of the tribulation, when the man of sin is finally revealed for who he really is (Daniel 9:27, II Thessalonians 2:3–10). So Jesus is speaking to the generation of Christians who will see the "abomination of desolation" being placed in the temple.

Jesus goes on to warn believers not to be fooled by any false Christ or false prophets because it will be impossible to miss his return. No one will have to tell you Christ has returned; the whole world will see it together. He goes on to say:

"At that time if anyone says to you, 'Look, here is the Messiah!' or, 'There he is!' do not believe it. For false messiahs and false prophets will appear and perform great signs and wonders to deceive, if possible, even the elect. See, I have told you ahead of time.

"So if anyone tells you, 'There he is, out in the wilderness,' do not go out; or, 'Here he is, in the inner rooms,' do not believe it. *For as lightning that comes from the east is visible even in the west, so will be the coming*

of the Son of Man. Wherever there is a carcass, there the
vultures will gather."

— Matthew 24:23–28

So the disciples Jesus speaks of in Matthew 10:17–23 and the
disciples Jesus speaks of in Matthew 24:3–35 are the same group.
They will face extreme persecution and suffering in the great
tribulation. They are the ones who will see the return of the Son of
Man.

Finally, Jesus gives a direct and unambiguous answer to the
question of when he will return. He says:

> *"Immediately after the distress of those days* 'the sun will
> be darkened, and the moon will not give its light; the
> stars will fall from the sky, and the heavenly bodies will
> be shaken.'
>
> "Then will appear the sign of the Son of Man in
> heaven. And then all the peoples of the earth will mourn
> when they see the Son of Man coming on the clouds of
> heaven, with power and great glory. And he will send
> his angels with a loud trumpet call, and they will gather
> his elect from the four winds, from one end of the heav-
> ens to the other."
>
> — Matthew 24:29–31

Four things will happen together at the return of Christ. First,
the sun, moon, and stars will fall from the sky. Second, the Son of
Man will visibly return, and every eye on earth will see him. Third,
the trumpet call of the Archangel will be heard around the world.
And fourth, the rapture of the saints will take place at the same time
as the resurrection of the dead. All this will occur simultaneously on
the "day of the Lord," at the end of the age. The rapture of the saints
is not a separate event which happens seven years before everything

else. It cannot be separated from the falling of the stars from the sky, or from the public return of Christ at the end of the age.

Jesus goes on in Matthew 24:36–25:46 to give the disciples warnings and exhortations concerning their personal preparedness for the times of trouble that lay ahead for the church. But before he does that he makes certain they understand the signs of his return. He says:

> "Now learn this lesson from the fig tree: As soon as its twigs get tender and its leaves come out, you know that summer is near. *Even so, when you see all these things, you know that it is near, right at the door.* Truly I tell you, **this generation** will certainly not pass away until all these things have happened. Heaven and earth will pass away, but my words will never pass away."
>
> — Matthew 24:32–35

The generation that sees the worldwide hatred of the church, the appearance of the Antichrist and the revelation of his true nature, and the abomination of desolation: this is the generation that will see the culmination of the age and the return of Christ.

In Luke's version of the Olivet Discourse, he mentions the same events taking place at the end of the tribulation, and then he adds, "When these things begin to take place, [stars falling from the sky and Jesus appearing in the clouds] stand up and lift up your heads, because your redemption is drawing near" (Luke 21:28). This will fulfill the prophecy of Isaiah 18:3, which says, "All you people of the world, you who live on the earth, when a banner is raised on the mountains, you will see it, and when a trumpet sounds, you will hear it." Jesus will be seen by every nation on earth when he comes.

Notice that everything Jesus has said in this prophecy is based solidly on Old Testament prophecy. He quotes from Isaiah repeatedly. Why then do so many insist this is a new revelation?

Why do they insist the rapture comes seven years before the public return of Christ? As Paul taught his young disciple, Timothy:

> For the time will come when people will not put up with sound doctrine. Instead, to suit their own desires, they will gather around them a great number of teachers to say what their itching ears want to hear. They will turn their ears away from the truth and turn aside to myths.
>
> — 2 Timothy 4:3–4

The pretribulational rapture is a myth that millions want to be true. I wish it was true as well, but it is not. If you have been deceived by this teaching, you have been misled by angels of darkness masquerading as angels of light. Please go back and look again at every passage of Scripture used by teachers of a pretribulational rapture to support their teaching. Are they using a literal interpretation of every verse, or have they used symbolic and metaphorical interpretations whenever it is convenient? Will you be honest enough with yourself to take a second look?

ENDNOTES

1   W. Bauer, *A Greek-English Lexicon of the New Testament*, pg. 635

CHAPTER NINE

Prophecy in the Epistles

There is a passage that is the centerpiece of the pretribulational theory. This passage is found in I Thessalonians 4:13–17, which says:

> Brothers and sisters, we do not want you to be uninformed about those who sleep in death, so that you do not grieve like the rest of mankind, who have no hope. For we believe that Jesus died and rose again, and so we believe that God will bring with Jesus those who have fallen asleep in him. According to the Lord's word, *we tell you that we who are still alive, who are left until the coming [parousia] of the Lord, will certainly not precede those who have fallen asleep. For the Lord himself will come down from heaven, with a loud command, with the voice of the archangel and with the trumpet call of God, and the dead in Christ will rise first.* After that, we who are still alive and are left will be caught up together with them in the clouds to meet the Lord in the air. And so we will be with the Lord forever.
>
> — I Thessalonians 4:13–17

This passage begs the question: Was Paul restating a truth of Old Testament prophecy, or was he giving a new prophecy? Paul, like the apostle John, seems to base his statements of doctrine squarely on the Old Testament. Paul knew his Old Testament well; after all, it was the only Bible he had, and he believed every word of it. His prophecy in I Thessalonians 4:13–18 is a direct reference to Isaiah 27:12–13, which says:

> In that day the LORD will thresh from the flowing Euphrates to the Wadi of Egypt, *and you, Israel, will be gathered up one by one. And in that day a great trumpet will sound.* Those who were perishing in Assyria and those who were exiled in Egypt will come and worship the LORD on the holy mountain in Jerusalem.

The context of Isaiah 27 is the day of the Lord and God's rescue of Israel after they have been through the tribulation. The word "gathered" in this passage of Isaiah is the word *laqat*, which means "to glean." Gleaning is done by hand-picking chosen heads of grain, not by using a sickle or threshing machine. This is the gathering of the saints as promised by Moses, Isaiah, Jeremiah, and Ezekiel. In this case it is done by the angels of God, just as Jesus promised the disciples in Matthew 24:31. And the gleaning is done after the harvest is over. Remember the parables in Matthew 13? Furthermore, notice that Israel's gathering is promised to be accompanied by a great trumpet sound, just as Paul promised in I Thessalonians. There is nothing secret about the sound of this trumpet. The entire world will hear it (Isaiah 13:1–13, and Isaiah 18:3).

Furthermore, there is nothing secret about the Son of Man appearing in the sky at that time. Paul uses the word *parousia* to describe this event, emphasizing the fact that this is a public appearance. Again, that will happen at the end of the tribulation, when Christ destroys the kingdom of the Antichrist (Daniel 7:7–28).

His appearance will also be in conjunction with the resurrection of the dead at the end of the tribulation, on the day of the Lord (Ezekiel 37:1–14). In order for this to be a new prophecy, we are forced to believe there will be two rescues of the saints of God, two appearances of Christ, two trumpet blasts, and two resurrections of the dead. If that is the case, there must be a rapture at the beginning of the tribulation that doesn't include all the events prophesized in Scripture, followed by a rapture at the end of the tribulation that does.

That "great trumpet sound" is again referred to by Paul in I Corinthians 15:51–56, which says:

> Listen, I tell you a mystery: We will not all sleep, but we will all be changed—in a flash, in the twinkling of an eye, at the last trumpet. *For the trumpet will sound, the dead will be raised imperishable, and we will be changed.* [Clearly, this is a reference to the same event spoken of in I Thessalonians 4:13–18.] For the perishable must clothe itself with the imperishable, and the mortal with immortality. When the perishable has been clothed with the imperishable, and the mortal with immortality, then the saying that is written will come true: "Death has been swallowed up in victory."
>
> "Where, O death, is your victory? Where, O death, is your sting?"
>
> The sting of death is sin, and the power of sin is the law.

This is the same trumpet referred to by Jesus in Matthew 24:31. Both happen on the day of the Lord and in conjunction with the resurrection of the dead. The last trumpet is mentioned by Isaiah numerous times, and it always comes on the day of the Lord. For example, Isaiah 18:3 says, "All you people of the world, you who live on the earth, when a banner is raised on the mountains, you will see it, and when a trumpet sounds, you will hear it."

In other words, those who combine the miraculous gathering of Israel at the last trumpet, the resurrection of the dead, and the public appearance of the Messiah on the day of the Lord, and call it a "secret rapture" are just a little confused. They have taken several Old Testament teachings and claim they only apply to the Gentile church while turning a blind eye to the context of the Old Testament passages Paul is referring to.

II Thessalonians 2:1–7 is also used as proof of a pretribulational rapture. This passage says:

> Concerning the coming of our Lord Jesus Christ and our being gathered to him, we ask you, brothers and sisters, not to become easily unsettled or alarmed by the teaching allegedly from us—whether by a prophecy or by word of mouth or by letter—asserting that the day of the Lord has already come. *Don't let anyone deceive you in any way, for that day will not come until the rebellion occurs and the man of lawlessness is revealed, the man doomed to destruction.* He will oppose and will exalt himself over everything that is called God or is worshiped, so that he sets himself up in God's temple, proclaiming himself to be God.
>
> Don't you remember that when I was with you I used to tell you these things? And now you know what is holding him back, so that he may be revealed at the proper time. For the secret power of lawlessness is already at work; *but the one who now holds it back will continue to do so till he is taken out of the way."*

Two things make the pretribulational theory impossible to support from this passage. First of all, the rapture cannot occur until after the man of lawlessness is revealed, which will not happen until the halfway point of the tribulation. Until that point, the man of lawlessness will be thought of as a man of peace. He will negotiate a peace treaty (*hudna*) with Israel (Daniel 9:27), and be hailed as a great hero at the beginning of the tribulation. That event will mark the start of the seven-year period known as the great tribulation. "'Peace, peace,' they say, when there is no peace" (Jeremiah 6:14).

He will break the covenant halfway through the tribulation and be revealed as the man of lawlessness. Only after this point can the rapture occur according to II Thessalonians 2:3. That would seem to leave the door open for a midtribulation rapture, but Revelation 12 leaves that option out as well, because that is when the Two Witnesses are killed and the extreme persecution of Gentile Christians begins. Satan turns away from his efforts to pursue Israel and turns to persecuting Gentile Christians instead.

The other proof of the pretribulational rapture taken from this passage is the belief that the "one who now holds it back" is the Holy Spirit. II Thessalonians 2:7 says that person will be taken out of the way. They believe if the Holy Spirit of God is removed, the church must be raptured, because the Holy Spirit dwells in every Christian.

I have to ask: Do you have a box big enough to put God in? Where do you put an omnipotent, omnipresent God if you take him off the earth? And who moves him out of the way? Are God the Father and God the Son going to put God the Holy Spirit in a time-out for seven years? Look at John 14:16: "And I will ask the Father who will give you another comforter to be with you *forever.*" When does forever stop? Will this Scripture become null and void for the sake of the pretribulational rapture?

There will be multitudes of believers who go through the tribulation; that is apparent from chapter after chapter of Revelation. If they do not have the Holy Spirit in them, then John 14:16 is a lie. The truth is, the "one who now holds back" the plans of Satan and the Antichrist is Michael, the archangel (Daniel 10:13). He is the protector of Israel. When the Antichrist is given free rein for 4,200 days, Michael will temporarily step aside.

The last verse I will mention is Revelation 3:10: "Since you have kept my command to endure patiently, I will also keep you from the hour of trial that is going to come on the whole world to test the inhabitants of the earth." This is the message given to the church of Ephesus. Because it is the sixth of seven churches listed, teachers of a pretribulation rapture speculate these are metaphorical churches, and are to be understood as Church Ages. Understood this way, the church of this sixth Church Age will be raptured, leaving the church of the seventh Church Age to go through the tribulation.

Part of this supposition is based on the meaning of the Greek preposition *ek* used in the phrase "I will also keep you *from*. . ." *Ek* can mean "out of" or "from." Believers in a pretribulation rapture argue this is proof of a promised rapture of the church, taking us *out of* the world and keeping us *from* the tribulation that is about to come on the people of the world. That sounds like a strong argument, but it is only possible if the passage is understood as an allegory and not directed to seven real churches in Asia Minor.

However, these are not fictional churches, nor are they symbolic of Church Ages. History shows John wrote to real churches, not to symbols. Their ruins are visited by thousands every year.

If you do believe these are Church Ages, I have to ask you: When did each Church Age begin and end? Can you name these supposed Church Ages and tell me who the leaders of each age were? What challenges did they face that separated them from previous Church Ages? Why was each Church Age unique enough to be seen as different in the eyes of God?

The fact that no one can answer these questions should tell you this theory is based on an allegorical interpretation. You could name a thousand possible dates, and none can be proven to be right or wrong.

The entire argument goes back to the basic question of how you interpret the Bible. Do you stick to the literal, historical, grammatical, and contextual meaning of Scripture, or do you resort to allegorical interpretation when it supports your argument? Do you allow yourself to see "hidden messages" in Scripture that can only be understood by the "super-spiritual"? Are you willing to base your faith on the shifting sand of allegory, or is the Bible our solid rock, the words of which will not pass away until every jot and tittle is fulfilled?

Allegorical interpretation must be rejected if we are to base our faith on the word of God. And, with it must go the idea the sixth Church Age as a promise of a pretribulational rapture. You can argue about the meaning of "*ek*" until you are blue in the face. It doesn't matter. If there is no allegorical meaning of a sixth Church Age in Revelation 3:10, there is no pretribulational rapture.

We have looked at all the passages of the New Testament epistles that are commonly used to support the pretribulational theory. In every one of them, we have seen a common technique used by the teachers of this theory. The literal interpretation of the passages is set aside and an interpretation relying on allegory or metaphor is substituted. This is combined with an interpretation method which takes what it wants from the Old Testament and rejects what it does not want; appropriating the blessings promised to Israel while rejecting their judgments. We make the claim of being children of Abraham while forgetting that makes us Jews in the eyes of God.

Please consider very carefully this last passage from Paul:

> If some of the branches have been broken off, and you, though a wild olive shoot, have been grafted in among the others and now share in the nourishing sap from the olive root, do not consider yourself to be superior to those other branches. If you do, consider this: You

do not support the root, but the root supports you. You will say then, "Branches were broken off so that I could be grafted in." Granted. But they were broken off because of unbelief, and you stand by faith. Do not be arrogant, but tremble. For if God did not spare the natural branches, he will not spare you either.

Consider therefore the kindness and sternness of God: sternness to those who fell, but kindness to you, provided that you continue in his kindness. Otherwise, you also will be cut off. And if they do not persist in unbelief, they will be grafted in, for God is able to graft them in again. After all, if you were cut out of an olive tree that is wild by nature, and contrary to nature were grafted into a cultivated olive tree, how much more readily will these, the natural branches, be grafted into their own olive tree!

I do not want you to be ignorant of this mystery, brothers and sisters, so that you may not be conceited: Israel has experienced a hardening in part until the full number of the Gentiles has come in, and in this way all Israel will be saved. As it is written:

"The deliverer will come from Zion; he will turn godlessness away from Jacob. And this is my covenant with them when I take away their sins."

— Romans 11:17–27

We are grafted in as a branch of the cultivated olive tree of Israel. All of the promises made to Israel apply to us just as much as they still apply to Israel, and vice versa. "Jesus Christ is the same yesterday, today and forever" (Hebrews 13:8), and the same is true of his Word. The prophecies of future redemption for the saints of God apply to all the saints, Old Testament and New. As members of the New Testament church, we must remember our cherished promises of a rapture and being with Christ forever are based upon our being a grafted-in branch of Israel. If we ignore that fact, we are guilty of considering our branches to be superior and are therefore in danger of being broken off.

Stop and consider for a moment: Has anything new been added by the teaching of the apostles? Is the teaching in the New Testament of the resurrection, the rapture, the last trumpet, and the return of Christ on the day of the Lord, a new teaching? To whom were those promises made? Why, then, would we believe they only apply to us, and not to Israel?

CHAPTER TEN

Introduction to the Book of Revelation

The Revelation of John is unique among New Testament books, being the only book that rivals the Old Testament prophets in purpose and content. John's style of writing shows a cyclical-progressive pattern from vision to vision. This writing style echoes the style found in the book of Daniel, where each new vision refers to, and builds upon, the previous vision.

John records three series of judgments which include the wrath of God being poured out on those who follow the god of this world. They include seven seals, seven trumpets, and seven bowls. Each series of judgments builds upon the previous judgments, intensifying the wrath of God upon the earth. Jesus Christ proves the Psalmist right (Psalm 2:9) by opening the first seal and beginning the process of judging the earth.

The seals, trumpets, and bowls all end with a reference to the day of the Lord, which means each series of judgments will continue from its opening until the end of the tribulation. God's wrath will grow in intensity as each new series of plagues is poured out. The seal judgments destroy one-quarter of the earth and its people, and the trumpet judgments destroy another one-third. However, there is no limitation placed on the bowl judgments.

The judgments do not begin on the day Israel signs a peace treaty with the Antichrist. According to Daniel's prophecy in Daniel 9:27, that day marks the first day of a seven-year period known as the "great tribulation." But the wars that bring the ten-nation coalition to power will begin before that point. The head of the coalition will be replaced by the "little horn," who is the Antichrist. That is why there are no indications of time on the pouring out of the three series of judgments, but there is a time indicator given for Antichrist's reign.

The tribulation can be divided into two halves. The ministry of the Two Witnesses lasts for 1,260 days, followed by the 1,260 days Satan and the Antichrist chase after Israel while God protects her in the wilderness. The day the *hudna* is signed will mark the first day of the ministry of the Two Witnesses. Three and one-half years later, the Antichrist will enter the Temple to proclaim himself as God; that will mark the beginning of the second three and one-half years.

For centuries, the book of Revelation has been seen as a book of doom and gloom; first for the world, as the three series of judgments destroy the people of the earth, and second, for the church, as the Antichrist destroys the Christians. The church has dreaded the thought of the tribulation as being a time without God's help, when uncountable numbers of Christians will be slaughtered. But in fact, the Holy Spirit will be more active on behalf of the saints then than at any time since the first century.

Revelation 1:3 promises a "blessing" to everyone who reads and takes to heart the message of the book. Very few seem to have discovered what that blessing is, because they are so focused on the smaller details that they don't see the bigger picture and purpose. The blessing is to know Satan's game plan from start to finish. If you know what your enemy plans to do, you can prepare. To be forewarned is to be forearmed. You may ask, how can Christians prepare for Satan taking over the world? The answer is very simple: by following the commands of the New Testament, and implementing the principles that helped the church survive the troubles of the past. Those principles include intense prayer, total dedication to Jesus Christ, sharing with other Christians, and self-sacrifice.

The real message of Revelation is not found in the wrath of God and Satan being poured out on the earth. It is found in the *parentheses*. These parentheses are changes in the visions John sees which are not directly related to the judgments of the seals, trumpets, or bowls. The parentheses are there not to further the storyline of the tribulation, but to give insight to believers. They are John's way of applying the visions of the coming troubles to the lives of the saints, by way of warnings, exhortations and encouragements. They include very stern warnings not to accept the mark of the beast, along with exhortations to remain faithful even though the situation looks dire. But even more importantly, they also include repeated visions of saints being rewarded, and visions of the final victory of Jesus Christ over Satan and the Antichrist. These parentheses provide great hope and incentive for the saints to endure. This is John's real purpose for writing Revelation.

Each of the letters to the churches of Asia promise a reward. Each of those rewards is handed out in later parentheses to the saints who have overcome. That is the heart of John's message: it is an open letter of encouragement to the saints, promising that a huge number of believers will endure and overcome, and that they will receive a great reward from God at the coming of Jesus Christ. This is not a book of doom and gloom for the future of Christianity. Yes, it's a story of the trial of our faith, but that trial will result in the ultimate victory of Jesus Christ and his saints over the forces of evil. This is not an allegory; it is a fact you can count on every bit as much as you can believe your salvation rests in the trustworthy hands of Jesus Christ. These are his words, after all, delivered by a theophany—an appearance of Jesus in a form visible to a human being.

The key verses for understanding Revelation are Revelation 10:6–7, which are given to John through an angel. These verses say:

> And he [the angel] . . . said, "There will be no more
> delay! But in the days when the seventh angel is about
> to sound his trumpet the mystery of God will be ac-
> complished, *just as he announced to his servants the
> prophets.*"

The phrase "just as he announced to his servants the prophets"
is the key. It tells us that Revelation is based on the writings of the
Old Testament prophets and that it is the culmination of all biblical
prophecy. Everything promised by God through the prophets is
fulfilled in the pages of Revelation. There are 348 references to the
prophets in John's twenty-two chapters. Without a solid knowledge
of those prophecies, Revelation is an unsolvable mystery. Once you
understand that John's book is based on the solid foundation laid
down by Moses and the prophets, the book will unfold for you.

The outline of John's book is given to him, and in turn to us, by
Jesus Christ in Revelation 1:19. John is told to write "what you see,"
"what is now," and "what must take place later."

"What he sees" is the vision of the angel of Jesus Christ appearing
to him on the Isle of Patmos (Revelation chapter 1). "What is now"
are the seven churches of Asia (Revelation chapters 2–3). And "what
must take place later" is the actual prophetic section dealing with
the coming tribulation (Revelation chapters 4–22).

We are introduced to the prophetic section by a vision that is a
repeat of a vision seen by Daniel. The Revelation prophecy says:

> After this I looked, and there before me was a door
> standing open in heaven. And the voice I had first heard
> speaking to me like a trumpet said, "Come up here, and
> I will show you what must take place after this." At once
> I was in the Spirit, and there before me was a throne in
> heaven with someone sitting on it. And the one who sat

there had the appearance of jasper and ruby. A rainbow that shone like an emerald encircled the throne. . . .

Then I saw in the right hand of him who sat on the throne a scroll with writing on both sides and sealed with seven seals. And I saw a mighty angel proclaiming in a loud voice, "Who is worthy to break the seals and open the scroll?" But no one in heaven or on earth or under the earth could open the scroll or even look inside it. I wept and wept because no one was found who was worthy to open the scroll or look inside. Then one of the elders said to me, *"Do not weep! See, the Lion of the tribe of Judah, the Root of David, has triumphed. He is able to open the scroll and its seven seals."*

— Revelation 4:1–3 and 5:1–5

This is an expanded version of the vision that was seen by Daniel in 7:9–14. Daniel 7:13 plays a crucial role in understanding the New Testament. It is the source of the name Son of Man, which Jesus chooses to call himself seventy-six times in the gospels. The Son of Man takes authority from the hand of the Almighty Father and then overthrows the kingdom of the final beast in Daniel 7:23–27.

Jesus Christ quotes this verse in his Olivet Discourse as he explains to his four disciples when he will return and set up his kingdom. He also quotes this same verse to the high priest when Caiaphas demands to know if he is the son of God. Jesus replies, *"Yes! It is as you say"* (Matthew 26:64). Jesus is the Son of Man.

The coming of the Son of Man to take authority from the hands of God the Father is also predicted by Paul in I Corinthians 15:22–28, which says:

For as in Adam all die, so in Christ all will be made alive. But each in turn: Christ, the firstfruits; then, when he comes, those who belong to him. Then the end will come, when he hands over the kingdom to God the Father after he has destroyed all dominion, authority and power. For he must reign until he has put all his enemies under his feet. The last enemy to be destroyed is death. For he "has put everything under his feet." Now when it says that "everything" has been put under him, it is clear that this does not include God himself, who put everything under Christ. When he has done this, then the Son himself will be made subject to him who put everything under him, so that God may be all in all.

— 1 Corinthians 15:22–28

Chapter 5 of Revelation is John's vision of Jesus taking authority from God the Father and pouring out of the wrath of God on the world by opening the seals of judgment. Likewise, chapter 21 of Revelation shows Jesus handing authority back to the Father as the Father and Son reign in the New Jerusalem. In other words, Revelation confirms Daniel 7, and Daniel 7 and I Corinthians 15 will be fulfilled exactly as they were written.

I want to point out that Jesus Christ never leaves the earth once he returns in power and great glory with the hosts of heaven on the day of the Lord. In fact, the only time he ever leaves Jerusalem is to fight the Antichrist at the battle of Armageddon. There is no prophecy anywhere in the Bible of Jesus returning to heaven once he appears in the sky with the host of heaven to redeem the saints of God. That means Jerusalem is the "heaven" where Jesus Christ will reign as King of Kings. If we are to reign with Jesus Christ, it will be in Jerusalem. Please understand this point: we will not spend eternity someplace in the clouds playing harps. We will be on the new earth with its King of Kings and Lord of Lords. That is why the parables of Matthew 13 all indicate the "good" crops remain and the "bad" crops are removed.

Because of space considerations, this will not be a verse-by-verse study of John's Revelation. Instead, we will approach Revelation as we did the Old Testament prophets, mentioning only those portions necessary in order to understand the authors theme.

CHAPTER ELEVEN

The Seven Seals
Revelation 6:1–8:1

Chapter 6 begins the actual prophecy section of Revelation. Jesus Christ, the Son of Man, was found to be the only one in heaven and earth who is worthy to open the scroll containing the pronouncements of God's judgment upon the earth. We see that judgment poured out through John's eyes as seal after seal is broken.

> I watched as the Lamb opened the first of the seven seals. Then I heard one of the four living creatures say in a voice like thunder, "Come!" I looked, and there before me was a white horse! Its rider held a bow, and he was given a crown, and he rode out as a conqueror bent on conquest.
>
> — Revelation 6:1–2

> When the Lamb opened the second seal, I heard the second living creature say, "Come!" Then another horse came out, a fiery red one. Its rider was given power to take peace from the earth and to make people kill each other. To him was given a large sword.
>
> — Revelation 6:3–4

When the Lamb opened the third seal, I heard the third living creature say, "Come!" I looked, and there before me was a black horse! Its rider was holding a pair of scales in his hand. Then I heard what sounded like a voice among the four living creatures, saying, "Two pounds of wheat for a day's wages, and six pounds of barley for a day's wages, and do not damage the oil and the wine!"

— Revelation 6:5–6

When the Lamb opened the fourth seal, I heard the voice of the fourth living creature say, "Come!" I looked, and there before me was a pale horse! Its rider was named Death, and Hades was following close behind him. They were given *power over a fourth of the earth* to kill by sword, famine and plague, and by the wild beasts of the earth.

— Revelation 6:7–8

When he opened the fifth seal, I saw under the altar the souls of those who had been slain because of the word of God and the testimony they had maintained. They called out in a loud voice, "How long, Sovereign Lord, holy and true, until you judge the inhabitants of the earth and avenge our blood?" Then each of them was given a white robe, and they were told to wait a little longer, until the full number of their fellow servants, their brothers and sisters, were killed just as they had been.

— Revelation 6:9–11

The message of the seven seals is that one quarter of the earth and its people will be destroyed by the plagues and wars which are poured out at the command of Christ. This is the opening round of God's wrath. However, this will not be the beginning of the great tribulation. That will begin on the day the Antichrist signs the peace treaty with Israel. In Jesus' Olivet Discourse, he spoke of "wars and rumors of wars" in Matthew 24:6. These are the wars which will bring the ten-nation coalition to power. Jesus says in Matthew 24:8, "These are the beginnings of birth pains." The actual seven-year period of the tribulation will not begin until the Antichrist takes over that coalition. The wars of the coalition do not mark the beginning of the final seven years of the tribulation; that beginning is marked by the signing of the peace treaty with Israel.

Many Christians will be killed during the tribulation. We cannot hide that fact. But each death is a victory for that saint and a testimony to the church. In many cases, these are the ones who "overcome" and are rewarded. They are given white robes, as promised in Revelation 3:4, and are told to wait until they are joined by all of their brothers and sisters who will be killed. This book is a warning to us of what the church must face. That warning is part of our blessing if we use it to prepare for what is ahead. John says:

> I watched as he opened the sixth seal. There was a great earthquake. The sun turned black like sackcloth made of goat hair, the whole moon turned blood red, and the stars in the sky fell to earth, as figs drop from a fig tree when shaken by a strong wind. The heavens receded like a scroll being rolled up, and every mountain and island was removed from its place.
>
> Then the kings of the earth, the princes, the generals, the rich, the mighty, and everyone else, both slave and free, hid in caves and among the rocks of the mountains. They called to the mountains and the rocks, "Fall

on us and hide us from the face of him who sits on the
throne and from the wrath of the Lamb! For the great
day of their wrath has come, and who can withstand it?"
— Revelation 6:12–17

In Revelation 6:12–17, John uses a series of references taken
from the prophecy of Isaiah. They refer to Isaiah chapters 2, 24,
and 34. Please go back to Isaiah and reread those chapters if you
have forgotten what they say. All three passages refer to the very
end of time, specifically the day of the Lord. That is the day of the
coming of the Messiah to judge the earth. These Isaiah passages,
quoted here by John, are some of the same verses quoted by Jesus in
his Olivet Discourse (Matthew 24–25). The implication is that all of
the plagues mentioned above will continue from the time the seal
judgments are poured out until the end of the tribulation period.
The plagues of trumpets and bowls, which will start at a later date,
will do the same. This will be longer than a seven-year period, but
how long no one can say.

Now we come to the first of the parentheses of Revelation. This
is where we find the true heart of John's message to the church. I
call these visions parentheses because they are not directly related
to what is going on with the plagues of the seals, trumpets, and
bowls of God's wrath; however, they are taking place at the same
time. They are reminiscent of what we find in Hollywood movies,
where there is more than one story line and the scene changes as
characters come and go. The plagues are directed at the world. The
parentheses are meant for us. In them we find stern warnings, great
encouragement, and visions of reward for those who overcome.

After this I saw four angels standing at the four corners of the earth, holding back the four winds of the
earth to prevent any wind from blowing on the land
or on the sea or on any tree. Then I saw another angel

coming up from the east, having the seal of the living God. He called out in a loud voice to the four angels who had been given power to harm the land and the sea: *"Do not harm the land or the sea or the trees until we put a seal on the foreheads of the servants of our God."*

— Revelation 7:1-3

God will not desert the church during the tribulation. All of the seal judgments are put on hold until the foreheads of the saints are marked with a mark that only the angels bringing the plagues can see. In this case, this applies to the 144,000 saints mentioned in the next verses. But as we keep reading, we see it also applies to all the saints living in the tribulation period. God makes no distinction between Jewish and Gentile saints, not even with sanctifying marks.

The only difference God sees is between the saints and the people of the world. The saints are not affected by the plagues. It was the same situation during the exodus of the children of Israel from Egypt. Moses repeats seven times in Exodus 8-12 that God made a distinction between the children of Israel and the Egyptians. The plagues of God's wrath were being poured out on Egypt. The saints (the children of Israel) who lived through the Egyptian plagues were not harmed, nor were they raptured. That will be the case with the saints during the tribulation. They will not be harmed by God's wrath, but they will not be raptured until the end of the tribulation period.

Then I heard the number of those who were sealed: 144,000 from all the tribes of Israel. From the tribe of Judah 12,000 were sealed, from the tribe of Reuben 12,000, from the tribe of Gad 12,000, from the tribe of Asher 12,000, from the tribe of Naphtali 12,000, from the tribe of Manasseh 12,000, from the tribe of Simeon 12,000, from the tribe of Levi 12,000, from the tribe of

> Issachar 12,000, from the tribe of Zebulun 12,000, from the tribe of Joseph 12,000, from the tribe of Benjamin 12,000.
>
> — Revelation 7:4–8

Israel will turn back to God and worship Jesus Christ as their Messiah. We have already seen this promise in Deuteronomy 30, Isaiah 56, and Jeremiah 31. The same promise is made in Joel 2 and Zechariah 12. The veil will be lifted from their eyes. Their turning will be preceded by a wave of evangelism which will sweep through Israel and through Jewish communities around the world. That wave will be started by these 144,000 chosen Jews.

> After this I looked, and there before me was *a great multitude that no one could count*, from every nation, tribe, people and language, standing before the throne and before the Lamb. They were wearing white robes and were holding palm branches in their hands. And they cried out in a loud voice:
> "Salvation belongs to our God, who sits on the throne, and to the Lamb."
> All the angels were standing around the throne and around the elders and the four living creatures. They fell down on their faces before the throne and worshiped God, saying:
> "Amen! Praise and glory and wisdom and thanks and honor and power and strength be to our God for ever and ever. Amen!"
>
> — Revelation 7:9–12

The great multitude that no one could count is the result of the evangelism of the 144,000. "And so all Israel will be saved" (Romans 11:26). The church has grown to a number that only God can count. The fact that they are fellow believers in Jesus Christ is unquestionable.

> Then one of the elders asked me, "These in white robes—who are they, and where did they come from?"
>
> I answered, "Sir, you know."
>
> And he said, *"These are they who have come out of the great tribulation; they have washed their robes and made them white in the blood of the Lamb.* Therefore, "they are before the throne of God and serve him day and night in his temple; and he who sits on the throne will shelter them with his presence. Never again will they hunger; never again will they thirst. The sun will not beat down on them, nor any scorching heat. For the Lamb at the center of the throne will be their shepherd; he will lead them to springs of living water. And God will wipe away every tear from their eyes."
>
> — Revelation 7:13–17

I prefer the reading of the New American Bible for Revelation 7:14, which makes the meaning easier to understand.

> I said to him, "My Lord, you are the one who knows."
> He said to me, "These are the ones who have survived the time of great distress; they have washed their robes white in the blood of the Lamb."[1]

The phrase "time of great distress" is actually "time of great ϑλίψιη," or "time of great tribulation." These saints have been through the great tribulation and survived! This is not a message of doom and gloom for the church. This is a book of great hope for those who overcome. There will be an uncountable number of survivors who will not give up their testimony of Jesus. Yes, there will be many who are martyred, but that number will pale in comparison to those who survive. That is good news!

However, the question has to be asked: How will they survive? I believe the answer is found in the Bible. The advice of Isaiah is: "Go, my people, enter your rooms and shut the doors behind you; hide yourselves for a little while until the wrath has passed by" (Isaiah 26:20). And I can hear the words of Jeremiah echoing in my ears: "Oh that I had an inn in the wilderness for wayfarers, where I might flee from my people!" (Jeremiah 9:2a, KJV). And Jesus advises, "then let those who are in Judea flee to the mountains. Let no one on the roof of his house go down to take anything out of the house. Let no one in the field go back to get his cloak" (Matthew 24:16–18).

The answer is to flee. But flee to where, and how, and with whom? Those answers are not so easy. Nevertheless, we must do our best to be prepared. A good start is to become financially independent. Pay off your debts as soon as possible. We must also become independent regarding food and water, so plant a garden and fruit trees, and learn to can and preserve foods. If you can, dig a well and install a storage tank. All of these things are good, but they may not be the answer if we have to flee in the night. We might end up as small bands of believers living communally away from the general population.

Our church life will definitely change. The day of the mega-churches is coming to a swift end. They will be easy targets for any government that wishes to get rid of Christians. And of course, all church buildings will eventually face the same problem. It will start with taxing church property. The excuse will be the need to raise taxes to solve the financial crisis. Then it will move on to confiscation of church property and imprisonment of Christians, just like it did in Russia.

However, we have an example to refer to and learn from. The church of the first three centuries faced persecution, first from the Jews and later from the Roman government. History records that at least eleven separate Roman rulers did their best to stamp out the Christian religion by persecuting the church. People were arrested and tortured to death by various means. Property was confiscated, which either became state property or it was sold to the highest bidder. Tertullian records:

> If the Tiber rises as high as the city walls, if the Nile does not send its waters up over the fields, if the heavens give no rain, if there is an earthquake, if there is famine or pestilence, straightway the cry is, "Away with the Christians to the lion."[2]

Each time persecution broke out, the church went underground. Yet the church grew in numbers through all the hell that man could throw at it. And not only did they survive, they thrived.

How did they do it? We are told how in Acts 2:

> They *devoted themselves to the apostles' teaching* and to *fellowship*, to the *breaking of bread* and *to prayer.* Everyone was filled with awe at the many wonders and signs performed by the apostles. All the believers were together and had everything in common. *They sold property and possessions to give to anyone who had need.* Every day they continued to meet together in the temple courts. They broke bread in their homes and ate together with glad and sincere hearts, praising God and enjoying the favor of all the people. And the Lord added to their number daily those who were being saved.
> — Acts 2:42–47

You might think that was too simple and mundane to be a plan for survival, but it was not. The persecution had not yet started when that statement was made. The church was basking in the glow of the resurrection of Christ, and no one had chased them away from the Temple as yet. No one could deny the miracle that had taken place in their midst. New converts were being made by the thousands. They didn't realize it at the time, but the actions they took then prepared them to face the persecution that was just around the corner. That persecution began not long after the feast of Pentecost in the first year of the new church.

With the approval and authority of the high priest, the Christian Jews were arrested and removed from the synagogues. Their property was confiscated, and some were killed. The apostle Paul was one of the persecutors. In those first few decades after the resurrection, the church survived by going underground. Many fled to neighboring countries. Those who stayed in Judea didn't meet in synagogues; they met in house churches. Meeting out of sight of the authorities, small groups of Christians helping other Christians were able to survive and thrive. The evangelism continued unabated, and finally the church became the only religion of the Roman world. That is a picture of what is in store for the church in North America. Our wonderful church buildings may become things of the past, but the church will grow stronger than ever if we are faithful and follow the command of Christ to evangelize as we go.

A closer look at Acts 2 will reveal just how the church survived. First, they followed the teaching of the apostles and the word of God. Nothing can be more important for the church than reading and believing what the Bible says.

Beyond that, they took action that guaranteed the survival of the majority. They did that by eating together every day. How does that help our survival? It helps us to become the family that we are supposed to be. Close fellowship will be needed to get through the tribulation. Nothing grows fellowship like eating, sharing, playing, praying, and working together. That is how we really get to know our brothers and sisters in Christ.

Furthermore, when we really get to know our Christian brothers and sisters, our prayers for them are sincere and specific. The early church prayed for each other every day. They learned to love each other and pray for each other as they shared their needs with one another. And all of this stemmed from eating together every day. They knew each other's needs and prayed for them like they were their own needs. That is what close fellowship does for a church.

Finally, they shared with each other as each one had a need. This should never be seen as a plan for government action. This was not Christian communism; it was one Christian brother meeting the needs of another Christian brother. Yes, they used the apostles to distribute the funds to keep pride in check, but it was never an official church policy. Nor was it giving your money to a government to waste as they please. So how would someone know what the needs of another Christian are? By eating together, and fellowshipping together, and praying together every day. What a simple plan! I wish I could take credit for it, but I can't. It's God's plan for those of us who will go through the tribulation. And it's a remake of the plan used by the early church.

Frances Chan, in his book *Forgotten God*, tells the story of a gang member who joined a church in Southern California. He came regularly for about six months and then stopped coming. After a few months of not seeing the man, the pastor called him to find out what had happened. The man told him that in his gang, people were true family. They did everything together and would do anything for each other. That is what he expected to find in the church, but it wasn't there.

That story touched my heart. Nothing could be more damning of the church of North America than that statement. We are supposed to be a body and to be a part of each other. We are supposed to love each other as brothers and sisters. Yet, in nearly every church in America, most church members can't even name everyone in the congregation. We treat church as if it was a one-hour entertainment program for Sunday mornings. We come in, sit down, have a few laughs, listen to a good story, and then get up and head for the door. You might see the pastor as you leave, but don't count on ever seeing him during the week. He's too busy for that! If that describes your church experience, then you and your church are headed for trouble.

Let's start preparing now. Get financially solvent as soon as possible. Pay off your mortgage if possible. Plant a garden. But most of all, make good friends, very good friends, with your brothers and sisters in Christ. Learn their needs, share with them your needs, and pray for each other daily. If you are a member of a large church, find a dozen other Christians in that church and form a close fellowship with them. Meet together on a regular basis, after church or some other time. To help you meet other Christians in your church, ask your pastors to form dinner groups that meet at least every other week. Look for people that have the same interests as you do away from church. Maybe that involves sports, or collectables, or some other interest.

Start building your friends now. I believe the future of the church in North America will only be found in the home church: very small, very tight groups who share and help each other as they have needs. That is the way the early church survived. Furthermore, that is how churches in countries where persecution has been strong have survived. I can think of Russia, China, and several Muslim countries just off the top of my head. Get going now.

John ends his vision of the seven seals with a vision of the calm that will flood the earth after the wave of wrath. "When he opened the seventh seal, there was silence in heaven for about half an hour" (Revelation 8:1).

We are promised a day of rest when we enter the Promised Land. Joshua first made the promise way back when the children of Israel were about to enter the Promised Land. We are reminded again by the writer of Hebrews that the offer of a day of rest still stands and awaits us in heaven. Here it is! Those who were rewarded for their faithfulness in the sixth seal now receive rest in the last seal. But the peace and quiet last only a short time, then the next round of judgment begins.

ENDNOTES

1   United States Conference of Catholic Bishops, editors. *New American Bible, Revised Edition*

2   Ibid.

CHAPTER TWELVE

THE SEVEN TRUMPETS
Revelation 8:2–11:19

The cyclical-progressive nature of John's Revelation becomes apparent with the sounding of the seven trumpets. The plagues of the seven seals have not stopped, but now seven more plagues are poured out to increase the suffering of the people of the earth. They too will end with a reference to the day of the Lord, creating a cyclical pattern that expands upon what has already happened.

> And I saw the seven angels who stand before God, and seven trumpets were given to them.
>
> Another angel, who had a golden censer, came and stood at the altar. He was given much incense to offer, with the prayers of all God's people, on the golden altar in front of the throne. The smoke of the incense, together with the prayers of God's people, went up before God from the angel's hand. Then the angel took the censer, filled it with fire from the altar, and hurled it on the earth; and there came peals of thunder, rumblings, flashes of lightning and an earthquake.
>
> Then the seven angels who had the seven trumpets prepared to sound them. The first angel sounded his

trumpet, and there came hail and fire mixed with blood, and it was hurled down on the earth. *A third of the earth was burned up, a third of the trees were burned up, and all the green grass was burned up.*

— Revelation 8:2–7

The second angel sounded his trumpet, and something like a huge mountain, all ablaze, was thrown into the sea. A third of the sea turned into blood, a third of the living creatures in the sea died, and a third of the ships were destroyed.

— Revelation 8:8–9

The third angel sounded his trumpet, and a great star, blazing like a torch, fell from the sky on a *third of the rivers and on the springs of water*—the name of the star is Wormwood. A third of the waters turned bitter, and many people died from the waters that had become bitter.

— Revelation 8:10–11

The fourth angel sounded his trumpet, and a *third of the sun was struck, a third of the moon, and a third of the stars, so that a third of them turned dark.* A third of the day was without light, and also a third of the night. As I watched, I heard an eagle that was flying in midair call out in a loud voice: "*Woe! Woe! Woe* to the inhabitants of the earth, because of the trumpet blasts about to be sounded by the other three angels!

— Revelation 8:12–13

The fifth angel sounded his trumpet [the first woe], and I saw a star that had fallen from the sky to the earth. The star was given the key to the shaft of the Abyss. When he opened the Abyss, smoke rose from it like the smoke from a gigantic furnace. The sun and sky were darkened by the smoke from the Abyss. And out of the smoke locusts came down on the earth and were given power like that of scorpions of the earth. *They were told not to harm the grass of the earth or any plant or tree, but only those people who did not have the seal of God on their foreheads.* They were not allowed to kill them but only to torture them for five months. And the agony they suffered was like that of the sting of a scorpion when it strikes. During those days people will seek death but will not find it; they will long to die, but death will elude them.

The locusts looked like horses prepared for battle. On their heads they wore something like crowns of gold, and their faces resembled human faces. Their hair was like women's hair, and their teeth were like lions' teeth. They had breastplates like breastplates of iron, and the sound of their wings was like the thundering of many horses and chariots rushing into battle. They had tails with stingers, like scorpions, and in their tails they had power to torment people for five months. They had as king over them the angel of the Abyss, whose name in Hebrew is Abaddon and in Greek is Apollyon (that is, Destroyer).

The first woe is past; two other woes are yet to come.

— Revelation 9:1–11

Just as with the plagues of the seven seals, the plagues of the seven trumpets are poured out upon the people of the world, but not on those who have the seal of God on their forehead. This is a mark that can be seen by the angels, but not by humans. It is the opposite of the mark of the Antichrist, which can be seen by all. Through repetition, John emphasizes that we will not be the target of God's wrath in the tribulation. There will be a separation made between the saints of God and the people of the world which will protect us from God's wrath.

Trumpets one through four add to the misery of the world by killing one-third of the living things on earth. Adding that to the one-quarter of living things killed by the first seven plagues means one-half of all living things will die by these plagues. Yet even as the population of the non-believing world is dying at an astounding rate, the population of the believers is growing at an equally astounding rate. The evangelism explosion set off by the pouring out of the Holy Spirit of God on the 144,000 servants of God will swell the number of saints to an "uncountable number."

The fifth trumpet is the first of three "woes." Evil beings are created out of the smoke that comes out of the Abyss, which is another name for hell. Their leader is an angel from hell. Joel 2:1–11 prophesized this plague would come upon the earth in the last days. John expands on Joel's vision by telling us they are creatures of torment who inflict injuries that are not fatal, but are terribly painful. Their leader is named *Abaddon* in Hebrew, and *Apollyon* in Greek. Both names mean "destroyer."

In this same prophecy of Joel (Joel 2:28–32), we have the promise of the pouring out of the Holy Spirit of God on his saints in the last days. Peter repeats this message on the day of Pentecost, thinking the pouring out of the Holy Spirit on the apostles meant Jesus would be returning at any moment. That event was a typical fulfillment of Joel's prophecy. The true fulfillment will happen during the tribulation, as we see in Revelation 7, and again here in Revelation 9:

> The sixth angel sounded his trumpet [the second woe], and I heard a voice coming from the four horns of the golden altar that is before God. It said to the sixth

angel who had the trumpet, "Release the four angels who are bound at the great river Euphrates." And the four angels who had been kept ready for this very hour and day and month and year were released to kill a third of mankind. *The number of the mounted troops was twice ten thousand times ten thousand.* I heard their number.

The horses and riders I saw in my vision looked like this: Their breastplates were fiery red, dark blue, and yellow as sulfur. The heads of the horses resembled the heads of lions, and out of their mouths came fire, smoke and sulfur. *A third of mankind was killed by the three plagues of fire, smoke and sulfur that came out of their mouths.* The power of the horses was in their mouths and in their tails; for their tails were like snakes, having heads with which they inflict injury.

The rest of mankind who were not killed by these plagues still did not repent of the work of their hands; they did not stop worshiping demons, and idols of gold, silver, bronze, stone and wood—idols that cannot see or hear or walk. Nor did they repent of their murders, their magic arts, their sexual immorality or their thefts.

— Revelation 9:13–21

Again, John emphasizes that the plagues of God's wrath will kill the people of the world who don't repent. That means they won't be killing Christians. We will be protected by the mark of God on our foreheads, which will be seen by the angels of the plagues. Don't be fooled by those who tell you the Holy Spirit will be gone and the believers with him. The Holy Spirit of God will be more active during the tribulation than at any time since the ministry of Jesus Christ.

Then the angel I had seen standing on the sea and on the land raised his right hand to heaven. And he swore by him who lives for ever and ever, who created the heavens and all that is in them, the earth and all that is in it, and the sea and all that is in it, and said, *"There will be no more delay! But in the days when the seventh angel is about to sound his trumpet, the mystery of God will be accomplished, just as he announced to his servants the prophets."*

— Revelation 10:5–7

The major significance of this passage, which is missed by so many, is that the angel announces the plan of God's wrath will be complete when the seventh trumpet sounds (the third woe), and it will happen *just as it was announced to the prophets.* There is no more important verse in the entire book of Revelation for knowing how to understand it. John is summarizing everything the Old Testament prophets said about the redemption of Israel and the wrath of God. He is not inventing a new scenario. John is simply repeating what was said by the Old Testament prophets. The new material revealed by John does not change God's plan in any way; it only helps to explain it.

We now come to the major parenthesis in this section of Revelation. It is the vision of the Two Witnesses. They are sent to preach in the courtyard of the new Temple of God that has been rebuilt next to the Dome of the Rock. The signing of a peace treaty between the Antichrist and Israel and the building of the temple mark the beginning of the first half of the tribulation's seven years.

I was given a reed like a measuring rod and was told, "Go and measure the temple of God and the altar, with its worshipers. But exclude the outer court; do not measure it, because it has been given to the Gentiles. They will trample on the holy city for 42 months. *And I will appoint my two witnesses*, and they will prophesy for *1,260 days*, clothed in sackcloth." They are the two olive trees and the two lampstands, and they stand before the Lord of the earth. If anyone tries to harm them, fire comes from their mouths and devours their enemies. This is how anyone who wants to harm them must die. They have power to shut up the heavens so that it will not rain during the time they are prophesying; and they have power to turn the waters into blood and to strike the earth with every kind of plague as often as they want.

Now when they have finished their testimony, the beast that comes up from the Abyss will attack them, and overpower and kill them. Their bodies will lie in the public square of the great city—which is figuratively called Sodom and Egypt—where also their Lord was crucified. For three and a half days some from every people, tribe, language and nation will gaze on their bodies and refuse them burial. The inhabitants of the earth will gloat over them and will celebrate by sending each other gifts, because these two prophets had tormented those who live on the earth.

But after the three and a half days the breath of life from God entered them, and they stood on their feet, and terror struck those who saw them. Then they heard a loud voice from heaven saying to them, "Come up here." And they went up to heaven in a cloud, while their enemies looked on.

At that very hour there was a severe earthquake and a tenth of the city collapsed. Seven thousand people were killed in the earthquake, and the survivors were terrified and gave glory to the God of heaven.

The second woe has passed; the third woe is coming soon.

— Revelation 11:1–14

The period of time the Two Witnesses are allowed to preach is clearly given in the text as 1,260 days, or forty-two months, which is three and one-half years. Satan and the Antichrist are then allowed to have an equal number of days to rule unhindered by Michael, the archangel. This will fulfill II Thessalonians 2:5–7, but will not remove the protection from the plagues God has granted to his saints during this time. These two equal time periods allow us to divide the tribulation in half, and to know when it will start.

Yes, the Antichrist will be allowed to kill millions of Christians during his forty-two months of rule. But the number of martyred saints will pale in comparison to the "uncountable" number of saints who will survive to see the Lord coming in the air. The deaths of these saints will ensure their final victory. They will receive the seven rewards promised to the seven churches of Asia.

The seventh angel sounded his trumpet [the third woe], and there were loud voices in heaven, which said:

"The kingdom of the world has become the kingdom of our Lord and of his Messiah, and he will reign for ever and ever."

And the twenty-four elders, who were seated on their thrones before God, fell on their faces and worshiped God, saying:

"We give thanks to you, Lord God Almighty, the One who is and who was, because you have taken your great power and have begun to reign.

"The nations were angry, and your wrath has come. The time has come for judging the dead, and for rewarding your servants the prophets and your people who revere your name, both great and small— and for destroying those who destroy the earth."

Then God's temple in heaven was opened, and within his temple was seen the ark of his covenant. And there came flashes of lightning, rumblings, peals of thunder, an earthquake and a severe hailstorm.

— Revelation 11:15–19

The seventh plague brings us to the final outcome for Satan and the Antichrist, and for those who follow them. The lightning, thunder, hailstorm, and earthquake refer to the wrath of God being poured out at the appearance of Jesus Christ on the day of the Lord.

The three chapters of Isaiah referred to at the end of the seven seals are referred to again here at the end of the seven trumpets:

Whoever flees at the sound of terror will fall into a pit; whoever climbs out of the pit will be caught in a snare.

The floodgates of the heavens are opened, the foundations of the earth shake. The earth is broken up, the earth is split asunder, the earth is violently shaken.

The earth reels like a drunkard, it sways like a hut in the wind; so heavy upon it is the guilt of its rebellion that it falls—never to rise again.

— Isaiah 24:18–20

But the full extent of God's wrath on that day is not revealed until we get to Revelation 19.

This final scene of the second round of plagues reminds us that no matter what happens here on earth, even if all the churches are closed and the temple is inhabited by Satan, the word of the Lord will stand forever. Those who are willing to put their lives on the line and stand with the Lord will be the final victors. The lake of fire holds no terror for them, but the it will be the "reward" for the Antichrist and all who follow him.

CHAPTER THIRTEEN

The Protagonist, the Antagonists, and the Victors
Revelation 12:1–14:20

Revelation chapters 12 through 14 are a series of visions unrelated to the seals, trumpets, or bowls. Their purpose is to reveal who the characters at the center of the tribulation will be, to exhort us to remain faithful, and to ensure us of final victory. In essence, what we have in these parentheses is a CliffNotes™ version of the entire book of Revelation. Not only are we told who the good guys and bad guys are, we also get to peek at the finale to see what happens in the end. Let's start with the story of the protagonist and the first antagonist.

The Protagonist — Israel

> A great sign appeared in heaven: a woman clothed with the sun, with the moon under her feet and a crown of twelve stars on her head. She was pregnant and cried out in pain as she was about to give birth.
>
> — Revelation 12:1–2

The woman is our heroine. She and her child are identified for us in the context by the two obvious references to the Old Testament. The woman is Israel. The reference is to Genesis 37:9–10. Joseph had a dream in which he saw the sun, moon, and eleven stars bow down to him. His father, Jacob, interprets the dream as follows, "What is this dream you had? Will your mother and I and your brothers come and bow down before you?" (Genesis 37:10). The fact that the woman in this vision has twelve stars at her feet means that Joseph is now counted as one of the stars. So the woman is the nation of Israel. She gives birth to a son "who will rule the nations with an iron scepter" (Revelation 12:5); the son she gives birth to is the Son of God, Jesus Christ, the Messiah.

THE FIRST ANTAGONIST — SATAN

> Then another sign appeared in heaven: an enormous red dragon with seven heads and ten horns and seven crowns on its heads. Its tail swept a third of the stars out of the sky and flung them to the earth. The drag-on stood in front of the woman who was about to give birth, so that it might devour her child the moment he was born. She gave birth to a son, a male child, who will rule all the nations with an iron scepter. And her child was snatched up to God and to his throne.
>
> — Revelation 12:3–5

In Revelation 12:9, we are told the red dragon is Satan, so there is no mystery there. He has taken one third of the angels of heaven as his followers, and they now are doing his will here on earth. Satan and his clan tried to kill the baby Jesus when he was born but did not succeed. Revelation 12:5 is taken directly from Psalm 2:9, referring to the time when Christ will rule the world from the throne of David in Jerusalem. But that will not happen until after he is "snatched up to God and to his throne," which happened at the ascension in Acts 2. Psalm 2:9 will be literally fulfilled with his second earthly appearance.

> The woman fled into the wilderness to a place prepared for her by God, where she might be taken care of for 1,260 days.
>
> — Revelation 12:6

It is the halfway point in the tribulation, and halfway through John's Revelation. The ten-nation coalition of the empire of Babylon is ruling the world, and the Antichrist is now ruling over that coalition. The *hudna* (peace treaty) he signed with Israel is broken and the Two Witnesses are dead. Satan is leading the Antichrist to carry out his ancient plan of killing off every Jew on earth so that a Jewish Redeemer cannot appear. But that plan doesn't work, just like killing all the babies in Bethlehem didn't work. God protects Israel by letting them escape into the "wilderness." We are not told where that will be, for obvious reasons.

> Then war broke out in heaven. Michael and his angels fought against the dragon, and the dragon and his angels fought back. But he was not strong enough, and they lost their place in heaven. The great dragon was hurled down—that ancient serpent called the devil, or Satan, who leads the whole world astray. He was hurled to the earth, and his angels with him.
>
> Then I heard a loud voice in heaven say: "Now have come the salvation and the power and the kingdom of our God, and the authority of his Messiah. For the accuser of our brothers and sisters, who accuses them before our God day and night, has been hurled down. They triumphed over him by the blood of the Lamb and

by the word of their testimony; they did not love their
lives so much as to shrink from death. Therefore rejoice,
you heavens and you who dwell in them! But woe to
the earth and the sea, because the devil has gone down
to you! He is filled with fury, because he knows that his
time is short."

— Revelation 12:7–12

Michael is the archangel and guardian of Israel, and it is he who
was holding back the evil one in II Thessalonians 2:6. Satan had
been restrained for three and one-half years, but now he is back—
and with a vengeance! His time is very limited, and he knows it. He
loses his place in heaven. He is no longer welcome, and he is tossed
out on his ear. There remains no one in heaven to accuse the saints
before God for our many sins. Hallelujah!

When the dragon saw that he had been hurled to the
earth, he pursued the woman who had given birth to
the male child. The woman was given the two wings of
a great eagle, so that she might fly to the place prepared
for her in the wilderness, where she would be taken care
of for a time, times and half a time, out of the serpent's
reach. Then from his mouth the serpent spewed water
like a river, to overtake the woman and sweep her away
with the torrent. But the earth helped the woman by
opening its mouth and swallowing the river that the
dragon had spewed out of his mouth. *Then the dragon
was enraged at the woman and went off to wage war
against the rest of her offspring—those who keep God's
commands and hold fast their testimony about Jesus.*

— Revelation 12:13–17

When Satan cannot get to his primary target—Israel—he is

filled with anger which must be vented somewhere. He turns his attention to us, the other children of Israel. We are his secondary target. If you question the relationship between the church and Israel, it is explained in this verse. We are the non-Jewish offspring of our Jewish mother.

Satan will have to make do by releasing his anger on "those who keep God's commands and hold fast to their testimony about Jesus" (Revelation 12:17). That is you and me, if you are a Gentile Christian. This is not a division made in the body of Christ by God. There is "no difference between Jew and Gentile—the same Lord is Lord of all and richly blesses all who call upon him, for everyone who calls upon the name of the Lord will be saved" (Romans 10:12–13). The distinction is made by Satan.

The Qur'an is filled with hatred for the Jews, and contains numerous predictions of their demise at the hands of the Islamic Redeemer. But in fact, his persecution of the Jews will only serve to bring millions of Jews into a personal relationship with God. Gentile Christians are only secondary targets of wrath in the Qur'an. Nevertheless, we will take most of Satan's wrath during the final three and one-half years of the tribulation.

THE SECOND ANTAGONIST — THE ANTICHRIST

It is at this point in our study of Revelation that our understanding of Daniel and Islam becomes very important. The description of the dragon who comes out of the sea is taken directly from Daniel 7, and matches exactly with the description of al-Mahdi in Islamic prophecy. He will come from Babylon (Khorasan) with a huge army and conquer Jerusalem. Then he will demand to be worshipped and do his best to kill all the saints of God, both Jew and Gentile.

> The dragon stood on the shore of the sea. And I saw a
> beast coming out of the sea. It had ten horns and seven

heads, with ten crowns on its horns, and on each head
a blasphemous name. The beast I saw resembled a leopard, but had feet like those of a bear and a mouth like
that of a lion.

— Revelation 13:1–2a

The description of this beast should not be a surprise to anyone.
The beast has ten horns, but only seven heads; this means the ten-
nation coalition is in its final stage. The Antichrist has replaced
the ruler who started the ten-nation coalition and has revealed his
true nature. He has changed from the man of peace to the man of
lawlessness. If I am correct, the initial ruler of the coalition will be
Ayatollah Khomeini. He will die of old age, and his replacement
will be Muhammad ibn Mansur, al-Mahdi. But three nations will
protest his appointment, and war will break out between the nations
of the coalition. Three nations will be defeated: Egypt, Sudan, and
Libya. Then the Antichrist will be completely in charge. That is the
prediction of Daniel 11:41–43, and that is the situation we find here
in John's vision of Revelation 13:1–2.

In Daniel 7:1, four beasts come out of the sea. They are a lion,
a bear, a leopard, and the indescribable fourth beast. In Revelation
13:2a, the first three beasts from Daniel 7:1 are combined into one
terrible beast. That's because this final ruler of the kingdom of
Babylon will rule all the lands that were controlled by those four
beasts. This is also why all of the prophets condemn the nations
surrounding ancient Israel. They will all be the targets of God's
wrath on the day of the Lord. But the gang-leader of these enemies
of Israel is the nation of the Antichrist—Babylon.

The dragon gave the beast his power and his throne and
great authority. One of the heads of the beast seemed to
have had a fatal wound, but the fatal wound had been

healed. The whole world was filled with wonder and followed the beast. People worshiped the dragon because he had given authority to the beast, and they also worshiped the beast and asked, "Who is like the beast? Who can wage war against it?"

The beast was given a mouth to utter proud words and blasphemies and to exercise its authority for forty-two months. It opened its mouth to blaspheme God, and to slander his name and his dwelling place and those who live in heaven. It was given power to wage war against God's holy people and to conquer them. And it was given authority over every tribe, people, language and nation.

— Revelation 13:2b–7

Satan is the one who gives this beast its power. That means Satan and Allah are the same person. The beast is the coalition of ten nations. The head with the fatal wound is the Antichrist, and he is the ruler of the beast. It is this head whose number equals 666. Distinguishing between the ten-nation coalition beast and the individual beast is what makes Revelation 13 and 17 so difficult to understand. The human beast seems to have been killed and has come back to life. Satan is the source of his deceptive "fatal wound." His resurrection, or return from occultation (suspended state), will deceive millions.

This beast will blaspheme Jehovah and everything that is holy. Again, we should not be surprised, because it was predicted by both Isaiah and Paul. As a Satan-indwelt, resurrected man, he will have one purpose in mind: to kill as many of the saints of God as possible. He is given forty-two months (1,260 days, or three and one-half years) to accomplish this task. Some people have speculated the forty-two-month period will be longer than the 1,260 days given to the Two Witnesses. However, we know the final days of suffering will be cut short because of Jesus' statement in Matthew 24:22. So, no man can know or predict the day or hour of Christ's return.

At this point, the Antichrist will have authority over every government on earth. That means the end of the Christian church as we know it. There will be no more cathedrals, sanctuaries, or even little churches on the corner with white steeples. Survival will depend upon going underground and helping your fellow Christians, just as the church did in its early days. I know this is repetitious, but it is coming faster than many of us believe. You had better be ready. You won't be able to go to a book store to buy a new Bible. In fact, you might not have access to any Bible. You had better get the word of God into your heart and keep it there, starting now.

> *All inhabitants of the earth will worship the beast—all whose names have not been written in the Lamb's book of life,* the Lamb who was slain from the creation of the world.
>
> Whoever has ears, let them hear.
>
> "If anyone is to go into captivity, into captivity they will go. If anyone is to be killed with the sword, with the sword they will be killed.
>
> *This calls for patient endurance and faithfulness on the part of God's people."*
>
> —Revelation 13:8–10

John refers to Jeremiah 15:2, warning us that many Christians will suffer imprisonment and death at the hands of al-Mahdi. There is no way to make this pretty. The death total will be in the millions. Ask yourself: How strong is my faith? Will I be willing to die for my faith? What is the alternative? Think about that. Is saving this life your goal? The answer doesn't lie in a false confession, trying to trick people into believing you worship Allah. Nor does it lie in buying assault rifles and lots of ammunition. The only real answer can be found in patience, endurance, and faithfulness to Jesus Christ at any cost.

THE THIRD ANTAGONIST — THE FALSE PROPHET

The beast who comes out of the earth, described in Revelation 13:11–18, is not mentioned in Old Testament prophecy, but his description matches exactly with the predicted protégé of al-Mahdi, known as Isa in Arabic. Isa comes out of the dust of Saudi Arabia in Islamic prophecy.

> Then I saw a *second beast, coming out of the earth.* It had two horns like a lamb, but it spoke like a dragon. It exercised all the authority of the first beast on its behalf, and made the earth and its inhabitants worship the first beast, whose fatal wound had been healed. And it performed great signs, even causing fire to come down from heaven to the earth in full view of the people. Because of the signs it was given power to perform on behalf of the first beast, it deceived the inhabitants of the earth. It ordered them to set up an image in honor of the beast who was wounded by the sword and yet lived. The second beast was given power to give breath to the image of the first beast, so that the image could speak and cause all who refused to worship the image to be killed. *It also forced all people, great and small, rich and poor, free and slave, to receive a mark on their right hands or on their foreheads,* so that they could not buy or sell unless they had the mark, which is the name of the beast or the number of its name.

> This calls for wisdom. *Let the person who has insight calculate the number of the beast, for it is the number of a man. That number is 666.*
>
> — Revelation 13:11–18

The third antagonist is called the False Prophet. He is an impersonator of Jesus Christ; he calls himself Jesus (Isa), Son of Mary. According to the Qur'an and *hadiths*, the work of Isa will be to correct the misconceptions caused by his first appearance two thousand years ago. This imposter will declare that he didn't mean to imply that he was really God, or the Son of God. He was just another of God's prophets with a message of peace. If you do not believe his message this time you will be killed! That's a message of peace?

He has two horns, which make him look like a lamb, but he speaks like a dragon because he is a false Christ empowered by Satan/Allah. He has the same ability to call down fire from heaven as the Two Witnesses had previously. Furthermore, he creates a statue in honor of al-Mahdi, much like the giant statue of Sadaam Hussein which was torn down by American troops in Bagdad. Isa will cause the statue to speak, deceiving millions. When the Ark of the Covenant is found and the Qur'an is found inside, the deception will be too great for most to resist. This is the deception that will be so convincing that it will "deceive even the elect—if that were possible" (Matthew 24:24).

Isa will preach a new gospel message (Galatians 1:8) which proclaims al-Mahdi as the true Redeemer of the world. But Isa doesn't come to save people from their sins; he comes to make Islam the only religion in the world and to kill those who will not believe. He will mark the foreheads of those who believe, and he will kill those who will not convert. It is Isa who removes the option of *jizya* (tax for non-Muslims). Islamic prophecy tells us that he will make the faces of the believers to shine so those who do not believe will be much easier to spot. The fact that Christians will not be able to buy or sell should give us incentive to become financially solvent and self-sustaining for food production. But remember to grow enough to share with other Christians in need.

Revelation 13:18 has been a mystery to believers for centuries, but it shouldn't be. The number 666 is said to be the number of a man. In the first place, we know the Arabic name of the man who will be brought back from occultation by Satan. He is Mohammad ibn Mansur, called al-Mahdi, or the Redeemer. However, John could not have known that name, nor could any saint who was born before AD 785. We should look for a name that would be known by all the followers of Jesus Christ, both in John's day and now. The numerology system that was used by John and the first century church has died out and is gone. We cannot hope to recover it.

However, by putting together the clues from several scriptural passages, I believe we can come up with a possible name for this last ruler of Babylon. First, we know that he will be a man who is resurrected by Satan. Second, from his description, which is so similar to Satan that they are hard to tell apart, we know that he will be indwelt by Satan. Third, from Revelation 17:8, we know that he will be resurrected out of hell (the Abyss). And fourth, from Daniel 9:26, we know that it was this person who enabled the Jews to kill Jesus at his first coming.

If we put all these clues together with the names of the candidates that fit all four criteria, we come up with the name Judas Iscariot. We know from Luke 22:3 that Judas was indwelt by Satan, which explains the closeness of descriptions between Satan and the Antichrist in Revelation. We know that Judas is the one who betrayed Jesus and enabled the Sanhedrin to kill him, which fulfills Daniel 9:26. The apostle Peter quotes from Psalm 69:25 regarding Judas. In that same Psalm, verses 20–28 indicate that the one being spoken about is to be destroyed and never have a part in salvation. Therefore, Judas went to hell when he died. And the final piece of evidence is that the Qur'an says that it was Judas who died on the cross, not Jesus (Sura 4:152–157). All of this is nothing more than speculation on my part. But the pieces of the puzzle do seem to fit. I believe that Judas Iscariot will be resurrected from hell by Satan, impersonate Muhammad ibn Mansur (al-Mahdi), and become the Antichrist.

THE VICTORS — THE 144,000

All the believers who overcome the suffering and deceptions of the tribulation and remain faithful to Jesus Christ are victors, and they will be rewarded with the same rewards mentioned by Jesus in the letters to the seven churches of Asia. But the 144,000 Nazirites who will be sent out to the cities of Israel, and give their lives in doing so, are the true victors in this parenthesis.

> Then I looked, and there before me was the Lamb, standing on Mount Zion, and with him 144,000 who had his name and his Father's name written on their foreheads. And I heard a sound from heaven like the roar of rushing waters and like a loud peal of thunder. The sound I heard was like that of harpists playing their harps. And they sang a new song before the throne and before the four living creatures and the elders. No one could learn the song except the 144,000 who had been redeemed from the earth. These are those who did not defile themselves with women, for they remained virgins. They follow the Lamb wherever he goes. They were purchased from among mankind and offered as

firstfruits to God and the Lamb. No lie was found in their mouths; they are blameless.

— Revelation 14:1–5

Sometimes serving God means giving up your life for the sake of your testimony. Millions of saints have done this through the centuries. These men were especially chosen to be Nazirites; they never tasted wine or experienced women. Their mission was to go through the towns and villages of Israel spreading the gospel, knowing that the consequences would be imprisonment and death. These are the men for whom the warning of Matthew 10:17–23 was intended. They completed that mission, and now they receive their reward. The rest of chapter 14 is filled with the messages of six angels. All are important, but because of space, we will look only at the message of the third angel.

A third angel followed them and said in a loud voice: "If anyone worships the beast and its image and receives its mark on their forehead or on their hand, they, too, will drink the wine of God's fury, which has been poured full strength into the cup of his wrath. They will be tormented with burning sulfur in the presence of the holy angels and of the Lamb. And the smoke of their torment will rise for ever and ever. There will be no rest day or night for those who worship the beast and its image, or for anyone who receives the mark of its name." *This calls for patient endurance on the part of the people of God who keep his commands and remain faithful to Jesus.*

Then I heard a voice from heaven say, "Write this: *Blessed are the dead who die in the Lord from now on."*

"Yes," says the Spirit, *"they will rest from their labor,*

for their deeds will follow them."

— Revelation 14:9–13

The message of the third angel to the saints is the strongest warning yet: we must hold on to our faith and not surrender to the Antichrist. You cannot make a false confession and take the mark of the beast in order to escape the power of al-Mahdi and Isa. If you do, God will treat you just like you are one of them. Jesus said:

> "Whoever acknowledges me before others, I will also acknowledge before my Father in heaven. But whoever disowns me before others, I will disown before my Father in heaven."
>
> — Matthew 10:32–33

God wants us saints to clearly see the difference between this life and the next and to stand up for God. Living conditions on earth will be almost unbearable at this point, but if they kill you, you are the winner. Your reward will be the same as the 144,000.

CHAPTER FOURTEEN

THE SEVEN BOWLS
Revelation 15:1–16:21

Before we look at the final round of God's judgments on the earth, there is a preview given of the final destruction of God's enemies. The angel of the revelation uses the metaphor of a grape harvest to draw a word picture of that destruction in Revelation 14:18–20. The grapes are harvested and thrown into God's wine press, resulting in blood flowing from "the city" up to the bridle of a horse for 1,600 stadia. That is five feet deep for 168 miles. The city cannot be Megiddo, because Megiddo is too small for that much blood. Besides, the entire nation of Israel is only 145 miles long. The city must be Babylon, which is in a broad valley and has a large population. This preview of Babylon's demise is further detailed in Revelation 17–18. But before the angel takes us there, the earth will have to endure one more round of plagues.

> I saw in heaven another great and marvelous sign: seven angels with the seven last plagues—last, because with them God's wrath is completed. And I saw what looked like a sea of glass glowing with fire, and standing beside the sea, those who had been victorious over the beast and its image and over the number of its name. They

held harps given them by God and sang the song of God's servant Moses and of the Lamb:

"Great and marvelous are your deeds, Lord God Almighty. Just and true are your ways, King of the nations. Who will not fear you, Lord, and bring glory to your name? For you alone are holy. All nations will come and worship before you, for your righteous acts have been revealed."

After this I looked, and I saw in heaven the temple—that is, the tabernacle of the covenant law—and it was opened. Out of the temple came the seven angels with the seven plagues. They were dressed in clean, shining linen and wore golden sashes around their chests. Then one of the four living creatures gave to the seven angels *seven golden bowls filled with the wrath of God*, who lives for ever and ever. And the temple was filled with smoke from the glory of God and from his power, and no one could enter the temple until the seven plagues of the seven angels were completed.

Then I heard a loud voice from the temple saying to the seven angels, "Go, pour out the seven bowls of God's wrath on the earth."

The first angel went and poured out his bowl on the land, and ugly, festering sores broke out *on the people who had the mark of the beast and worshiped its image.*

The second angel poured out his bowl on the sea, and it turned into blood like that of a dead person, and every living thing in the sea died.

The third angel poured out his bowl on the rivers and springs of water, and they became blood. Then I heard the angel in charge of the waters say:

"You are just in these judgments, O Holy One, you who are and who were; for they have shed the blood of your holy people and your prophets, and you have given them blood to drink as they deserve."

And I heard the altar respond:

"Yes, Lord God Almighty, true and just are your judgments."

The fourth angel poured out his bowl on the sun, and the sun was allowed to scorch people with fire. They were seared by the intense heat and they cursed the name of God, who had control over these plagues, but they refused to repent and glorify him.

The fifth angel *poured out his bowl on the throne of the beast, and its kingdom was plunged into darkness.* People gnawed their tongues in agony and cursed the God of heaven because of their pains and their sores, but they refused to repent of what they had done.

— Revelation 15:1–16:11

Two things stand out as we look at the final round of plagues. First, notice there is no limitation put on these plagues. Second, notice how specific these plagues are on those who worship the beast and are a part of his kingdom. There is no mention of the effect of the plagues on the saints of God because the saints will not suffer from these plagues. During the plagues in Exodus, a darkness that was so deep "it could be felt" fell on Egypt, but "all the Israelites had light in the places where they lived" (Exodus 10:23). That will be the situation with all these plagues.

The throne of the beast will be Jerusalem. The beast will be sitting in the temple, claiming to be God, but God will show him and the world who is really in charge. This is why Jerusalem will have to be rebuilt when Christ returns.

John writes this book both as a warning and as an encouragement to the saints of God. We will survive and come out of the tribulation victorious. God will not give us abundance and great wealth; that would only make us targets for the people of the world. But he will sustain us as the world around us suffers from his wrath. I am reminded of the children of Israel in the desert for forty years. God provided just enough manna, quail, and water to see them through. I am also reminded of Elijah and the widow of Zarephath. God provided enough oil and flour to make three cakes of bread every day for three years. God sustained them but did not give them great abundance. That will be the same with us in the tribulation.

As another example, God promised Hezekiah he would rescue him from the hand of Sennacherib, but not with great abundance. He said: "This year you will eat what grows by itself, and the second year what springs from that. But in the third year, sow and reap, plant vineyards and eat their fruit" (Isaiah 37:30). The scarcity from Sennacherib's raid lasted for two years, and God provided enough to get by. He will do that for us in the tribulation. Remember, the plagues of the seals, trumpets, and bowls are for the world. The anger of God and his wrath are poured out on the people of the world. But with each series of wrath there is at least one parenthesis of hope. It is the messages in the parentheses that are meant for us!

> The sixth angel poured out his bowl on the great river Euphrates, and its water was dried up to prepare the way for the kings from the East. Then I saw three impure spirits that looked like frogs; they came out of the mouth of the dragon, out of the mouth of the beast and out of the mouth of the false prophet. They are demonic spirits that perform signs, and they go out to the kings of the whole world, to gather them for the battle on the great day of God Almighty.
>
> "Look, I come like a thief! Blessed is the one who stays awake and remains clothed, so as not to go naked and be shamefully exposed."

Then they gathered the kings together to the place
that in Hebrew is called *Armageddon*."
— Revelation 16:12–16

Revelation 16:16 is the one and only place in the Bible that
mentions the name Armageddon as the place of the final battle at
the second coming of Jesus Christ. It is the Greek equivalent of the
Hebrew name "Mountain of Megiddo." Could Megiddo be the place
in the wilderness that God uses to protect Israel from the Antichrist?
(See Revelation 12:6.) Ask yourself: Why is the Antichrist at Megiddo
with a massive army gathered from all the Muslim lands? We know
he will be searching the world to find the place where God is hiding
the Jews. Will he hear a rumor that the Jews are at Megiddo? Will
he go there with all his army, including the massive army from the
East, to finally destroy all of Israel?

Even though the number of fighters from various Muslim
nations will be huge, the battle will be over in a matter of minutes.
Islam will disappear in a river of blood and mangled corpses, which
will become a feast for the birds of prey. The Antichrist and the False
Prophet will be taken alive and thrown into the lake of fire.

The final step in the outpouring of God's wrath will be the
separate judgment of the city of Babylon, the archenemy of God's
people.

The seventh angel poured out his bowl into the air, and
out of the temple came a loud voice from the throne,
saying, "It is done!" Then there came flashes of lightning, rumblings, peals of thunder and a severe earthquake. No earthquake like it has ever occurred since
mankind has been on earth, so tremendous was the
quake. The great city split into three parts, and the cities of the nations collapsed. *God remembered Babylon*

the Great and gave her the cup filled with the wine of the
fury of his wrath. Every island fled away and the mountains could not be found. From the sky huge hailstones,
each weighing about a hundred pounds, fell on people.
And they cursed God on account of the plague of hail,
because the plague was so terrible.

— Revelation 16:17–21

The seventh bowl of judgment is a direct reference to the judgment of Babylon on the day of the Lord, as prophesied in Jeremiah 50-52. A vast human army will attack and destroy the city and the area known in ancient times as Babylon. My hope is that the armies of America will resist the pressures put on us by the ten-nation coalition of the Antichrist, but the Bible is silent on what America will do. There are many who see a reference to America in the "ships of Tarshish" (Jeremiah 51:24-29) or in the "islands of the sea" (Daniel 11:30). However, unless you believe the Phoenicians had a trading route that took them across the Atlantic Ocean to America, this is not a probable theory.

I think it is best to say we don't know if America will be an ally of the Antichrist or just another nation that is temporarily subjected to his power. As things look right now, it could go either way. We as a nation are compromising more and more with Islam and Shariah Law. How far will we drift before the Christians of this nation stand up and say, "enough"? Please pray for our nation.

CHAPTER FIFTEEN

THE WHORE OF BABYLON
Revelation 17:1–18

Revelation 17 and 18 are actually a parenthesis following the judgments of the seven bowls. The material in these two chapters is taken almost exclusively from the Book of Daniel, with a great deal more detail added.

I am amazed by people who read the Book of Revelation from 1:1 to 17:18 and say Babylon is a code word which means Rome. Haven't you noticed the many times throughout the Old Testament and Revelation where Babylon has been referenced? Have you noticed that Rome has never been referenced even one time? There are only two cities that are the focus of the prophecy of Revelation 4–22: Jerusalem and Babylon. Jerusalem will be rebuilt, and Babylon will be destroyed. Babylon is not a code word that means Rome. Babylon means Babylon.

> One of the seven angels who had the seven bowls came and said to me, "Come, I will show you the punishment of the great prostitute, who sits by many waters. With her the kings of the earth committed adultery, and the inhabitants of the earth were intoxicated with the wine of her adulteries."

> Then the angel carried me away in the Spirit into a wilderness. There I saw a *woman sitting on a scarlet beast* that was covered with blasphemous names and had *seven heads and ten horns.* The woman was dressed in purple and scarlet, and was glittering with gold, precious stones and pearls. She held a golden cup in her hand, filled with abominable things and the filth of her adulteries. The name written on her forehead was a mystery: *BABYLON THE GREAT THE MOTHER OF PROSTITUTES AND OF THE ABOMINATIONS OF THE EARTH.*"
>
> — Revelation 17:1–5

The enmity between God and Babylon goes all the way back to Gilgamesh and the founding of Babylon. It was the source of the fertility goddess myth that became the cornerstone of all pagan religions. The Tower of Babel was built at Babylon to create a "high place" for performing sexual rites the gods could not ignore. God prevented that by sending chaos among the people through the confusion of languages. However, the scattering of the nations simply spread the fertility goddess myth to every ancient civilization on earth. This is why John calls Babylon the "Mother of Prostitutes."

> I saw that the woman was drunk with the blood of God's holy people, the blood of those who bore testimony to Jesus.
>
> When I saw her, I was greatly astonished. Then the angel said to me: "Why are you astonished? *I will explain to you the mystery of the woman and of the beast she rides,* which has the seven heads and ten horns."
>
> — Revelation 17:6–7a

The woman who sits on the beast is not an individual; she is the city of Babylon. The beast she sits on is the ten-nation coalition (see

Revelation 17:18). The false religion of this woman will demand the death of all who do not convert to the religion of the Antichrist who rules the earth. The woman and the beast will use this false religion to persecute Christians during the tribulation period. The spirit of Islamic *jihad* will be the rallying point that gives this woman her power. That is why she rides on the back of the beast. She is drunk with the blood of the saints she has martyred.

> "The beast, which you saw, once was, now is not, and yet will come up out of the Abyss and go to its destruction. The inhabitants of the earth whose names have not been written in the book of life from the creation of the world will be astonished when they see the beast, *because it once was, now is not, and yet will come.*"
>
> — Revelation 17:7b–8

Chapter 17 is the most confusing and difficult to understand of all the visions of Revelation. That is because there are two beasts in this vision with nearly the same description. One is a man and the other is a ten-nation coalition. We first saw this situation in Daniel 7. Daniel described a beast that is a ten-nation coalition with a boastful little horn as its leader; the leader is also a beast. Together they are the final beast of Babylon. We saw the same situation in Revelation 13 with the beast that comes out of the sea: it is a combination of the kingdoms that ruled over Babylon from Nebuchadnezzar to the Antichrist. It also has a head that is a beast. In both cases, the little horn or head (the leader of the coalition) and the coalition of nations are combined as the final beast of Babylon.

Verses 7–8 of Revelation 17 describe one of those beasts. It is a man who once was, now is not, and is still to come. This man is the same beast we saw in Revelation 13:3–10. He is the Antichrist. He will be resurrected by the power of Satan, and he will still show the evidence of the fatal wound that was healed. We know he is resurrected by Satan, because Satan has been given three and one-half years to do as he pleases. This beast is Satan's best weapon against the people of God.

> "This calls for a mind with wisdom. The seven heads are seven hills on which the woman sits. *They are also seven kings. Five have fallen, one is,* the *other has not yet come;* but when he does come, he must remain for only a little while."
>
> — Revelation 17:9–10

Now comes the confusing part. The focus of the prophecy shifts from the man who is a beast to the ten-nation coalition that is a beast, but with the same description. To make things even harder to understand, Revelation 17:9 contains what I consider to be a bad translation that needs to be understood correctly. John uses the word ὄρη (oray) to describe where the woman sits. Ὄρη means "mountains," and is always translated as "mountains," especially when it is used symbolically of kings or kingdoms.

Furthermore, in Revelation 17:9 we are told that the seven ὄρη are seven kings, so there should be no confusion: this is a symbolic use of the term ὄρη. Yet here it is translated as "hills." That fact has led many to believe John is talking about a city built on seven hills, and this has led many to jump to the conclusion that Rome will be the home of the Antichrist. Even though the entire Book of Revelation has made Babylon the center of God's wrath, people are still looking at Rome as the villain. We need to stop spiritualizing the text and believe what is says, as it is written.

However, the point of these verses is the woman (Babylon) sits on these seven kings, or kingdoms, five of which have fallen, one is currently reigning, and another is to come (as of AD 95). This is where it is important to understand the political history of Satan's Babylonian empires. We know from Daniel 2:36–39 that the heads of state who ruled Satan's past empires started with Nebuchadnezzar. In the vision of the four beasts of Daniel 7, we are told there would be four rulers over Babylon until the day Christ comes to destroy that kingdom and set up his own. If you follow the visions through the book of Daniel, you will find the third kingdom is divided into two parts: that of Alexander, then the Four Generals. These rulers are followed by the Seleucids. We are not told, but it is implied in the context, that there will be a significant gap between the last ruler of Seleucus' kingdom mentioned in Daniel 11:21 and the Antichrist's kingdom mentioned in Daniel 11:40. It is the Antichrist's kingdom which becomes the final beast of Daniel's visions.

However, all biblical prophecy is progressive, and Revelation is no exception. John's vision of Revelation 17:9–11 gives us a political history which helps to fill in the gap we find in Daniel 11:21–40. If you will recall from our discussion of Daniel's prophecy, there were to be five kingdoms of Babylon, followed by a gap, and then the final kingdom of Babylon would arise, making a total of six kingdoms and a gap. The angel of Revelation now reveals what will happen in that gap.

He says to John, "Five have fallen" (Revelation 17:10). Each of the five who have fallen is one of the kings who founded one of the past empires of Babylon. The first of the five was the kingdom of Nebuchadnezzar, 612–539 BC. The second was the kingdom of Cyrus, 539–332 BC. The third was the kingdom of Alexander, 332–322 BC. The fourth was the shared kingdom of the Four Generals, 322–312 BC. And finally, the fifth kingdom was established by the Seleucids, who ruled from 312 BC to 138 BC. This should not be a surprise to anyone. These are the same kings who were listed by Daniel.

Then the angel tells John "one is" (Revelation 17:10). This is the gap-filler that was not mentioned, but was implied, by the angel in Daniel. It is Arsacid dynasty of the Parthian kingdom. The Parthians were a tribe of Persians who began taking back the territory of the Seleucids in the third century BC. In 247 BC, they overthrew the Seleucid governor of the Persian province of Parthia and declared their independence as a nation. The generals who led the revolt were the brothers Arsaces and Tiridates. Arsaces became king and established the Arsacid dynasty. Over a period of more than one hundred years, the Parthians re-established the Persian Empire. In 138 BC, the Persians finally drove the last of the Seleucus clan out of Babylon and reclaimed their homeland. They ruled the Mesopotamian area from the border of Arabia to Armenia, and east to the Indus River. Their first capital was Babylon; however, when Babylon fell into ruins, they built the city of Ctesiphon, thirty-five miles from Babylon. In John's day, the ruler of Parthia was Pacorus II (AD 78–105); he is the "one who is."

During the Parthian era, the Jews revolted against the Romans three times. After the third revolt, during the reign of Caesar Hadrian, the Jews were forced out of Judah and not allowed to return. So after AD 135, there was no nation of Israel for Satan to destroy. The Jews were scattered around the world, making them far harder for Satan to attack. But on May 18, 1948, the nation of Israel was reborn by edict of the UN. In other words, the visions of both Daniel and John stop counting the "beasts of Babylon" from 135 to 1948; during that time, the nation of Israel did not exist and Jerusalem was in the hands of the Gentiles. Now that the nation of Israel has been re-established, the prophecy of John is ready to be fulfilled!

The angel goes on to say, "The other has not yet come" (Revelation 17:10). At this point, the angel is talking about the kingdom, not the man. In Daniel's prophecy, there were six beasts (kingdoms) and a gap. Now, the gap is filled by another kingdom, making seven kingdoms of Babylon from Nebuchadnezzar until the return of Christ. Today we are waiting to see the emergence of the ten-nation coalition which will fulfill the prophecy of the ten toes of the statue in Daniel 2, as well as the ten horns on the head of the beast in both

Daniel 7 and Revelation 13. It is my personal belief we will see this coalition come to power and exert its influence on the world in the very near future.

According to Daniel 7 and 11, that coalition will be made up of the territories of the final King of the North and King of the South. Iran began forming the Federation of Islamic States when Ayatollah Khomeini came to power on the 1970s. The goal of the Federation is to establish a caliphate to rule all Islamic states, and eventually to rule the world. So far, four other Islamic countries have joined with Iran. Who will be next?

The city of Babylon will not have to be rebuilt in order to fulfill this prophecy. Throughout history, the area in question has been known as Sumeria, Chaldea, Babylonia, Khorasan, Parthia, Persia, and Iraq/Iran. The name Khorasan plays a large part in Islamic prophecy as the homeland of al-Mahdi. It is a region, not just a city.

Then the angel goes on to say, "but when he does come, he must remain for only a little while" (Revelation 17:10). We know how long the Antichrist will last because of John's statement in Revelation 13:5. He will be granted the authority to rule for three and one-half years. That is not long for a world power to rule the world, but it will seem longer because of the plagues of God's wrath and the unbridled brutality.

> "The beast who once was, and now is not, is an *eighth king*. He *belongs to the seven* and is going to his destruction."
>
> — Revelation 17:11

Now the focus shifts from the ten-nation beast to the human beast. This is the final ruler of the final kingdom of Babylonia. He is of the seven, but he is counted separately because the final Babylonian empire will already be in existence when he arrives to take over. When the Islamic Federation reaches ten members, the next event to look for on the prophetic radar will be the rise of the Islamic Redeemer from the territory of Khorasan (Babylonia). He will be the boastful "little horn" spoken of by Daniel in 7:8. In keeping with the masquerade that Islam is a peaceful religion, he will sign a peace treaty with Israel; this is predicted in Daniel 9:27. When that happens, it will signal the beginning of the end of the world as we know it. He is the Antichrist, and it is his empire that carries the Whore of Babylon on her back. The fact that he "once was" means this man will be resurrected by Satan. He will be the al-Mahdi (Redeemer) for whom Islam is waiting. The Muslims believe he is now in occultation (a suspended state). However, Revelation 17:8 tells us that he is actually in hell, and that is where he is heading again!

> "The ten horns you saw are ten kings who have not yet received a kingdom, but who for one hour will receive authority as kings along with the beast. They have one purpose and will give their power and authority to the beast. "
>
> — Revelation 17:12–13

Of course, the eighth king, who has not yet arisen, will use this coalition of the ten nations to rule the world. We should see that united kingdom begin to form any day now. They will have plenty of money from oil revenues, while all the countries of the West are on the verge of bankruptcy. The strangulation of our oil supplies will put us over the edge. It is not that we don't have our own oil supplies, but greed and environmentalist concerns have kept us from using our own oil resources. That shortsightedness will turn the nations of the West into powerless blowhards as the ten-nation coalition rises to power.

"They will wage war against the Lamb, but the Lamb will triumph over them because he is Lord of lords and King of kings—and with him will be *his called, chosen and faithful followers.*"

— Revelation 17:14

Here, at last, is the rapture! The timing of this event is spelled out for us in the text. It happens as Jesus Christ comes back to destroy the Antichrist after he has had his three and one-half years of rule. It is at the end of the tribulation. No, Jesus Christ does not do a U-turn in the sky and head back to heaven with his saints for seven more years. The myth of a pretribulational rapture is destroyed by this passage.

Don't breeze over this verse lightly. The entire purpose of John's writing of Revelation is summed up in Revelation 17:14. When Jesus appears in the sky to destroy Babylon and its final king, he will have his "called" (κλητοί) with him. This is the root of the word "church" (ἐκκλησία). In the Old Testament (Septuagint), ἐκκλησία is used to refer to the entire nation of Israel. In the New Testament, the word "church" (ἐκκλησία) refers to the entire congregation, some of whom are saved and some of whom are not, as we saw in the letters to the churches of Asia in Revelation 2 and 3. In Revelation 17:14, John makes it clear Jesus does not come with the whole church, but only with the portion of the church that is called, chosen, and faithful.

The fact that Jesus does not come with the entire church is strongly emphasized by the adjectives "chosen" and "faithful." Jesus Christ will come with the *chosen* (ἐκλεκτοί), which means "the finest portion." Likewise, he will be accompanied by those who have been *faithful*; these are the ones we have seen rewarded in the various parentheses of Revelation.

In Matthew 22:1–14, Jesus tells the parable of a king who held a wedding banquet. The first guests invited (Israel) refused to come.

So a second invitation is given to one and all (the church). But one man is spotted at the feast without a wedding garment. He is tossed out, and Jesus exclaims, "For many are invited, but few are chosen." It is the chosen who will accompany Christ on that day.

In Matthew 24:12–13, Jesus said the love of *most* would grow cold. Many people believe they are saved because they were baptized at some point in their life. They live their lives with one foot dangling over the brink of hell wondering just how close they can get. But Jesus adds "he who stands firm to the end will be saved." The entire host of the ἐκκλησία will not be at the Wedding Supper of the Lamb; only the chosen and faithful will. John's purpose in writing Revelation is to warn both the seven churches of Asia and us: those who turn away when the troubles begin will not be there in the end.

According to Isaiah, Jeremiah, Ezekiel, and Daniel, the enemy Jesus comes to destroy will be Babylon and its final ruler. It is the day of the resurrection for the saints of God and the miraculous gathering of the living saints of God. If you have forgotten those promises, please review chapter three. This is the day the Son of Man will make his public appearance (see Matthew 24:30). The Antichrist will be thrown into the lake of fire and his army destroyed at Christ's return.

CHAPTER SIXTEEN

THE DAY OF THE LORD
Revelation 19:1–21

Revelation 19 begins with four Hallelujahs. The first three Hallelujahs bring the tribulation period to an end by coming full circle, returning to John's vision of things in heaven in Revelation 4 and 5, when Christ said, "Come up here, and I will show you what must take place later" (Revelation 4:1). Only this time the creatures of heaven give praise to Jesus for having accomplished what he set out to do when he took the sealed scroll from the hand of God. The praise comes from a multitude of saints, the twenty-four elders, and from the throne of God.

> After this I heard what sounded like the roar of a great multitude in heaven shouting:
>
> "*Hallelujah!* Salvation and glory and power belong to our God, for true and just are his judgments. He has condemned the great prostitute who corrupted the earth by her adulteries. He has avenged on her the blood of his servants.
>
> And again they shouted:

> *"Hallelujah!* The smoke from her goes up for ever
> and ever."
> The twenty-four elders and the four living creatures
> fell down and worshiped God, who was seated on the
> throne. And they cried:
> *"Amen, Hallelujah!"*
> Then a voice came from the throne, saying:
> "Praise our God, all you his servants, you who fear
> him, both great and small!"
>
> — Revelation 19:1–5

Everything has been accomplished. The wrath of God has been
poured out. The only thing left to accomplish is the destruction of
the Antichrist and his army, but that will have to wait for a moment.
Right now is the time for the saints to celebrate.

The fourth Hallelujah and the vision of the rider on the white
horse that follows gives us the sequence of events for the second
coming of Jesus Christ. Many Christians know that Christ will fight
the battle of Armageddon when he returns, but they are unable to
say what else will happen and place those events in order. Revelation
19:6–20 gives us that order of events. This last Hallelujah, like the
first, is shouted by a great multitude of saints whose combined
voices are so loud they sound like thunder.

> Then I heard what sounded like a great multitude, like
> the roar of rushing waters and like loud peals of thun-
> der, shouting:
> *"Hallelujah!* For our Lord God Almighty reigns. Let
> us rejoice and be glad and give him glory! For the wed-
> ding of the Lamb has come, and his bride has made her-
> self ready. Fine linen, bright and clean, was given her to

wear." (Fine linen stands for the righteous acts of God's
holy people.)

Then the angel said to me, *"Write this: Blessed are*
those who are invited to the wedding supper of the Lamb!"
And he added, "These are the true words of God."

— Revelation 19:6–9

The New Testament saints have been raptured and the dead Old
Testament saints have been raised. The deafening sound of praise
comes from those who have overcome and are about to be rewarded
with the finest meal of their lives. They are dressed in white because
their sins have been forgiven by the grace of their Messiah, the
Jewish Redeemer. All the rewards promised to those members of
the seven churches who overcame by their faithfulness to Christ are
handed out to this multitude.

Now it's time to eat, and this is not your average church potluck!
It is the Wedding Supper of the Lamb. The Wedding Supper of the
Lamb is a reference to Isaiah 25:6–8, which is the passage Jesus
referred to in Matthew 8:11–12. In the Isaiah passage, the menu is
listed as a "feast of rich food," "a banquet of aged wine," and "the
best of meats." The phrase "a banquet of aged wines" reminds us of
the wedding in Cana where Jesus changed the water into the finest
of aged wines. Notice in the Matthew 8:11–12 passage that the Jews
who do not believe in Christ are not invited to the banquet, but the
Gentiles who do believe are there to take their place.

We have to return to the gospels and the Old Testament in order
to understand why this event is placed where it is. We are told that
we cannot know the date of the day of the Lord, but we can know
the sequence of events which will occur on that day. That sequence
is made clear for us by Matthew 21, Acts 2, Ezekiel 43, and here in
Revelation 19.

The first time Jesus entered through the Eastern Gate, he was accompanied by his disciples. This last time, he will be accompanied by a multitude of disciples who have been either resurrected or caught up alive. Why? Jesus doesn't need our help to cleanse the temple. The answer is simple: Jerusalem will be the new home of the saints (see Hebrews 11:8–16). Isaiah 66:6–9 tells us that, in a single day, Jerusalem will be miraculously rebuilt and the nation of Israel reborn.

So the *parousia*, or public appearance, of Jesus will involve the resurrection of the Old Testament saints as promised by the prophets, and the rapture of the living New Testament saints as promised by Paul.

The second event of the day of the Lord is the cleansing of the temple. This is immediately followed by the third event of the day of the Lord, which is the miraculous rebuilding of the city and re-establishment of the nation of Israel.

Furthermore, the resurrected and raptured saints are accompanying Christ because they are on the way to the Wedding Supper of the Lamb. This is the fourth event that will take place on that day.

After the saints have been fed and sequestered out of harm's way in their new home, Jerusalem, Christ heads north to the mountain of Megiddo with his army of angels; that will be the fifth event that takes place on the day of the Lord. No, we are not that army.

Will there be a time delay between the banquet and the battle? We don't know, it doesn't say, but that is a possibility. All of this does not have to be accomplished in "the twinkling of an eye," or even in twenty-four hours, to fulfill the promises of the day of the Lord.

This might be the "silence in heaven" that lasts for about half an hour (Revelation 8:1). It might refer to the peace the saints will experience because of the banquet and the rest that follows. But that rest is interrupted by John's vision of the return of Christ from heaven on his white charger. John says:

> I saw heaven standing open and there before me was
> a white horse, whose rider is called Faithful and True.
> With justice he judges and wages war. His eyes are like
> blazing fire, and on his head are many crowns. *He has a*
> *name written on him that no one knows but he himself.*
> — Revelation 19:11–12

The rider on the white horse is Jesus Christ. This is the second coming that every saint, from Abraham to you and me, has been waiting for. It happens as the last act of the tribulation. It is an event that will be seen by the entire world, and there is nothing secret about it. The name written on him is something that no one knows. When we see that name, it will reveal the true relationship between the Father and the Son, which no one fully comprehends today.

> He is dressed in a robe dipped in blood, and his name
> is the Word of God. *The armies of heaven were following*
> *him*, riding on white horses and dressed in fine linen,
> white and clean.
> — Revelation 19:13–14

"The armies of heaven" is not a reference to the raptured saints who are now in Jerusalem. We are not the armies of heaven. This is referring to the angels who will be with Jesus (see Jude 14–15). Jesus is not going to ask the saints, who have been told to turn the other cheek, now to take up arms and kill our enemies. Besides that, the weapon Christ will use to destroy the Antichrist will be his word. It is called a sword that comes out of his mouth because his word is more powerful than any weapon.

That brings up the question: how should we respond when we see the enemy coming with weapons to kill us? Should we respond with AK-47s and RPGs? I used to think so until I read Tertullian's *Apology*. Tertullian tells Marcus Aurelius (Caesar) that the number of Christians in his realms is so great, they could take up arms and defeat the Romans if they so desired, but to do so would deny the very gospel message they were dying for. Defending one's family is understandable, but trying to become God's army is not.

Revenge is not a Christian option. Jesus didn't say, "If your enemy slaps you on the cheek, kill him." When we avenge ourselves, we usurp the authority of Jesus. We replace him as God and Judge and take that role upon ourselves. That is the very reason why Jesus is coming back. The Antichrist will be usurping the authority of God. He will be taking the place of God in the temple, and Jesus Christ is coming back to kill him. Let God be God.

> *Coming out of his mouth is a sharp sword with which to strike down the nations.* "He will rule them with an iron scepter." He treads the winepress of the fury of the wrath of God Almighty. On his robe and on his thigh he has this name written:
> KING OF KINGS AND LORD OF LORDS.
> — Revelation 19:15–16

The sword out of Jesus' mouth is metaphorical language. Jesus does not have a literal sword in his mouth, but he has the power of a sword in his words. It was by the word of God that the world was created. "God said, 'Let there be light,' and there was light" (Genesis 1:3). It is this power that will be in the mouth of Christ. The Antichrist has no hope against such power. With the power in his words to both create and destroy worlds, Jesus is KING of KINGS and LORD of LORDS.

> And I saw an angel standing in the sun, who cried in a loud voice to all the birds flying in midair, "Come, gather together for the great supper of God, so that you may eat the flesh of kings, generals, and the mighty, of

horses and their riders, and the flesh of all people, free and slave, great and small."

— Revelation 19: 17–18

There are two great suppers mentioned in the Old Testament. The first one we have already seen. That was the Wedding Supper of the Lamb mentioned in Isaiah 25, which is the awards banquet for all the saints who have overcome. But never let it be said that Jesus is not an animal lover. We know his eye is on the sparrow; now he takes the time to feed the eagles, vultures, ravens, and other carrion eaters.

This is the feast mentioned in Ezekiel 39:17–20, and it takes place on the day of the battle of Armageddon. Verses 17–18 of Revelation are nearly an exact quote from the Ezekiel 39 passage. On the menu is *Hamon Gog*, which means the "multitude of Gog." In John's day, Gog was located in the region of the Caucasus Mountains and northward into the steppes of Russia. This multitude of Gog will become suet for the birds of the air.

> Then I saw the beast and the kings of the earth and their armies gathered together to wage war against the rider on the horse and his army. But the beast was captured, and with it the false prophet who had performed the signs on its behalf. With these signs he had deluded those who had received the mark of the beast and worshiped its image. *The two of them were thrown alive into the fiery lake of burning sulfur.* The rest were killed with the sword coming out of the mouth of the rider on the horse, and all the birds gorged themselves on their flesh.
>
> — Revelation 19:19–21

Isaiah 14:19–20 and Isaiah 30:32–33 will be fulfilled by this event. The Antichrist and the False Prophet are tossed into the lake of burning sulfur. Good riddance! Their comrades-in-arms, however, will have to wait for their judgment. They are killed and buried. We will see their judgment in chapter 20.

> And I saw an angel coming down out of heaven, having the key to the Abyss and holding in his hand a great chain. He seized the dragon, that ancient serpent, who is the devil, or Satan, and *bound him for a thousand years.* He threw him into the Abyss, and locked and sealed it over him, to keep him from deceiving the nations anymore *until the thousand years were ended.* After that, he must be set free for a short time."
>
> — Revelation 20:1–3

The term "millennium" comes from verse 3. It is the thousand-year period when Satan is bound in hell and Jesus Christ reigns on earth as the sovereign king of all. If you believe the word of God is to be understood literally, as I do, then this is the fulfillment of the premillennial hope. Furthermore, it is the completion of all Old Testament prophecies. Jesus Christ, the Messiah of Israel, has returned to earth to rescue Israel and begin his reign as King. Now God's promise to Abraham will be fulfilled. The earth will be returned to a Garden of Eden state at this time, and every man will sit under his own fig tree in peace and safety (see Isaiah 9:2–7, 11:1–9, and 65:17–25). However, the length of this Garden of Eden state is not revealed in the Old Testament. We find in Revelation this period will last for a thousand years, at which time the Father will create a new heaven and earth, and he will take back the role of leadership from Christ. That fact is revealed for us by Paul in I Corinthians 15:20–28. Abraham's promise will be kept, but it will be kept in a new and eternal Promised Land.

I saw thrones on which were seated those who had been given authority to judge. And I saw the souls of those who had been beheaded because of their testimony about Jesus and because of the word of God. They had not worshiped the beast or its image and had not received its mark on their foreheads or their hands. They came to life and reigned with Christ a thousand years. (The rest of the dead did not come to life until the thousand years were ended.) *This is the first resurrection.* Blessed and holy are those who share in the first resurrection. The second death has no power over them, but they will be priests of God and of Christ and will reign with him for a thousand years.

— Revelation 20:4–5

These are the thrones the mother of James and John requested Jesus to reserve for her sons. Will James and John be sitting on two of those thrones? Maybe; we don't know. Notice that those who are part of the first resurrection are the ones who overcame the Antichrist and gave their life for their testimony. They are resurrected now and will reign with Christ for a thousand years. Also notice it is only Christians who gave their lives for Christ during the tribulation who take part in this first judgment and are universally rewarded. It is called the first resurrection because there will be a second resurrection for those who died from the plagues and wars of the tribulation. Anyone who takes part in this first event will be eternally blessed because this judgment is based on grace. If your name is written in the Lamb's Book of Life, you will reign with Christ and never face another judgment.

The millennium will be the strangest time in the world's history. The earth will return to a Garden of Eden state. Isaiah 11:6–9 says:

The wolf will live with the lamb, the leopard will lie down with the goat, the calf and the lion and the yearling together; and a little child will lead them.

The cow will feed with the bear, their young will lie down together, and the lion will eat straw like the ox.

The infant will play near the cobra's den, the young child will put its hand into the viper's nest.

They will neither harm nor destroy on all my holy mountain, for the earth will be filled with the knowledge of the LORD as the waters cover the sea.

— Isaiah 11:6–9

In other words, violence in the animal kingdom will be a thing of the past.

That will be true of mankind as well. Habakkuk 2:14 says, "For the earth will be filled with the knowledge of the glory of the LORD as the waters cover the sea." Wars will cease; mankind will acknowledge Jesus Christ as King of Kings and Lord of Lords as he reigns over the world from the Holy City of Jerusalem. But the thing that will make the millennium so strange will be the mixture of humanity. Those people of the nations who survived the tribulation, and presumably are followers of Christ, will repopulate the earth.

However, we who are raptured at the second coming of Christ will be changed into new bodies, as Paul says in I Corinthians 15:

Listen, I tell you a mystery: We will not all sleep, but we will all be changed—in a flash, in the twinkling of an eye, at the last trumpet. For the trumpet will sound, the dead will be raised imperishable, and we will be changed. For the perishable must clothe itself with the imperishable, and the mortal with immortality. When the perishable has been clothed with the imperishable, and the mortal with immortality, then the saying that

is written will come true: "Death has been swallowed
up in victory."

"Where, O death, is your victory? Where, O death,
is your sting?"

— I Corinthians 15:51–55

That means some people will still have mortal bodies and some
people will have immortal bodies; some people will be making
babies, while others will not. This is the main reason a second
resurrection and judgment are necessary. No one will escape this
life without facing the judgment seat of Christ.

John goes on to say:

When the thousand years are over, *Satan will be released
from his prison and will go out to deceive the nations in
the four corners of the earth*—Gog and Magog—and to
gather them for battle. In number they are like the sand
on the seashore. They marched across the breadth of
the earth and surrounded the camp of God's people,
the city he loves. But fire came down from heaven and
devoured them. And the devil, who deceived them, was
thrown into the lake of burning sulfur, where the beast
and the false prophet had been thrown. They will be
tormented day and night for ever and ever.

— Revelation 20:7–10

This is the part I struggle with understanding. Have you ever
said to yourself, "If I were God I would. . ."? Well, that is what I
have said many times, especially when I read this passage. If it was
up to me, I would have killed Satan in the Garden of Eden. All of
the suffering of humanity for all these centuries could have been
avoided. But now, after the tribulation, why let him go? I have to
confess, I do not understand the mind of God. I guess that is why he

said to Isaiah, "As the heavens are higher than the earth, so are my ways higher than your ways and my thoughts than your thoughts" (Isaiah 55:9).

Gog and Magog will give it another try. They will raise another army to fight the last battle of history. This one is mentioned in Ezekiel 38:3–9. There are two battle scenes with Gog and Magog in Ezekiel. The last battle is mentioned first, but don't let that throw you. The Old Testament prophets did not fully understand everything they wrote. That is why the chronological order of events is confused in the prophets, yet what they said will be fulfilled. This is Hamon Gog's second try at overthrowing God. However, the result is the same both times. Some people never learn.

The angel of the revelation does not dwell on the battle scene. It seems to be over before it started. The only thing of importance about this battle is the final demise of Satan. He is thrown into the lake of fire to join the Antichrist and the False Prophet. We then come to the scene of the second resurrection:

> Then I saw a great white throne and him who was seated on it. The earth and the heavens fled from his presence, and there was no place for them. And I saw the dead, great and small, standing before the throne, and books were opened. Another book was opened, which is the book of life. The dead were judged according to what they had done as recorded in the books. The sea gave up the dead that were in it, and death and Hades gave up the dead that were in them, and *each person was judged according to what they had done.* Then death and Hades were thrown into the lake of fire. *The lake of fire is the second death. Anyone whose name was not found written in the book of life was thrown into the lake of fire.*"
>
> — Revelation 20:11–15

The great white throne judgment concludes the millennium. There is only one judge this time: God the Father. The apostle Paul tells us in I Corinthians 15:22–28 that Jesus will reign until he has put all enemies under his feet, and then he will turn the kingdom back over to the Father. This is that point in history. Gone is the panel of twenty-four judges who were all human beings and fellow believers. This is superior court, and those being judged are those who were born during the millennium, along with those who died without Christ before the millennium began. The only witnesses allowed are the Book of Life and the Book of Works. If your name is in the first book you will enter heaven. If your name is not in the Book of Life, you will be judged by the Book of Works.

There will be many who come out of this judgment with rewards and white robes. They will be considered fellow saints with all those who were resurrected at the first resurrection.

However, the army of the Antichrist who died at the battle of Armageddon, and all those who died without Christ throughout the ages, will now stand before the Father for trial. This is the second resurrection.

Islam, the religion of the Antichrist, teaches that every man will be judged by his works. Well, God is going to give them what they have asked for. The supporters of the Antichrist will come forward for judgment and a search will be made in the Book of Life, but their names will not be recorded there. That means that the outcome of the trial will be based solely on works without grace. As a result, those who fought against Christ at Armageddon, and who are resurrected for this judgment, will die a second time. That is why it is called the second death. The second death is the lake of fire.

CHAPTER SEVENTEEN

THE NEW JERUSALEM
Revelation 21:1–22:21

In the final two chapters of Revelation, John sees a new vision. It is not a parenthesis, but rather the culmination of all the promises of the entire Bible. It is the eternal age. The old order of things has passed away, and there is no longer any time. The apostle Peter was given a glimpse of this event in II Peter 3:7 and 10, which say:

> By the same word the present heavens and earth are reserved for fire, being kept for the day of judgment and destruction of ungodly men. . . .
> But the day of the Lord will come like a thief. The heavens will disappear with a roar, the elements will be destroyed by fire, and the earth and everything in it will be laid bare."

Revelation doesn't give us any details to determine if John saw this event happen; he simply records the results, which are a new heaven and earth.

> Then I saw a new heaven and a new earth, for the first heaven and the first earth had passed away, and there

was no longer any sea. I saw the Holy City, the new Jerusalem, coming down out of heaven from God, prepared as a bride beautifully dressed for her husband. And I heard a loud voice from the throne saying, "Look! God's dwelling place is now among the people, and he will dwell with them. They will be his people, and God himself will be with them and be their God. He will wipe every tear from their eyes. There will be no more death or mourning or crying or pain, for the old order of things has passed away."

He who was seated on the throne said, "I am making everything new!" Then he said, "Write this down, for these words are trustworthy and true."

He said to me: "It is done. I am the Alpha and the Omega, the Beginning and the End. To the thirsty I will give water without cost from the spring of the water of life. Those who are victorious will inherit all this, and I will be their God and they will be my children. But the *cowardly, the unbelieving*, the vile, the murderers, the sexually immoral, those who practice magic arts, the idolaters and all liars—*they will be consigned to the fiery lake of burning sulfur. This is the second death.*"

— Revelation 21:1–8

Everything that has been said in the word of God from Genesis to the Apocalypse has now been accomplished. The combination of heaven and earth together into one eternal dwelling for the saints is the only thing that was not promised, but it could have been surmised by the promises made to Abraham and David. How else could Abraham and his children live in the Promised Land forever, and we Christians be with Christ forever? How else could the man

David reign on the throne of God forever? All those promises fall into place with the joining of heaven and earth into one eternal dwelling.

One of the seven angels who had the seven bowls full of the seven last plagues came and said to me, "Come, I will show you the bride, the wife of the Lamb." And he carried me away in the Spirit to a mountain great and high, and showed me the Holy City, Jerusalem, coming down out of heaven from God. It shone with the glory of God, and its brilliance was like that of a very precious jewel, like a jasper, clear as crystal. It had a great, high wall with twelve gates, and with twelve angels at the gates. *On the gates were written the names of the twelve tribes of Israel.* There were three gates on the east, three on the north, three on the south and three on the west. *The wall of the city had twelve foundations, and on them were the names of the twelve apostles of the Lamb.*

The angel who talked with me had a measuring rod of gold to measure the city, its gates and its walls. The city was laid out like a square, as long as it was wide. He measured the city with the rod and found it to be *12,000 stadia in length, and as wide and high as it is long.* The angel measured the wall using human measurement, and it was 144 cubits thick. The wall was made of jasper, and the city of pure gold, as pure as glass. The foundations of the city walls were decorated with every kind of precious stone. The first foundation was jasper, the second sapphire, the third agate, the fourth emerald, the fifth onyx, the sixth ruby, the seventh chrysolite, the eighth beryl, the ninth topaz, the tenth turquoise, the eleventh

> jacinth, and the twelfth amethyst. The twelve gates were
> twelve pearls, each gate made of a single pearl. The great
> street of the city was of gold, as pure as transparent glass.
>   — Revelation 21:9–21

The New Jerusalem will be more beautiful than any city that was ever built on earth. This is the "city with foundations, whose architect and builder is God" (Hebrews 11:10). Abraham has been looking for this city for four thousand years. It will be made from precious jewels and paved with gold. Those who believe the Jewish and Gentile Christians will have different futures need to look at verses 12 and 14 very carefully. The foundations of the walls are the twelve tribes of Israel, and the gates are the twelve apostles. We are one body with one Lord, and we have one future.

There is one feature of this city that is hard to imagine. It is 12,000 stadia (1,261 miles) in width, length, and height. That is a staggering amount of volume. Is the city built in layers? How would you visit with those living 12,000 stadia above you? Newton's laws of physics will be a thing of the past. Only those equipped with new bodies would be able to live in such a city. But if our new bodies are anything like the body of Jesus after the resurrection, the 12,000 stadia won't be a problem.

> I did not see a temple in the city, because the Lord God
> Almighty and the Lamb are its temple. The city does
> not need the sun or the moon to shine on it, for the
> glory of God gives it light, and the Lamb is its lamp. The
> nations will walk by its light, and the kings of the earth
> will bring their splendor into it. On no day will its gates
> ever be shut, for there will be no night there. *The glory
> and honor of the nations will be brought into it. Nothing
> impure will ever enter it,* nor will anyone who does what
> is shameful or deceitful, but only those whose names

are written in the Lamb's book of life.

— Revelation 21:22–27

Evidently, those believers of the nations who survived the second battle of Gog and Magog will live in their own countries outside the city of Jerusalem during the eternal age (see Isaiah 65:17–25). Those believing children born during the millennium will have stood before God the Father for judgment at the second resurrection. They will be able to return to their homes during the eternal state yet come and go as visiting saints. However, Jerusalem will be reserved for those who accepted Christ before the millennium began and remained faithful to him during the tribulation.

> Then the angel showed me the *river of the water of life*, as clear as crystal, flowing from the throne of God and of the Lamb down the middle of the great street of the city. On each side of the river stood the tree of life, bearing twelve crops of fruit, yielding its fruit every month. And the leaves of the tree are for the healing of the nations. No longer will there be any curse. The throne of God and of the Lamb will be in the city, and his servants will serve him. They will see his face, and his name will be on their foreheads. There will be no more night. They will not need the light of a lamp or the light of the sun, for the Lord God will give them light. And they will reign for ever and ever.
>
> — Revelation 22:1–5

In ancient times, the place of eternal dwelling was known as the underworld. It was divided into a realm for the good and a realm for the bad. In the parable of Lazarus and the rich man, Jesus indicated the good and the bad could see each other, but could not cross over from one realm to the other. John's vision of the eternal state repeats

that same idea, with the fires of hell being outside the walls of the
New Jerusalem.

> Outside are the dogs, those who practice magic arts, the
> sexually immoral, the murderers, the idolaters and ev-
> eryone who loves and practices falsehood.
>
> — Revelation 22:15

The lake of fire does not cease to exist in the eternal state. Some
have taught that God could never be so cruel as to punish people
forever. Instead, they teach the annihilation theory, saying those
thrown into the lake of fire will be burnt up and annihilated so that
their souls will no longer exist. That is not what this verse indicates.
The lake of fire was originally intended for Satan and the fallen
angels. Their punishment is eternal. All who follow them will suffer
the same fate.

The angel of the revelation gives one last admonition and
warning to the churches of Asia and all the future saints who read
John's book. What is said is true in every detail and will happen in
God's timing. In the meantime, the invitation to come to Christ still
stands. There is still time to repent. If you ignore that offer or change
the angel's message in any way, there is no hope for you.

> "I, Jesus, have sent my angel to give you this testimony
> for the churches. I am the Root and the Offspring of
> David, and the bright Morning Star."
>
> The Spirit and the bride say, "Come!" And let the
> one who hears say, "Come!" Let the one who is thirsty
> come; and let the one who wishes take the free gift of the
> water of life.
>
> I warn everyone who hears the words of the proph-
> ecy of this scroll: If anyone adds anything to them, God
> will add to that person the plagues described in this

scroll. And if anyone takes words away from this scroll of prophecy, God will take away from that person any share in the tree of life and in the Holy City, which are described in this scroll.

He who testifies to these things says, "Yes, I am coming soon."

Amen. Come, Lord Jesus.

The grace of the Lord Jesus be with God's people. Amen.

— Revelation 22:16–21

Yes, the invitation to "come" still stands. If you don't know Jesus as your personal savior, now is the time to get your heart right with God. Do it while you still can, the time is short! The decline of Europe and the Western powers is proceeding rapidly. The rising of the powers of the East and Middle East is becoming apparent. Don't be fooled by thinking God has chosen America to be the "light of the world." Our nation has, in large measure, rejected God, and he in turn has rejected our nation. But you are on his heart. The offer to "come" is meant for you. Please accept it.

Maranatha!

A Chronological Review
of Millenial Views

2000 BC: There was no understanding of a millennium in the days of the Old Testament saints. Abraham was promised the land of Canaan as his eternal reward because of his faith in God. The prophets who followed Abraham expanded on the promise of a future redeemer that was given to Adam and Eve in Genesis. They prophesied that a redeemer would rule the earth from the throne of David (Jerusalem), but there was never a time limit put on that redeemer's rule. Their limited understanding of prophecy ended with the appearance of a redeemer, as if that event would mark the beginning of eternity.

AD 30: *Premillennialism.* This was the New Testament apostles' belief about the future. It was a continuation of the Old Testament Jewish beliefs concerning the promises given by God to their Jewish fathers, but with much more clarity because of the indwelling of the Holy Spirit. Their belief in a resurrection and grace for salvation provided through a Messiah was greatly expanded upon by the apostle John in Revelation. His prophecy did not change the Old Testament belief; it expanded and explained it. The Revelation of

John explains what will happen in the seven years prior to the return of Jesus Christ, and reveals a millennium for the first time.

Because a literal reading of these events reveals that Christ will return before the millennium begins to defeat the Antichrist and then reign for a thousand years, this theology is known as premillennialism. In other words, Christ returns before the millennium starts. This was the universal belief of all early church leaders for the first three hundred years of church history. Several pretribulational teachers have tried to explain away this universal belief by saying there were ambiguous statements made by some of the early church leaders. That is true only if those statements are taken out of the context of the leader's total writings.

324: *Preterism.* Preterism is the second oldest view of the millennium and prophecy in general. Preterism was first preached by Bishop Eusebius Pamphili in AD 324, during the reign of Constantine. Eusebius taught that Constantine was the reincarnation of Jesus Christ, and the millennium started with his reign.[1] Therefore, the return of Christ was to be understood as being fulfilled allegorically. But the reign of Constantine lasted for only thirty years, and the kingdom he began lasted only another two hundred and fifty years. This belief was not widespread and vanished with the death of Constantine in AD 337. It was not heard of again until the Reformation, 1,150 years later.

420: *Amillennialism.* The Visigoths overran and sacked Rome in the years AD 409–10. The Roman people were devastated by this turn of events and demanded that the government reject Christianity and return to worshipping the old gods. In reply to the outcry, Augustine, Bishop of Hippo in Algeria, North Africa, wrote *The City of God.*[2]

Augustine argued prophecy should be understood as allegorical. The troubles of the tribulation period as described by John were symbolic of all of human history. Christians have always been, and will always be, persecuted by Satan, and this will continue until the end of history, whenever that might be. Likewise, the millennium of Revelation 20 was symbolic of the world peace which will be established in the end. This will happen very gradually as the City of God overtakes the City of Man. The millennium should not be understood as a specific period of time, just as the seven years of the tribulation should not be understood as a specific period of time; both are symbolic and indefinite.

Therefore, there is no millennium and no literal return of Christ; there is just an ultimate victory for Christianity. This belief became the standard teaching of the Roman Catholic Church from the sixth century until the present. Amillennialism is by far the most common belief among Christians today because Roman Catholics outnumber Protestants by two to one.

1500s: *Premillennialism returns with Protestantism.* It is widely acknowledged by church historians that the Reformation would have happened even if Martin Luther had not been born. Northern Europe was experiencing a widespread spiritual awakening at the time, and one of the major factors in this awakening was the Brotherhood of the Common Life, a group which existed a hundred years before Luther's birth. This group started home Bible-study groups which were interested in the literal meaning of the original Scriptures.

Because of the high rate of growth of these home Bible-study groups, the need for Bibles in the language of the people became a major factor in the drive to invent a new, faster way to print the Scriptures. It is no coincidence that the first Bibles printed by Gutenberg were meant to supply the needs for the home Bible-study groups of the Brotherhood.

It was through Luther's contact with the Brotherhood at Wartburg that Luther's eyes were opened to the gospel. However, since Luther was an Augustinian monk, he retained a modified form of Augustine's beliefs about the City of God and the City of Man with regard to the millennium. However, Luther was not the only reformer of the Reformation. Many Anabaptist groups were formed at the same time as the Lutherans. They had no desire to remain as a part of the Catholic church, as did Luther. It was through the many Anabaptist groups, followed several years later by the Baptists, that historic premillennialism made a comeback.

1521: *Preterism returns.* Martin Luther preached that the pope was the Antichrist and the trials and suffering he was going through were the tribulation period mentioned in Revelation. However, the Roman Catholic defenders of the pope claimed this could not be true since, based on what Eusebius had said, all prophecy had already been fulfilled. They argued that Nero had been the Antichrist and the tribulation was the persecution of Christians during his reign; never mind the fact that Nero died twenty-five years before John's prophecy about the future was written. Again, they fell back on allegorical interpretation and symbolism as a method of biblical interpretation.

1700s: *Conservative Postmillennialism.* Two hundred years of religious war in Europe, from 1521 to 1715, had killed one-third of the European population, and this left a very bitter taste in the mouths of those who survived this period of religious zeal and warfare. The Enlightenment, which began in 1687, led to a great deal of biblical criticism and disbelief. The Industrial Revolution, which followed on the heels of the Enlightenment, created a sense of accomplishment by mankind and generated a new twist on the old amillennial beliefs. Many believed that mankind would perfect the world through education, medical advancements, industrialization, and evangelism. These new advancements would spread to the entire world, bringing in the millennium. When the world was at peace and all mankind were believers, then Christ would return and reign as king. This is conservative postmillennialism, which taught a literal physical return of Christ to rule on earth once mankind had rid the world of evil.

1800s: *Liberal Postmillennialism.* This approach was favored by the German school of higher criticism. They believed mankind would continue to perfect itself through industry, medicine, education, and science to the point that man would become his own god. This view was best expressed by G. W. F. Hegel, who began teaching at the University of Berlin in 1818. The old mythology of a spiritual being called God was done away with and replaced with the ideas of the Absolute and the Übermensch, or Superman (namely, the German race). This liberal form of postmillennialism was also widely believed in Europe until the end of WWII. The disillusionment of two world wars and more than a hundred million deaths seems to have ended this postmillennial hope of mankind perfecting the world.

1840: *Pretribulational-Premillennialism.* A new twist on the old premillennial belief system of the apostles began as the result of a series of sermons by John Nelson Darby in 1840. Darby was a Plymouth Brethren pastor from England. He was invited to be the head speaker at a prophecy conference in Lausanne, Switzerland, where he revealed his new understanding of premillennialism for the first time. Darby's theory became the major belief system among conservative Christians in North America through the teaching of the Niagara Bible Conference movement from the 1870s to the 1890s. At the start of the twentieth century, pretribulational-premillennialism became the only acceptable view among the fundamentalists in North America.

1950s: *Modified Preterism.* The failure of mankind to bring in the millennium and to perfect the world has led many in the conservative postmillennial camp to turn to a modified preterist system. Many preterists believe all prophecies except for the return of Christ have been fulfilled. Furthermore, they believe there is no way to determine when Christ's return will happen since all biblical prophetic signs have been fulfilled. Again, a heavy reliance on allegory and spiritualizing is necessary for this system to work.

1950s: *Midtribulational-Premillennialism.* This is an offshoot of John Nelson Darby's pretribulational theory. The midtribulational theory states that the rapture of the Gentile saints will take place at the midway point of the tribulation. The main support for this view comes from II Thessalonians 2:3; however; this verse makes no statement as to the timing of the rapture. It simply rules out the possibility of a rapture *before* the midway point of the tribulation. Anything beyond that is pure speculation.

1960s: *Continuous Rapture Theory.* This is another recent offshoot of John Nelson Darby's theory. Those who hold to this view believe there will be a pretribulational rapture that will take all the Gentile saints who are prepared to meet the Lord at his return. Then, throughout the tribulation, individuals who are converted to Christianity will be raptured as well, creating a continuous series of raptures. The biggest problem with this theory is the total lack of Scripture to support it.

1960s: *Liberal Postmillennialism.* This theory, with a liberal twist, made a big comeback in the political realm with America's war on poverty and the government's support for unionization. This is strictly an agnostic/atheist movement among the liberal elite who have taken over the Democratic Party whose goals match those of G. W. F. Hegel.

PROBLEMS WITH THE THEORIES

As you can see, the children of God have had numerous views concerning prophecy through the centuries. Your view makes you neither saint nor sinner. It will in no way determine if your future is heaven or hell, unless you have chosen to follow the disciples of Hegel. However, each of the systems mentioned above has problems associated with it.

Amillennialism and postmillennialism both suffer from a fatal flaw. They can never reach their goal of world perfection because the "mission field" will never stop growing. Even if every person on earth was to earn a PhD, and had access to the best medical treatment, and was a member of the "church," there would still be many millions of children born every year who were not "perfect." Therefore, the "mission field" will never stop growing. In addition, population growth has always outpaced the growth rate of the church.

Preterism, on the other hand, pleads total ignorance and "your guess is as good as mine." It relies heavily on metaphor, allegory, and spiritualization to interpret Scripture passages as having been fulfilled in centuries past, which makes Scripture meaningless. So why bother with Scripture at all? Why not buy a newspaper and make your own predictions?

That leaves premillennialism, either the one developed in the first two centuries of the church, or one of the offshoots developed in the nineteenth and twentieth centuries. But which one? That question depends upon how many raptures you believe in, and when you believe they will occur in relation to the tribulation. Historic premillennialism believes in one rapture at the end of the tribulation. Darby's form of pretribulational-premillennialism believes in one rapture at the beginning of the tribulation.

Darby's theory requires that *dispensationalism* (a belief that God deals with believers differently in different eras of time) be true. But there is no biblical support for dispensationalism without the use of spiritualization and speculation. Those who do believe in dispensationalism differ on how many dispensations there have been. Different authors have suggested dispensations numbering from three to thirteen. Since every version is based on the solid foundation of speculation, you can guess as many as you like. However, each version of dispensationalism depends upon God reneging on his promise of a future miraculous gathering of the Jews. According to the pretribulationalists, that promise has been given to the Gentiles. This view calls into question the very nature of God, and it comes close to making God an anti-Semite who reneges on his promises.

Then there is the possibility one of the other pretribulational rapture theories developed in the twentieth century could be correct. Could there be a midtribulational rapture? There does seem to be one passage that gives some support to this theory, but it contradicts other Scripture passages.

How about the two-rapture theory, one at the beginning of the tribulation (for Gentiles) and one at the end (for Jews)? But where is the Scriptural support for two raptures? And as long as we are going to consider raptures that have no Scriptural support, how about the continuous rapture theory? Each person who converts during the tribulation will be immediately raptured. There could be millions of raptures, but where is the Scripture to back this theory?

There is only one way to solve this issue. We must agree to accept the literal, grammatical, historical, and contextual interpretation of each and every passage of Scripture without exception. That way we will know just what the Bible says. Then you can make your decision to believe it or not.

Endnotes

1   Pamphili, Eusebius, *Theophania*, available online at http://en.wikipedia.org/wiki/Theophania.

2   Augustine, "The City of God," in *Nicene and Post-Nicene Fathers of the Christian Church*, editor Philip Schaff

BIBLIOGRAPHY

Aslan, Reza. *No God but God: The Origins, Evolution and Future of Islam.* New York: Random House Publishing, 2006.

Augustine, "The City of God," in Nicene and Post-Nicene Fathers, Series 1, Volume 2, ed. Philip Schaff. Grand Rapids, MI: Eerdmans Publishing Co., 1956.

Bauer, W. *A Greek-English Lexicon of the New Testament and Other Early Christian Literature.* Chicago: University of Chicago Press, 1952.

Brown, F., S. R. Driver, and C. A. Briggs. *The Brown-Driver-Briggs Hebrew and English Lexicon.* Peabody, MA: Hendrickson Publishers, 2001.

Bunn, Davis T. *Riders of the Pale Horse.* Minneapolis: Bethany House Publishing, 1994.

Butler, Clark. *G.W.F. Hegel.* Boston: Twnage Publishing Co., 1977.

Cohen, Abraham. *Everyman's Talmuc: The Major Teachings of the Rabbinic Sages.* New York: E. P. Dutton and Penguin Books, 1949.

Durant, Will. *The Age of Faith*. New York: Simon & Schuster, 1954.

George, Andrew. *The Babylonian Gilgamesh Epic: Introduction, Critical Edition with Cuneiform Texts*. Oxford: Oxford University Press, 2003.

Gray, John. *Near Eastern Mythology: Mesopotamia, Syria, Palestine*. London: Haqmlyn Publishing, 1969.

Harris, Horton. *The Tubingen School: A History and Theological Investigation of the School of F. C. Bauer*. Grand Rapids: Baker Books, 1975.

Herodotus. *The Histories*. trans. by M. Marincola and Aubrey DeSelincourt. New York: Penguin Classics, 1996.

International Bible Society. *New International Study Bible*. Grand Rapids, MI: Zondervan, 2010.

Jacobsen, Thorkild. *The Sumarian Kings List*. Chicago: University of Chicago Press, 1939.

Lewis, Bernard. *Islam in History: Ideas, People, and Events in the Middle East*. Chicago: Open Court Publishing, 1993.

Nicholson, R. A. *Translations of Eastern Poetry and Prose*. Cambridge: Cambridge University Press, 1922.

Pamphili, Eusebius, *Theophania*, http://www.tertullian.org/fathers/eusebius_theophania_02book1.htm

Ramm, Bernard. *Protestant Biblical Interpretation, A Textbook of Hermeneutics*. 3rd ed. Grand Rapids, MI: Baker Books, 1970.

Richardson, Donald. *Secrets of the Koran*. Ventura, CA: Regal Books, 2003.

Richardson, Joel. *Antichrist, Islam's Awaited Messiah*. Enumclaw, WA: Pleasant Word (a division of Wine Press Publishing), 2006.

Sahil Bukhari. Available at http://thejerusalemfund.org and http://jihadwatch.org.

Sahil Muslim. Available at http://thejerusalemfund.org and http://jihadwatch.org.

Salahi, Adil. *Muhammad: Man and Prophet, A Complete Study of the Life of the Prophet of Islam*. New York: Barnes and Noble Books, 1995.

Shoebat, Walid, and Joel Richardson. *God's War on Terror: Islam, Prophecy and the Bible*. Top Executive Media, 2008.

Sunan Abu Dawud. Available at http://thejerusalemfund.org and http://jihadwatch.org.

Sunan al-Sughra. Available at http://thejerusalemfund.org and http://jihadwatch.org.

Sunan al-Tirmidri. Available at http://thejerusalemfund.org and http://jihadwatch.org.

Tertullian. "The Apology." In *Latin Christianity*, by A. C. Cox. New York: Charles Scribner's Sons, 2008.

The Holy Qur'an, trans. by A. Yusuf Ali, Ahmadiyya Anjuman Isha'at Islam Lahore Inc.

The Holy Qur'an: Text, Translation, and Commentary. New York: Khalil Al-Rawal, 1938.

Toews, John Edward. *Hegelianism: The Path Toward Dialectical Humanism.* 2nd ed. Cambridge: Cambridge University Press, 1985.

United States Conference of Catholic Bishops, editors. *New American Bible, Revised Edition.* Washington, DC: Catholic World Press/World Bible Publishers, 2010.

Wright, Archie T. *The Origin of Evil Spirits: The Reception of Genesis 6:1-4 in Early Jewish Literature.* Tubingen, Germany: Mohr Siebeck, 2005.